IN DIVERS MANNERS

A St Mary's Miscellany

I

IN DIVERS MANNERS

A St Mary's Miscellany

to commemorate the 450th anniversary of
the founding of St Mary's College,
7th March, 1539

Edited by D.W.D. Shaw

Published 1990 by

St Mary's College
University of St Andrews
St Andrews
Fife KY16 9AL
Scotland

ISBN 0 9516136 0 X

Designed, typeset and printed by
University of St Andrews Reprographic Services

CONTENTS

CONTENTS

FOREWORD

The covers of this small volume cannot hope to contain the life and times of St Mary's College in the University of St Andrews. That is not its purpose. But this collections of lectures and essays does provide for us a glimpse through some of the windows of our College's history and may perhaps whet our appetite to open other almost-forgotten doors for ourselves.

The College has had a long and notable history and we are fortunate that within the last generation its history has attracted the attention of distinguished scholars, some of whose work is included here. Staff and students, past and present (and others too!) now have the chance to retain, in collected form, words spoken on various occasions to different listeners.

This book is produced to mark the College's 450th anniversary. These years have been, at times, distinguished, stirring and troubled. They have reflected the life of the nation. The years ahead, for the College, promise to be no less challenging. The St Mary's College Fellowship (membership of which is open to all who have studied at the College) is happy to be associated with this time of celebration and to offer modest help in the publication of these papers.

David W.Clark,

Helensburgh,
December, 1989

President,
St Mary's College Fellowship

INTRODUCTION

It has been my great privilege to be Principal of St Mary's College in the University of St Andrews during the year 1989 when the College celebrated the 450th anniversary of its foundation. St Mary's Fellowship, whose president has graciously contributed a foreword, wished to play its part in the celebrations and decided to commission a volume of essays or lectures to commemorate the occasion. This little book is the outcome.

The main celebrations took place on Tuesday, 7th March, 1989. The day (gloriously sunny!) began with staff and students of the College processing from South Street to St Salvator's, the College Chapel, for a service of thanksgiving. The preacher at this service was Professor Jan Milic Lochman, of the University of Basel, and I am proud to be able to include his sermon as the opening chapter of this book. After luncheon in the Lower College Hall, there was a University Graduation Ceremony in the Younger Hall, presided over by the University's Principal and Vice-Chancellor, Professor Struther Arnott, at which honorary degrees were awarded as follows:

D.D. - Professor Lochman
   The Rt Reverend Professor J.A.Whyte, Moderator of the General Assembly of the Church of Scotland
   The Most Reverend and Rt Hon Robert Runcie, Archbishop of Canterbury and Primate of All England

LL.D.- Lord Mackay of Clashfearn, Lord Chancellor of Great Britain
   Professor A.J.Forty, Principal and Vice-Chancellor of the University of Stirling
   Professor M.J.Hamlin, Principal and Vice-Chancellor of the University of Dundee.

After the graduation ceremony, the company moved to the Buchanan Theatre to hear Professor G.H.M.Posthumus Meyjes of the University of Leiden lecture on the position and function of the Doctor of Divinity in mediaeval society and church. He has kindly consented to the inclusion here of this fascinating lecture (Chapter II). The day of celebration ended with a reception in Parliament Hall and a Senate Dinner in St Salvator's Hall. Celebrations continued, however, with a residential re-union and Summer School in July in University Hall (see Chapter IV), and ended with a Carol Service organised by the students of St Mary's in Holy Trinity Parish Church, St Andrews, on Sunday, 10th December (subsequently broadcast by the B.B.C.).

The chapters of this book reflect the title, being lectures delivered at various times over the last seven years. In 1983, the then Principal of St Mary's, Prof. William McKane, inaugurated the St Mary's College Lectures, a series of lectures delivered during the Candlemas term. He delivered the first series himself and these among others happily found their way into print as a contribution to this anniversary year as *Selected Christian Hebraists* (Cambridge University Press, 1989). Many of the lectures here were originally delivered as St Mary's Lectures (e.g. Chapters VIII, IX and XII). Others (e.g chapters IV and VII) were delivered to the St Mary's Summer School (a residential course held over five days each summer) or as the public Opening Lecture of the academic session (Chapter X).

1987 marked the centenary of the birth of that great St Mary's theologian, D.M.Baillie, 1986 having seen the centenary of the birth of his famous brother John. The Baillies' contribution to Scottish theology and Church was righly celebrated in St Andrews and form the subject of a special section here. This accounts for the presence of two 'guest' contributors, Professor A.C.Cheyne, emeritus Professor of Ecclesiastical History, and Professor John McIntyre, emeritus Professor of Divinity, both of New College in the University of Edinburgh, and to them I am deeply grateful for their permission to include their lectures.

It is appropriate that a volume such as this should tell at least something of the story of St Mary's College, and the "Historical" section accordingly includes a trilogy of lectures on the first century of the College's existence. 'Biblical' and 'Theological' sections complete the volume.

My fellow contributors and I have every reason to be grateful to the St Mary's College Fellowship for the support they have given this project. We should also like to acknowledge the generous support received from the managers of the A. & J. Deas Fund. Personally, I should like to thank Miss M.R.Blackwood and Miss S.M.Millar for their secretarial patience and skill, and Mr C.B.Bremner, of the University's Reprographic Services for his invaluable technical assistance.

St Andrews, December, 1989   D.W.D. Shaw

I. THE EXPERIMENT OF HOPE

- *A sermon preached by Professor Jan Milic Lochman, D.D., University of Basel, in the Collegiate Church of St Salvator on 7th March, 1989, on the occasion of the Commemoration of the 450th Anniversary of the Foundation of St Mary's College, University of St Andrews.*

I

When I was invited to preach on this solemn occasion a host of personal memories came alive for me. In my unforgettable academic year 1946-1947, this College and this Chapel became a place of lasting spiritual inspiration for me. The memories I am speaking about are, first of all, those of many faithful preachers - both from among my teachers like Principal Duncan, Professors Baillie, Dickie, Forrester . . . and of distinguished guest-preachers of those days like Reinhold Niebuhr and Emil Brunner. But there are also memories of the true atmosphere of worship in this Chapel, enriched by the treasury of music provided by the magnificent University Choir. And, last but not least, there are the happy memories of the regular Sunday pilgrimages from this Chapel to the harbour pier, to the place where the first missionaries were supposed to have landed.

In a sense, what I would like to do in this sermon is to issue an invitation to such a pilgrimage to the memorial of the first Christian missionaries, to the witness of their apostolic origins. I would like to attempt this by drawing attention to the apostolic word as it is written in 1 Timothy, 4.10: *'For to this end we toil and strive, because we have our hope set on the living God, who is the Saviour of all men, especially of those who believe.'*

The days in which these words were originally written were in many respects critical and dismal times. Culturally and socially, they were times of transition, of spiritual and moral crises and political threats. And for the small groups of Christians, there were additional bitter experiences of persecution from without and of spiritual agonies within. How often had those in charge of the Christian mission, the

Apostles, to ask frustrating questions: Why toil and why strive? Why not seek less dangerous and more rewarding walks of life?

With such questions as the background to our text the Apostle gives his answer: *'For to this end we toil and strive, because we have our hope set on the living God'.* It is amazing: those very people who had to face particularly painful agonies, the Apostles, were messengers of hope. They give a very clear reason for their attitude: *'We have our hope set on the living God '*. They confess the living God. And that confession changes their world view. The world as it is and with all its crises and destructive tendencies is still God's world. It has not sold out to the apocalyptic principalities and powers as so many contemporaries thought. Chaotic forces and blind fate did not have the ultimate say. As the story of Christ confirmed from its beginning to the end, this world is the sphere of God's concern and salvation. Therefore we cannot simply let it go, as fatalists would suggest. Christian mission is a resistance movement against fatalism. *'Therefore we toil and strive, because we have our hope set on the living God.'*

II

Am I mistaken, if I see traces of a similar spiritual orientation in the background of that particular event we are commemorating together today, the foundation of St Mary's College? The conditions 450 years ago were not particularly favourable. The post-mediaeval and pre-reformation period, was again an era of transition with typical uncertainties and dangers. Why toil and strive under such circumstances? Why not rather wait and see? The foundation (and, for that matter, the major part of the whole history) of St Mary's was and has remained an experiment of hope.

What was the *motivation* of our founding fathers to venture on this experiment? Centuries later, the words *In principio erat verbum* were incorporated in the St Mary's coat of arms. In this sentence, the motivation for our work in the College, for our toiling and striving in theology and education is well stated. It is, to start with, a double motivation. It points to the beginnings, to the origins, to the *principles of things* and pays respect to them. First things first: an academic enterprise is not a playground for volatile busybodies but a place of concentration on essentials. And these essentials are identified: In the beginning was *the Word.* An academic enterprise is a place where the word is honoured and the discipline of the word and devotion to the word is learned and practised. This is why the foundation and the work of a College is of such importance for the spiritual and moral climate of church and society. Particularly in these days of shaken values and of uncertain orientation, this is our mission in Colleges and Universities: to point to the ultimate values and principles and to the dignity of the word.

'In principio erat verbum' : this word reaches still deeper than what we have emphasised so far. This is the first sentence of St John's gospel. If we read it in the light of what follows we shall have to be more specific. This is not only a general statement about the first principles and the dignity of the word - this is the story of God's beginning and of its fulfilment in the Word that became flesh in Jesus Christ our Lord. In other words: this is the story of the *living God.* It is in this particular direction that the origins and the programme of our College point and focus our vision and our mission. This makes St Mary's in the deepest sense an experiment of hope. Forever, or rather, as long as the College lives and strives it will preserve and find its identity, its *raison d'être,* in this unmistakable orientation: *'For to this end we toil and strive, because we have our hope set on the living God ...'*

III

This is, no doubt, the essential message of the apostolic text. However, the text is not yet exhausted. It continues as follows: '... *who is the Saviour of all men, especially of those who believe'.* At first hearing, this is a curious sentence, a piece of rather awkward logic. The apostle states 'God is the Saviour of all', but then, as if he became less certain, he adds: 'especially of those who believe'. Yet precisely in this, let us say,'dialectic', he expresses something essential about the relation between the church and the world, about the unique vocation of Christ in its relation to our common human destiny. Both emphases have their importance.

7

That little word *'especially'*! There *is* a *special* vocation of Christians. To become and to remain Christian is not a simple matter, an easy road on which anything goes. It is a *militia Christi* - a struggle to remain faithful to that specific faith and hope and love to which the Apostles and the martyrs of all ages have borne their witness. In the footsteps of Jesus it is a narrow way on which specific initiatives of faith and hope and love have to be launched. A church which ever lost this Christ oriented distinctiveness would become as salt which had lost its savour. For the God of our salvation is related especially to those who believe.

And yet, that special vocation is in no way a privilege which Christians could preserve and enjoy for their private comfort only, monopolising it in a spirit of self-righteous separation. The hope of that special vocation is an open-ended hope. If really grounded in the living God, the exclusive hope of Christians initiates a process of all-inclusive compassion. The outstretched arms of the crucified Lord embrace the church *and* the world in a gesture of all-inclusive invitation. For the living God in Christ is *'the Saviour of all, especially of those who believe'*.

Once more I am thinking of the mission of St Mary's in this perspective. For the major part of its history, our College has been a Divinity school within the University. As such, it has served in response to its specific vocation. It has commemorated and interpreted the Christian message not only in the spirit of academic obligation and scholarly discipline but also in the spirit of devotion and commitment to the Truth of Christ. 1500 names of our former students are listed in our address list, working not only in Scotland and in the British Isles but also in many countries of Europe, both East and West, and on all the Continents of the world! This host of witnesses testifies to that special vocation as preachers, teachers and in all varieties of Christian action.

And yet, most of us are deeply grateful that this special preparation for this special vocation was offered to us not in separation from others but within the framework of the University. We have been enriched and challenged in contacts with our friends in other Colleges. We have taken away much and in manifold ways; and hope we have given something to this University as well. For the hope of our special vocation is the hope for all.

Hope for all - is it not the essential contribution which a theological College, faithful to its origins, can offer to its University? This has been at least my own personal experience and conviction particularly in the years in which I was privileged to act, as a theologian, as the head of my University of Basel (which is still, as St Andrews, an ancient European University).

All sciences and all scientists have their times of success and their times of failure. Every research institute echoes occasionally not only to the triumphant cry 'eureka! ' but also to the sighs of frustration and doubt. What's the point of it all? How frequently has the situation of a scientist - and that of modern man and woman generally - been likened to and interpreted in terms of the myth of Sisyphus: every day having to push the stone a little further up the hill of knowledge - only in the end to find that the stone rolls backward down the hill again.

A theological College has no ready-made solution to offer for such hope-less experiences. We participate in them and have our own agonies. Yet by pointing to the ultimate reality of God - remembering *In principio erat verbum!* - we recall the liberating dimension of an horizon of meaning that is not man-made and, therefore, not man-destructible. The horizon of meaning which encompasses every success and failure: 'Our eternal home'. With these visions it is never pointless and futile for us as human beings and as scientists toiling and striving in our Universities and research institutes to push or drag our small or huge stones a few paces up the hill. It is worthwhile to go ahead with our experiments of hope - in God's name and for humanity's sake. 'For to this end we toil and strive, because we have our hope set on the living God who is the Saviour of all men, especially of those who believe.'

*

One last word.   There is a Christian hymn which again and again has helped me on happy and less happy occasions.   I learned it, in its Czech version, as a young boy.   But it is a British hymn, one of those precious British gifts to ecumenical Christianity, which I learned in Scotland.   Let me recall its last words to conclude and, in a sense, to summarise, this sermon: our common prayer for the future way of the College we honour and love:

> O God, our help in ages past,
> Our hope for years to come,
> Be thou our guard while troubles last,
> And our eternal home.

II. QUASI STELLAE FULGEBUNT

'They will shine like the stars'

On the position and function of the Doctor of Divinity in mediaeval church and society

- G.H.M.Posthumus Meyjes

In 1516 a booklet was published in Paris on the subject of doctors holding a university degree and their privileges. Its author was a jurist called Pierre Lemonnier de Lesnauderie, rector of the University of Caen from 1505 till 1520. The introduction runs as follows: "Because the entire world is illumined by the learning of doctors and other scholars, and we should wander in darkness without those doctors who, as the saying goes, 'shine like the stars in the firament', I intend to tell something about them".[1] Making these words my own, I intend in my turn to give a brief account of the position and function of the theological doctor in mediaeval society and church. The connection with the book just mentioned can only be very partial, dealing as it does with juridical doctors rather than theological ones. The former were of an altogether different kind, distinct from the theologians if only because they were usually married. This condition occasioned Piere Lemmonier to treat a great number of questions which in no way applied to theologians, who indeed had opted for celibacy and therefore were not troubled with the kind of grotesque problems the rector of Caen had to rack his brains about, such as: "Should the *magister* call his wife *magistra*?" "Can he bestow donations to his concubine?" "Is it allowed for a doctor to beat his wife, clap her in irons, put her on bread and water?"[2] I am happy to

---

[1] **Opusculum de doctoribus et privilegiis eorundem**, Paris, 1516. It was reprinted under the title **De privilegiis doctorum** in **Tractatus illustrium..jurisconsultum**, Venetiis 1584, t.l8, fol 3v - 21r. The latter is the edition referred to throughout. The quotation in the introduction is to be found on fol.3v. Gabriel le Bras based his very copious article "Velut splendor firmamenti: le docteur dans le droit de l'Eglise médiévale", **Mélanges offerts à E. Gilson** (Toronto/Paris 1959), 372-388, on Pierre Lemonnier's booklet.

[2] Pierre Lemmonier de Lesnauderie, **De privilegiis doctorum**, pars I, q. XXXVI,fol.6v.

11

be in a position to disregard problems of that kind in all serenity, for the mediaeval theologians were far too lofty for such pedestrian casuistries. With true fortitude, they bore the sight of their juridical colleagues wrestling with them.

The high esteem in which the theologians were held in mediaeval society and the great influence they exerted on it are closely bound up with the then prevalent notion of order and hierarchy manifested in all contemporary institutions.[1] The Dutch historian Huizinga, in *The Waning of the Middle Ages*, remarks: "The notion of the subdivision of society into classes permeates all theological and political reflection in the Middle Ages." And he continues: "In all sectors of contemporary life this sense of hierarchy recurs." The terms used were "class", "order", "State", terms that covered a great number of groups which in our eyes are very heterogenous. They referred to social classes in our sense of the word, but also to professions. Current expressions were moreover "wedded state", "state of sin", "virginal state", "state of grace", and so on.[2]

This is not a detail we have to call special attention to in the present context. Suffice it to mention that each individual, no matter what his function was, belonged to a group which in its turn formed part of one all-comprising hierarchical whole. All "classes", "orders", and "states" were kept together by the notion that each separate group represented a divinely ordained arrangement and that it was both part of, and organically indispensable in, the divine world order, as essential and respectable as the thrones of heaven and the powers of the angelic hierarchy in the invisible world above.

Each class was assigned its proper function in the well-ordered ideal image of church and society; not necessarily consistent with its usefulness in daily life, but according to the degree of its sanctity, its

---

[1] For the following I am much indebted to the article by R. Guelluy, "La Place des théologiens dans l'Eglise et la société médiévales", **Miscellanea historica in honorem Alberti de Meyer** (Louvain/ Bruselles 1957), 571-589, which also offers a great deal of literature. Furthermore J.Leclerq, "L'idéal du théologien au Moyen Age", **Revue des Sciences Religieuses**, 21 (1947), 121-148.

[2] J. Huizinga, The **Waning of the Middle Ages**, London, 1924, 47ff.

commitment and proximity to the highest goal, God. Each social group had its proper task, accurately defined and laid down by statute. The purpose of this arrangement was to bring into harmony the distinct activities of the various individuals and groups with a view to the universal well-being desired by God. In the theoretical expositions of the mediaeval scholars on society, the equality by nature of all human beings was confessed on the one hand, while on the other the inevitable inequality as regards social ranking was upheld. Pope Gregory the Great (590 - 604), for instance, states that although all humans have by nature been created equal, yet at a later time a secret ordinance had been issued subordinating some people to others, according to the diversity of their talents. "This diversity", he says, "which is a consequence of sin, has been ordained by divine judgement."[1] Such a statement, to be multiplied at will, leads to the conclusion that social inequality was established and accepted both in theory and in practice in the Middle Ages; in contradistinction to modern times, in which it is being levelled out as much as possible - at least in principle. The hierarchically articulated structure of society corresponded to a specific mentality. The hierarchy of functions was regarded as postulated by God as well as by nature. This is the reason why, in spite of social inequality, there was nevertheless a relative measure of mutual respect; a respect that, at least initially, kept the discontent with the shortcomings of the leading classes within limits.[2]

All this has been brought up merely for the purpose of gaining a better insight into the role of the university in mediaeval social life. For us, who live in an age that allows us unlimited freedom to form an independent opinion on philosophical and theological questions, it is difficult to imagine a situation that was completely different. But different the situation in the Middle Ages certainly was. Scrutiny of reality and truth were seen as strictly socially determined functions, to be exercised by that specifically qualified institution that was the

---

[1] Gregory, Moralia, XXI.15 (**ML** 76, 203): "Omnes namque homines natura aequales sumus...omnes homines natura aequales genuit, sed variante meritorum ordine, alios aliis dispensatio occulta proponit. Ipsa autem diversitas, quae accessit ex vitio, recte est divinis iudiciis ordinata." Referred to by Walter Ullmann, **The Individual and Society in the Middle Ages**, Baltimore (1966), 14.

[2] Guelluy, a.c. pp. 571-581, Ullmann, o.c pp.15ff.

13

university. Corporately organized in faculties and nations, the university performed this duty in the public interest. Other groups and individuals had to steer clear of all investigation into reality and truth. And this was generally and ungrudgingly accepted, for, as was commonly thought, this was the order reflecting God's will and intention. The universities were established and safeguarded by rules and privileges enabling them to fulfill their duty. From the middle of the twelfth century onward, the universities had their specific Statutes, acknowledged by both the secular and the ecclesiastical authorities.

Now what was the position held by theological learning and its students in the mediaeval university? Theology took pride of place among all academic disciplines (arts, law, medicine). The theologians themselves contributed considerably to the composition of the mediaeval encyclopaedia of sciences, and I dare say they did not forget their own interests in the process. They designed an organic conception of sciences that was greatly influenced by Aristotle's philosophy.[1] In this conception, based on a hierarchy of principles, theology ranked first on the grounds of the fact that it was theology that meditated on and argued about the highest principle, God.

Corresponding to the hierarchy of sciences and learning there was a hierarchy of functions. Each scholar placed himself in the service of the particular kind of learning that best matched his function. Thus the theologian served the cause of the knowledge about Revelation and faith. That was his speciality, and to its exalted position he owed his prestigious standing within contemporary society. The doctors were treated with respect by princes, the great of the realm, people and church alike, because they had a thorough knowledge of Scripture and tradition. They kept watch over the hallowed heritage of the faith and divulged it for the benefit of church and society. Indeed was not theirs the superior learning because they had embraced the knowledge about God and made it the subject of their study? Moreover, since they were the professional interpreters of divine truth, they were supposed to be endowed with a very special grace. For with the hierarchy of functions corresponded a hierarchy of gifts of grace. And just as a prince was endowed with a special grace in order that he

---

[1] Guelluy, **a.c.**, 574-575

might rule, so also the theological doctor in order to expose the mysteries of salvation.[1]

Viewed against this background, it is hardly surprising that in the Middle Ages obdurate minds, heretics, were bound to be regarded as highly offensive. Indeed because they were convinced that they knew better than the scholars, they slighted the God-given hierarchical order of functions. Someone like Joan of Arc could not but meet with appalling misunderstanding from her interrogators - that happened in 1431 - because she refused to yield to the specialists and appealed to what she herself had witnessed. This was counted against her as a devilish intractability: an illiterate woman - an *indocta* - who vaingloriously thought that she could put her own good-for-nothing insight before the wisdom of the scholars. That was outrageous. Somebody like her deserved no better than to be swept from the face of the earth.[2]

So far I have mentioned the theological doctor mainly in connection with his social position and function. Let us now look more closely into his role in the church.

It may be posited that the comparatively independent doctor's position was a relatively late issue in history, for it did not exist prior to about 1200. Initially, the doctors constituted a unity with the ecclesiastical hierarchy, and it was only after and through the rise of the universities that the theological doctors as a body developed into a class of their own, also called masters, *magistri*. At the time of Pope Gregory the Great (590-604) the term *ordo doctorum*, the order of doctors, collectively denoted the bishops,[3] and continued to carry this meaning all along during the early Middle Ages, the period of feudalism, in which education was concentrated in the monastic and cathedral schools, and the ideal of ascesis and personal sanctity also determined

---

[1] Guelluy, **a.c.** 577-581

[2] Guelluy, **a.c.**, 572 n.2 (p.579). Notes 2.

[3] Yves M.-J. Congar, **Die Lehre von der Kirche,**. Von Augustin bis zum abendlaendische Schisma, Handbuch der Dogmengeschichte, ed. M. Schmaus et al., T.III fasc. 3c (Freiburg/Basel/Vienna 1971), 157ff.

the scholarly pursuit. Round about the beginning of the thirteenth century things began to change with the rise of the universities in the cities. The class of the *magistri* came into being, who together with the students pursued a totally novel scholarly ideal. The prime motive was now a rational exploration of truth and reality rather than personal sanctity and world renunciation. This was now the object of the dedication of the doctors who - essentially unlike their predecessors in this respect - no longer found satisfaction in reconciling the testimonies of Scripture and the Church Fathers. Instead, they introduced new authorities - Aristotle in particular - and in addition took the judgment of (recent) predecessors into consideration. Thus the Fathers joined the "moderns". Moreover, it was no longer grammar or rhetoric that came first, but logic. All this gave a wholly novel orientation to theology. Scholasticism was born, and it was the doctors who gave it birth.

They gave their lectures within the framework of the theological faculties. How they proceeded and what exactly their task implied will be discussed later on. At this point I should like to dwell for a moment on the more fundamental question of what their opinion was on instruction, its presuppositions and its limits. What does it actually mean when it is said that a teacher teaches a pupil? Is it at all possible for one person to teach someone else and call himself his master, teacher? Is not God the only one competent to do this? Such questions, brought up by all doctors, originated partly in philosophical, epistemological, and partly in theological contemplation. As to the latter, there is, for instance, a passage from the Gospel of St. Matthew that played a part: "You are not to be called rabbi, for one is your master, and you are all brethren" (Mt 23:8). To the people of the Middle Ages, the words "one is your master" (*unus est magister vester*, V.) signified that all knowledge and insight was inspired from on high, by God. But, this being so, what kind of role might have been reserved for a human intermediary of knowledge and insight? One may, moreover, well wonder what right such an intermediary might have to arrogate to himself the title of "master"! And, finally, in what way is this knowledge from on high received by man? How do his senses, his intellect, his soul, contribute to this process?

For our present purpose there is no need to elaborate on this issue. I only want to point out, in passing, that here as in so many other respects St Augustine has been the great source of inspiration. It was especially his early dialogue *de magistro* that for a long time determined the discussions on these problems.[1] Now St. Augustine was very close to Plato in that in his view knowledge and insight lie dormant in man's memory, to be awakened and activated by the kind of instruction that asks questions. In this process, the role of the teacher is only a modest one: he can only questioningly refer to the truth which has been present in the soul of the pupil all along. He may assist by smoothing the way for insight, but never will he be able to give or transmit knowledge. Very vividly and eloquently St.Augustine expresses his intention at the close of his *de magistro*, where he says: "Indeed do teachers teach with the intention of having their insights adopted and retained, and not the subjects as such which they pass on by means of words? Who, indeed, could have such an odd notion about knowledge that he should send his son to school in order to learn what the teacher thinks?... When being taught, the pupils will take counsel with themselves whether the truth is being told by, each according to his capacity, listening as closely as possible to the truth that lives in their innermost selves."[2]

Later theologians have often endorsed this pattern of St. Augustine's thought when they were occupied with epistemological problems, and in this context also put the question as to what, in fact, teaching amounted to. Thomas Aquinas, rather than following St. Augustine (and Plato) with regard to the theory of knowledge, clearly preferred to follow in Aristotle's footsteps; which, for that matter, makes little difference to his idea of what "teaching" implies. Far from denying that God, being the one and only true teacher, gives all knowledge and insight, he allows the human teacher more room besides. He compares the latter's function with that of a physician who, while not being able to create health, can contribute to it by aiding nature and by enabling her to conquer illness by her regenerative power. In a comparable way, he says, a human teacher can assist someone else's intellect by means of his words, his adequate use of language. A

---

[1] Text and translation of **de magistro** are to be found in **Oeuvres de Saint Augustin**, VI Dialogues philosophiques, III, ed. F.J. Thonnard (Paris, 1952, Bibliothèque Augustinienne), 14-121; "Notes complémentaires" 481-195.

[2] St Augustine, **de Magistro**, XIV, 45 (ed. Thonnard, 116).

teacher can show the way in order that the pupil's intellect will learn independently to discern truth from untruth.[1]

Let us now turn from this basic problem to one more familiar to us, a very modern problem in our eyes but one which in fact was already brought up in 1280 by a theologian from the Southern Netherlands called Henry of Gand. He hazards the harrowing question: can a woman be a Doctor of Divinity? In his answer, he distinguishes between being capable of teaching and being entitled to do so. As to the first he shows an astounding liberality, saying that everyone can teach - man or woman, young or old, regular or secular, cleric or lay, provided he/she has the required knowledge. This, to him, apparently is not the problem. The question, however, remains whether it is allowed for a woman to teach, whether she has the right to do so. How does he solve this problem?

In order to teach in one's official capacity, he argues, four stipulations must be met. The first requirement is steadfastness in a teacher, lest he turn away from the acknowledged truth foolhardily. Next, he should have perseverance. In the third place, he must have authority; and finally, he must be a person of vivid eloquence, in order that he may elevate his audience. Now our Henry discerns nothing of the sort in women. On the contrary. No perseverance in the proclamation of the faith, nor the strength to continue a work once begun. Moreover, she is far too weak by nature for her to dispute or otherwise appear in public. Nor does she dispose of the authority indispensable in any teacher, seeing that according to St. Paul she has been subordinated to the male prowess. The only thing - and now comes the sting - she incontestably does have is vivid eloquence, or less mildly put: garrulousness. But it is just too bad that in the case of women this gift does not meet its purpose, to wit: victory over sin, but, contrariwise, provokes it. In brief: no woman can be a Doctor of Divinity officially. Softening the blow somewhat, he hastens to add that of course women are very welcome teachers as long as it is a matter of teaching-duties on the basis of a benefice or for reasons of charity - always provided

---

[1] Thomas Aquinas, **de Veritate**, q. IX de magistro, a. 1: "Utrum homo docere alium possit et dici magister, vel Deus solus" in **Quaestiones disputatae**, I ed. Mandonnet(Paris 1925), 300-307 (304).

that her doctrine may be sound, her audience consist exclusively of women, and her teaching be not done publicly in a church.[1]

Reduced to a single formula, Henry of Gand's reasoning runs: *she*, a woman, *may* be able to teach, but it cannot be done, it just is not done. Indeed the structure of the world makes it impossible, a structure that is immovably fixed because it originates in God. And in this structure there is no room for female teachers; women have other duties apportioned to them. This is our scholastic's starting-point; and by his reasoning he tries to give it a rational basis. In other words, he works his way towards a system of values he sees as absolute, without letting himself be hampered by what we would call "claims of reality" or anything of the kind. He would not even understand what we are referring to, for "reality" in our sense of the word simply had no business to require anything in his view; it was something of the order of shapeless matter, and as such could only be passive and lie waiting for inspiration from above. Now this was the very process in which the theological doctors - and now I turn to the main issue of my argument - played such an important role. In what did their function actually consist?

Broadly speaking, the theological doctors were expected to have an active command of the knowledge of Revelation. They had to be able to explain the faith for the benefit of school and church, and to defend it against attacks from outside. The terms used for these and other doctoral activities were: *legere, disputare, determinare, praedicare* and *regere*. *Legere*, reading, meant: lecturing on the basis of Scripture, glosses, the Books of Sentences by Peter Lombard and the commentaries on them. *Disputare*, disputing, denoted both the accurate formulating of a problem and finding a solution to it by scholastic means. The entire process was also summarized with the term *determinare*, determining: the most appropriate and characteristic

---

[1] Henry of Gand, **Summae quaestionum ordinariarum**, Paris 1520 (reprint 1953), a. XI de doctore theologiae, 3: "Utrum mulier possit esse doctor". In my presentation I have used the article of M. Schmaus, "Der Lehrer und der Hörer der Theologie nach der Summa Quaestionum des Heinrich von Gent", **Universitas**. Dienst an Wahrheit und Leben, Festschrift für Bischof Dr. Albert Stohr, I (Mainz 1960), 3-16.

description of the doctrinal activity. Next to their teaching function, the doctors also had a preaching task. When they were being given their doctoral degree, they were explicitly authorized to preach, *praedicare*. The formal requirements which their sermons had to meet were highly complicated. A doctoral sermon had to consist of no less than 22 parts.[1] Due to these exacting requirements, the laborious pieces of work acquired what may well be called a Gothic structure. Finally - and how consoling this must sound to the present much-pestered successors to their mediaeval colleagues -, the doctors were also qualified to *administer (regere)*, and a great many of them have indeed discharged this duty.[2] I cherish the thought that they, like us, did so in deep gratitude for having been so favoured, no doubt without a flicker of self-pity or spite.

I shall now try to bring everything into greater relief by paying attention to a number of documents from the thirteenth and the beginning of the fourteenth centuries. By that time, the doctor's function was in full bloom. These documents express the doctors' responsibilities and duties in clear outlines. They belong to the so-called *disputationes de quolibet*, disputations on random subjects; debates very much like intellectual sparring matches. It was the custom at the Theological Faculty of Paris - at the time by far the most important one and in many respects the shining example for the University of St Andrews - to organize biannual disputations on random subjects. These so-called quodlibet disputations, supervised by a professor, were ordinarily held by senior students who acted as opponents and defenders respectively. The professor was charged with formulating a conclusive answer to the adduced pro- and contra-arguments. Mostly the audience provided the subjects, the purpose of which was to foster and at the same time give evidence of proficiency in one's optional subject.[3]

---

[1] Lowrie J. Daly, **The Medieval University 1200 - 1400** (New York 1961), 159. See also, besides the article of J. Leclercq mentioned in n.3, his "Le magistère du predicateur au XIIIe siècle", **Archives d'Histoire Doctrinale et Litteraire du Moyen Age**, 15 (1946), 105-147. Also M.-M. Davy, **Sermons universitaires parisiens de 1230-1231**, Paris, 1931.

[2] Cp. C.H.Haskins, **The Mediaeval Professor**, (New York 1923), 67.

[3] P.Glorieux, **La littérature quodlibétique de 1260 a 1320**, 2 vol. (Kain 1925, 1935). Daly, o.c., 150 ff.

Without overmuch imagination one can visualize the opportunities this procedure offered to prankishly or maliciously inclined students. Indeed it gave them a wonderful chance of embarrassing their teachers with ticklish, complicated or frivolous questions. So, for instance, Henry of Gand was faced with the question whether a freak that had been born with two heads should for that reason be baptized twice. On the other hand, one may assume that some teachers will have pounced with delight on such intellectual skirmishes, because of the opportunities they offered to prove their acumen and dexterity in combat. But this aspect of the quodlibet disputations is not primarily what makes them so interesting to us; it is rather the fact that in these debates not only theological but also topical questions came up for discussion to which the so-called quodlibetic literature owes its significance for us.

I can only touch upon the most important features out of the plethora this literature contains.[1] In the first place, there are a number of random questions pertinent to the responsibility of the academic theologian with regard to the ecclesiastical practice. One of the tasks of the doctors consisted in instructing the clergy. Often the clerics had been educated at the university, where they had been sitting at the doctors' feet. What they had learned from their teachers they transmitted to the faithful by the traditional means: administering the sacraments, worship, pastoral care, religious instruction (catechism), preaching. Such a process of transmission, smooth, habitual and well-defined, gives the impression of being uncomplicated and a matter of course. In practice, however, the education of the priests was often found wanting. Hence the question crops up time and again: are the doctors to be blamed for the ignorance of the priests and for what is lacking in their formation?[2]

Nowadays we would formulate the question differently, but its embarrassing content remains much the same. Apparently the tension between the requirements of university and church (or society), or rather between scholarly research and professional

[1] See the registers on the work of Glorieux, s.v. docteur.

[2] Leclercq, "L'Idéal", 123ff., giving the text of Guillaume Pierre de Falegar's **quodl. q.**15. according to BNlat. 14305 fol.152. Notes 3.

education, was felt as early as the thirteenth century. Characteristically, the negative answer was given in a strictly hierarchical reasoning. The argumentation ran as follows: the course of knowledge, like water in a Roman fountain, runs from the highest level - where the doctors sit enthroned - via the intermediate level to the lowest one, that of the priests. Now should the knowledge of the latter prove to be deficient, it is not the doctors who are accountable, but the fact that the priests concerned were simply not equal to the demands of the education they had received. They would have done better not to choose a teacher on the level of higher education but one from a lower level. So no blame attaches to the doctors whatsoever. On the contrary, for their position in the hierarchical structure allows them not to simplify matters. Indeed it is their very duty to treat only the more complicated problems of faith and ethics, an obligation they can not shirk without arrogating to themselves the duties assigned to others, i.e. the lower echelons. And that would be very wrong indeed, for had not Aristotle rightly stressed that the well-being of society is best served when everyone does what he is by nature intended to do?[1]

This argument testifies yet again to the preponderance of hierarchical thinking in the Middle Ages, and also shows that any tension between ideal and reality was neutralized in favour of the ideal. In the final analysis each deficiency of reality is explained by pointing to a neglect of the hierarchical order. This order it is that has the final say in the matter; this is the prince, and bleak reality remains the beggar.

In 1267, a certain Gérard d'Abbeville was asked why doctors spent more time on disputations than on preaching. Would it not be much more worthwhile to uplift the minds of the believers than to contradict the unbelieving? In his answer the author adopts a distinction made by St Augustine (*de Trin.* XIV, 1) and argues that there are two kinds of knowing (*scire*). One is an elementary kind of knowing which is transmitted by preaching, the other is a more reflective, theological knowing, acquired by means of reasoning and disputing. The former, he says, suffices for ordinary lay people, for, armed with the elementary religious knowledge passed on to them in the sermons, they can attain eternal life. But the matter does not end at that point. For it is

---

[1] Leclercq, "L'Idéal", 124.

necessary that the faith be defended and rationally elucidated vis-a-vis heretics. And this requires much more: scholarship is required. We cannot do without disputations, that is to say without a scientific method. In other words, it is imperative that there be doctors.[1] On the other hand - and yet again one question leads to another - indispensability presupposes that the subjects investigated and taught by the doctors are indeed useful and valuable. This being so, what about a doctor asking curious, improper (meaningless) questions (*questiones curiosae*)? Will he fall from grace?

Before giving an answer to this disturbing question, another author and colleague of Gérard d'Abbeville, Hervé de Nédellec, examines how one is to understand these "curious questions", among which he numbers all questions not directly relevant to salvation for three reasons: either they are contrary to salvation (black magic), or they are indifferent as regards salvation (geometrics), or, finally, they may be involved in it but as such do not relate to it (logic). On the basis of this distinction follows a very comprehensive answer, taking into consideration the doctor's intention in bringing up his "curious question". I shall give two examples. When he broaches a question of the kind with the intention of refuting an error, then sin is out of the question; on the contrary, such an investigation cannot but be called laudable. But if, conversely, he brings up such questions randomly or for reasons of personal vanity, then sin he does. And he is guilty of mortal sin when he, by giving all his time and attention to investigations of this kind, neglects his proper task altogether. Being a doctor, he is obliged to explain and defend the truth in the interest of universal well-being. Should he neglect this duty in order to serve his own purposes, he then fails to live up to his position, is untrue to his teachership (*magisterium*), indeed is wanting in love for God and his neighbour.[2]

The answer in its turn leads to a new problem, formulated explicitly by Godefroy de Fontaines (end of the thirteenth century), who puts the following questions: Is a doctor permitted to make doctrinal statements on matters that only the pope can pronounce on? and: may he make

---

[1] Leclerce, "L'Idéal", 128ff, **quodl**. X, q. 1, to **BN** lat. 16405 fol.79.

[2] Leclercq, "L'Idéal", 131ff. **quodl**. II, q. 16 (ed Venetiis 1513, fol 65v-66r).

a stand against an episcopal pronouncement when he is convinced that the opposite is true?[1] These questions touch on the complicated relationship between doctor and doctrinal authority in the Middle Ages. How did the authority of the doctors relate to that of the church in terms of hierarchy, priesthood and jurisdiction? How did their authority with regard to teaching relate to that of the pope in his capacity of the most qualified teacher? How were the limits and the differences defined?

As has been said before, the doctors were called to reveal and defend the truth in the public interest. That was the task assigned to them by medieval society and church alike. As a body, they formed a corporation of professional researchers of the truth whose rights and duties were contingent on the corporation.[2] But what matters here is that they had no hierarchical standing in the ecclesiastical sense. They were qualified to preach but had not been ordained in principle, and consequently were not entitled to administer the sacraments.[3] Individually they may have been ordained before or after taking their doctoral degree, but the doctorate as such was not intrinsically connected with priesthood, and therefore separate from the ecclesiastical hierarchy.

This, however, does not mean that they had no connection with the church at all. Indeed not, for they were members in their capacity of Christian believers, and often the connection also lay in their being beneficiaries holding a church living. Apart from this, however, the

---

[1] **Quodl.** III, q. 10, resp. **quodl.** VII q. 18 (ed. de Wulf/Pelzer, II, p. 218, pp.402-404). Cf. also **Johannes Brevicoxa** in **Johannis Gersonii Opera Omnia** (ed. Dupin), I, c.840.

[2] M.-D. Chenu, **Introduction à l'étude de St. Thomas d'Aquin** (Montreal/Paris 1954), 18ff. See also my **Jean Gerson, Zijn kerkpolitiek en ecclesiolgie** ('s-Gravenhage 1963), 267ff.

[3] Thomas Aquinas, **Contra impugnantes Dei dultum et religionem**, cap.II, An religioso liceat docere, in **Opuscula genuina theologica**, IV, (ed. Mandonnet, Parisiis 1927), p. 18: "(ad officium docendi) sacer ordo non requiritur". See further Pierre Lemonnier de Lesnauderie, **Dee privilegiis doctorum**, pars I, q. XXVII, fol. 6v: " Quaero an per doctoratum imprimitur character..quod non. Nam non datur hoc officium ex impresso charactere sed ex potestate officii. Et est quaedam authorizatio et declaratio, quo declaretur dignum ad officium doctrinae, et datur ei authoritas, ut doceat."

only formal bond linking them to the ecclesiastical hierarchy and the teaching profession consisted in the licentiate's oath they took before the chancellor of the university. The chancellor represented the pope, to whom he mostly owed his appointment; his main task was to guard over the orthodoxy within the university. I take my example from the form of licence used by the Chancellor of the University of St Andrews, which was copied from that of the University of Paris. Till 1560 the form of licence used at St Andrews to run as follows:

"I N.N. Chancellor of the University of St Andrews in the authority of God Almighty, of the Apostles Peter and Paul, and of the Apostolic See, confer on you the licence to read, to dispute, to administer, to preach and to exercise all other activities in a theological faculty, here and elsewhere on earth, in the Name of The Father ..."[1] - Thus, the licentiate's oath expressed obedience to the Apostolic See.

Now how did the authority of the theological doctor relate to the doctrinal authority of the pope? For an answer to this we have to look to the terminology. The term "authentic" was reserved exclusively for papal (and conciliar) doctrinal pronouncements, while statements by doctors were called "scholastic" or "magistral". In both cases the former was of an absolute nature and the latter was relative.

The range covered by the doctors' authority in lectures and disputations had its limits, the most important of which was, obviously defined by dogma. Once an issue had been established and declared an article of faith by papal or conciliar decree, the doctors had to leave it alone unless for the purpose of explaining or defending it. Conversely, the doctor was perfectly free to expand on any issue not - or not yet - declared a tenet of the faith. In that case he was free to formulate opinions and so initiate discussions between schools, scholars and orders. But he had to abandon his opinion as an error when persuaded by rational arguments that it was contrary to the established doctrine.[2]

---

[1] Robert Korr Hannay, **The Statutes of the Faculty of Arts and the Faculty of Theology at the period of the Reformation**, St Andrews 1910, (St Andrews University Publications no. VII), 69ff.

[2] W. Borth, **Die Luthersache** (causa Lutheri) **1517-1524** (Luebeck/Hamburg 1970), 22ff., and my "Het gezag van de theologische doctor in de Kerk der Middeleeuwen. Gratianus, Augustinus Triumphus, Ockham en Gerson", **Nederl. Archief voor Kerkgeschiedenis** 63 (1983), 105-128.

Taking stock of both forms of authority and their interrelationship, they can not be denied rationality. There is a logic in the distinctions and boundaries that precludes confusion. From the point of view of doctrinal development there was a reasonably harmonious relationship between the respective representatives. The doctors, for instance, were invariably included in the preparation of conciliar decisions, and also in other respects their special knowledge was duly being used to advantage. Yet it is remarkable that, especially in the later Middle Ages, a certain tension began to take shape between the doctors on the one hand and representatives of the hierarchy on the other. The doctors often sharply censured the church for tolerating a great many abuses. This criticism was mainly levelled at the church's secularization, her wealth, her bureaucratic, top-heavy administration, her extortionate fiscal system.

Now the remarkable thing is that the theological doctors were readily inclined to hold their juridical colleagues, the canonists, responsible. Indeed it can hardly be denied that the latter, ever since their group had grown into a separate class in the course of the twelfth century, had had exceptional opportunities to get their ideas accepted in the church. In this they had the strong support of the church leaders, who in those centuries (and long afterwards) virtually without exception used to be canonists and not theologians. The result of their activity was that the appearance of the church was changed considerably. Around 1300 the juridical features had become predominant. With her commandments and prohibitions the church dominated everybody, regardless of rank or position. She was an exclusive, strictly hierarchically organized institution, with her own highly developed law; a state above the states in which the clergy were the rulers and the lay people the subjects.[1]

Now the crucial point is that gradually the theologians began to take more exception to this church structure with its obsession with power and its pretension to be the highest norm, being deaf to considerations of piety and deeper learning. The theologians accused the canonists of having introduced an autonomous way of thinking in the church, a way of thinking that, heedless of theology and piety, speculated and

---

[1] H.E.Feine, *Kirchliche* **Rechtsgeschichte**, I (Weimar 1954), 266-267.

literally decreed *ad libitum*. William of Ockham, about 1330, reminds his pupils of the ways in which theologians thought of their contemporary canon lawyer colleagues:

"First of all I wish you to know that theologians in their hearts deeply despise contemporary canonists as being blockheads, presumptuous, imposters, deceivers, hairsplitters and ignoramuses."[1] Why this unbridled contempt? Because modern canonists, although they know all laws, are completely ignorant of natural science, moral science and theology. Obviously, also the church leaders were included in the criticism of the canonists.[2]

Thus, schematically, the background has been given of the how and why of the widening gulf between university and church, theologians and hierarchical authorities from the end of the thirteenth century onwards. The university - in particular that of Paris and her theological faculty - began to distance herself from papal interference and to take autonomous decisions with respect to doctrinal matters. When, in 1303, consulted by the French King Philip the Fair, who was at odds with Pope Boniface VIII, the university on her own initiative suggested the organization of a general council. Not very long after, she denounced certain notions expressed in a sermon by Pope John XXII. Ockham developed the thesis that doctors should not as a matter of course endorse a papal doctrinal decision but first examine it thoroughly. During the Schism (1378-1417), when western Christendom had to put up with two - and for some time even three - popes, it was yet again the University of Paris that, on its own initiative and authority, pronounced judgments on doctrinal questions through her teachers and doctors. Telling is also the broad delegation of theological doctors to the councils of Pisa, Constance and Basel. A unique phenomenon that was not greatly appreciated by the hierarchy - it was halted before it would develop into a custom.

These examples may serve to show that in the later Middle Ages the church increasingly lost its hold on theologians and theological

---

[1] Ockham, **Dialogus** I, 1 cap. 3 (ed. Goldast, 401.39-42)

[2] See my **Jean Gerson et l'Assemblée de Vincennes (1329)** (Leiden 1978), pp. 88ff and the literature mentioned there. For Ockham, see **Dialogus**, VII, cap. 42ff. (Goldast, pp. 696-709); c.14 (451).

faculties. Matters did not come to such a pass that it resulted in a breach, yet it should be noted that the university became more and more an instrument of civil power, certainly so in France. The splendid structure of learning designed and built up in preceding centuries began to show alarming cracks during this period. The relationship between faith and reason, theology and philosophy, lost much of its harmonious equilibrium in the course of the fourteenth and fifteenth centuries. On the other hand university education, increasingly concentrating on logic, no longer met the wishes of all educated people. Some of them resorted to the broad movement of humanism that in part flourished outside the universities. Others took refuge in mystical movements which existed apart from, if not hostile to, official scholarship.[1] In the sixteenth century these trends continued and developed, which resulted in drastic changes in the position and function in the then society and churches.

I have invited your attention for a subject belonging to an institution that may well be called one of the finest issues of the Middle Ages: the university. No need to hold forth on the changes since then. In any case the theological doctors have dropped the presumptuous notion of "shining like the stars in the firmament".[2] But, to continue and conclude in the same vein, they are still very much interested in the Sun - or, less metaphorically, the Source of illumination from on high.

---

[1] Guelluy, a.c., p. 582; Congar, **Die Lehre**, 158.

[2] The title of this article derives from Dan. 12:3, a passage that in the Middle Ages was often used in connection with the doctors. Cp Pierre Lemonnier de Lesnauderie, **De privilegis doctorum**, part II, q. 27, fol. 8r, and the references mentioned there. A 17th-century reminiscence is to be found in John Donne's "A Litany XIII, The Doctors" (**The Complete English Poems**, ed. A.J. Smith,Penguin, p. 321):

> "Their zeal may be our sin. Lord let us run
>
> Mean ways, *and call them stars*, but not the sun"

III. A Trilingual College for Scotland

The Founding of St Mary's College[1]

- James K.Cameron

The founding and erecting of Colleges as constituent parts of universities has been a significant feature throughout academic history, especially in the fifteenth and early sixteenth centuries. Among the universities of the continent colleges, as essentially "places in which students could live and have the necessary freedom for study and intellectual progress", formed a distinctive part of their early development. Colleges existed at French, Italian and German universities, and subsequently in the English universities. At both Oxford and Cambridge the development was particularly pronounced, where a somewhat independent pattern providing not only board and lodging but also instruction was followed.

The most highly celebrated college on the Continent was the House of the Sorbonne, founded by Robert de Sorbonne, for men who had already graduated in Arts and were entered on the long and arduous course leading first to the Bachelorship in Divinity and then the Doctorate. In the Italian Universities, during the sixteenth and first half of the seventeenth centuries colleges flourished. At Padua for example, some twenty such foundations were established between 1512 and 1653. In Germany we may cite the University of Heidelberg where the *Collegium Artstarum* founded by Conrad of Gelnhausen, the University's first chancellor, followed "the model of the Sorbonne". Similar developments appear to have taken place at Cologne and at Louvain where the university "retained the character of a federation of many colleges until the Reformation". Louvain also had four *paedagogia* "which (unlike the colleges proper) were under the direct

---

[1] In the preparation of this lecture I have greatly benefited from help most willingly given by Mr R.N. Smart, the University archivist and by Dr R.G. Cant. In the discussion of the writings of Archibald Hay I am particularly indebted to the article by Dr. E.K. Cameron, "Archibald Hay's 'Elegantiae'. Writings of a Scots Humanist at the College de Montaigu in the time of Budé and Beda", in **Acta Conventus Neo-Latini Turonensis**, ed. J-C. Margolin, Paris 1980, 277-301.

management of the faculty of arts". In Scotland similar developments followed the founding of its three mediaeval universities. St Andrews had at its outset a paedagogium under the direct control of the Faculty of Arts, which occupied the site on which Parliament Hall now stands. But when Bishop James Kennedy and his successor, Archbishop Stewart, founded their colleges, St Salvator's in 1450 and St Leonards in 1512, they were following an already well established academic pattern. At Glasgow Bishop Turnbull founded the university in 1451. It's pedagogy was frequently referred to as *Collegium facultatis*. Bishop Elphinstone founded the University of Aberdeen in 1495 and in 1500 began the erection of the College of St Mary in Nativity, now King's College. These Scottish plans of establishing colleges within university foundations were similar to developments in Spain, for example at Alcalà.

Universities and colleges have almost by their very nature an inbred conservatism, so that change can often only be brought about by confrontation, by the creation of a new and rival foundation. One of those forces which confronted and challenged the universities North of the Alps in the late fifteenth and early sixteenth centuries was the new Renaissance Humanism. Surprisingly enough the most significant beginnings were to be made in two of the most philosophically and theologically conservative of universities, Louvain and Paris, universities with which St Andrews University had had since its foundation the closest of relations. In 1517 Jerome Busleyden, a friend of Erasmus, bequeathed the bulk of his wealth, mainly derived from ecclesiastical sources, also his extensive collection of manuscripts and books, for founding in Louvain a centre dedicated to fulfilling the educational aims of northern Erasmian humanism. The name of the new centre, *Collegium Trilingue* clearly indicated its purpose.

The earliest use of the word *trilinguis* to refer to the Biblical tongues and to claim proficiency in them is found in Jerome's Apology against Rufinus. Erasmus, Jerome's most distinguished sixteenth century editor and advocate of educational, theological, and ecclesiastical reform, was deeply impressed by Jerome's emphasis on the study of the original languages and early texts of the Bible and espoused enthusiastically Laurentius Valla's philological and critical approach, in which he saw the instrument that would make possible the renewal of religious thought. Thus at Paris and in Oxford Erasmus began to form his own design "to reform the Church from within by a renewal of biblical theology, based on the philological study of the New Testament text and supported by a knowledge of patristics, itself renewed by the same methods". His programme demanded a knowledge of Hebrew, Greek, and Latin. This emphasis on the three languages as the essential philological basis for theological study and ecclesiastical renewal is the background to the foundation and development of the concept of the trilingual college. To achieve the objective of the northern humanists - the revitalisation of theology and of the church by the study of the scriptures in the original languages - it was necessary to provide colleges to aid the young students and to find scholars competent to teach them, colleges that were not to be dominated by the traditional philosophical and theological studies.

We have briefly mentioned the Collegium Trilingue at Louvain. In Spain Cardinal Ximines established the new university at Alcalà, which soon concentrated its attention on trilingual studies, and which was to give us the great Complutensian Polyglot Bible. However, a trilingual college did not come into being until 1528. In France King Francis I provided the Noble and Trilingual Academy, the College of Royal Lecturers, later known as the Collège de France. Mention must also be made of Bishop Fox's founding of Corpus Christi College in Oxford in 1517. At Cambridge "Lady Margaret, under the guidance of Bishop Fisher founded first Christ's and then St John's to be houses of the new studies". Louvain, Alcalà, and Paris rose rapidly to distinction. Similar attempts were made at other established centres, for example at the new University of Wittenberg, soon to blaze into prominence, and at Vienna, Leipzig, Heidelberg and Ingolstadt, all bastions of orthodoxy, and still others came into existence much later and in a quite different dress as academies of the Reformed Churches in Switzerland, the Rhineland, France, the Netherlands and Scotland. What, however, is not generally known is that as early as the third decade of the 16th century not only were proposals made to establish a trilingual College in Scotland's oldest university, but that the College, whose 450th foundation we now celebrate, was by some interested scholars intended from the outset to fulfil such a role.

At the beginning of the sixteenth century St Andrews had two foundations, the original pedagogy erected in 1412, and Bishop Kennedy's substantially built and richly endowed St Salvator's College dating from 1450. Partly as a result of this latter foundation and partly on account of its own inadequate endowment the fortunes of the pedagogy were on the wane. The young Archbishop Alexander Stewart, who had studied under Erasmus, conceived "a plan of reorganising and erecting it into a proper College" in 1509. There is no evidence that he planned for it a trilingual basis. He was in fact "diverted from his first intention by Prior John Hepburn" and "converted to his project of transferring the Hospital and Church of St Leonard" into a "College for Poor Clerks of the Church of St Andrews" - better known as St Leonard's College - whose principal objective was the provision of better education for novices of the Augustinian Order which served the metropolitan Church. Whatever plans Alexander Stewart might have had of introducing the new learning to his new college were terminated by his untimely death at Flodden in 1513.

However, St Leonard's College flourished, but the task of reviving the pedagogy remained until Archbishop James Beaton was translated from Glasgow to St Andrews in June 1523. If the new archbishop, returning to the seat of his own *alma mater*, wished to give in St Andrews practical expression of his academic interests as he had attempted at Glasgow and as Bishop Elphinstone had been doing at Aberdeen, then he needed to look no further than the Pedagogy for a suitable outlet.

The Archbishop put off little time in despatching a supplication to Rome for a licence to erect a college for the benefit of those poor priests and clerks of the archdiocese who wished to study *bonae artes et literae*. All that was requested, it has to be noted, conformed to the old pattern and there is no indication that Beaton had personally any intention of introducing the new learning. His nephew, and subsequently his coadjutor and successor, David Beaton, the future Cardinal, who had just returned from ten years in Paris, and who was fully aware of the academic changes that were being effected there, was undoubtedly behind the project. At Paris he must have known well the strong contingent of Scottish scholars who attended and taught within that university, and must have discussed with them the future of Scottish academic education, and as we shall see some of them were wholeheartedly committed to the new humanist educational programme. Further, in a period of rising Beaton fortunes it is not fanciful to see the Scottish Archbishop, who was also Chancellor of the Realm, as one who wished to emulate his English counterpart, Cardinal Wolsey, who in 1525 (the year of Beaton's Supplication to Rome) had begun work on his great college in Oxford - itself a reorganisation of an earlier foundation. Further within St Andrews "Eminent newcomers" such as George Lockhart (D.Theol. of Paris), John Major, "The mastermind among them" and Alexander Ayton who had "brought back the learning of Paris and Louvain" were also active and were associated at this time with the pedagogy. Looked at from a variety of perspectives the projected College of St Mary of the Assumption, the new name proposed for the re-vitalised pedagogy, may then be construed partly as an attempt of the Beatons to re-establish their prestige, partly as an attempt by distinguished scholars who had returned from abroad to bring new life to the oldest of the university's foundations, new balance to the university, and the benefits of education to a larger section of the priesthood, and partly as an attempt to provide in Scotland a base for the new humanist programme that had captured the minds of some of Scotland's aspiring young scholars at Paris.

These young men at Paris, representing the rising generation, had come under the influence of the new learning. They had been keeping a close eye on what was happening in St Andrews where they saw the opportunity to bring to Scotland the benefits of that new learning - an opportunity that should not be missed. At first encouraged by the efforts of Archbishop James Beaton in 1525, they found themselves frustrated in their expectations by his procrastination, by his failure to act, despite the fact that the Pope had granted his Supplication, which, however, had been rendered void by the death of the Pope. John Major gave up hope of being able to accomplish anything in the face of the delay and transferred to St Salvator's. However, negotiations with Rome were renewed a little over a decade after the Supplication of 1525 largely on account of pressure exerted by John and Archibald Hay, kinsmen of the Archbishop, and scholars at Paris.

John, who held the parsonage of Tyningham, returned to Scotland and to St Andrews and took legal steps to further the college plan. The original project had largely failed for lack of adequate endowment. The Archbishop had promised in his supplication to provide for it from his own income - *de bonis sibi a Deo collatis*. Hay arranged to resign his benefice by proxy at Rome in order that it, along with that of Tanadyce (held by the Archbishop's chamberlain, Henry Lumsden) be appropriated to the "new foundation". This action, which provided a means for securing the required endownment led to the issuing in February 1538 by Pope Paul III of a bull. This bull, which incorporates the second Supplication is in fact the appropriation of the two parishes, Tyninghame and Tanadyce, to the projected college. It also incorporates the licence sought by James Beaton for the erection of the college. The Archbishop had secured the right to found and to grant extensive powers to his college, powers that were equal in everything to those of the university - and by the annexation of the two parishes in perpetuity the required endowment. From other sources it is known that he was taking steps, in agreement with the metropolitan chapter, to annex to the College the parish of Inchbrayock, for which action he had not sought papal sanction.

Meanwhile in Paris John Hay's brother Archibald had been seeing through the press his *Oratio pro collegii erectione* addressed to his uncle, the Archbishop. It was published in September 1538 at Paris. Today it is indeed a rare document. The only known copy - in all probability Beaton's own - was for long in the Library of York Minster. It is now preserved with that Library in the Library of the University of York. Within a year of its publication the *Oratio* was followed by Hay's much longer and better known *Ad D(ominum) Davidem Betoun Panegyricus*. Hay had been incorporated in Paris in 1531 and obtained his licence in 1537; he became procurator of the German nation in 1539. His student days in Paris had been spent at the time when the Royal Lecturers had established for themselves a European reputation, and Hay had been enjoying a varied and successful career, first as a regent at the Collège de Montaigu and later at the Collège du Plessis. His literary activity at this time, showed Hay as "a convinced humanist in taste and doctrine".

In the *Oratio* and in the *Panegyricus* Hay set out his vision of the new St Andrews College that was in his expectation to arise from the ancient pedagogy. He advocated nothing less than the foundation of a Trilingual College markedly different from that proposed in the Supplications to Rome in 1525 and 1536, and the ensuing papal bulls.

"Hay saw the example of Europe as a clear prompting to encourage the building of a college on more humanist lines than those envisaged in the recent papal bull". In the *Oratio* he stressed the need to advance the study of letters, especially those that were conducive to piety and repeatedly mentions the great fame that the Archbishop would bring upon himself by erecting this *magnificum gymnasium*, which he later referred to as *egregium hoc domicilium Musarum*. Much is written to encourage the prelate by way of flattery and admonition, much in praise of those who support learning and of learning itself. *"Sed si quisquam literas sustulerit ipsum solem de mundo sustulisse videbitur, omnia sine his manca sunt, nihil permanens, nihil perfectum; neque aer quo vivimus tam est necessarius quam harum usus."*[1] If the Archbishop puts his hand to this work, he will be recalling all the clergy to a more praiseworthy form of life, he will be sustaining *politiores literas*, protecting them by his authority, adorning them with his splendour, and encouraging the most erudite professors by providing them with magnificent salaries; and, by building up a library of the most approved authors, his most generous *animus* will influence other princes to do the same.

In his outline of the curriculum *grammatica* formed "the basis of the whole pyramid" - the entrance leading to all sciences; poetry, part of grammar, was defined as *philosophia morum* and was praised in these words. *Nam heroicarum virtutum est buccinatrix navigationum, tumultuum bellorum, denique rerum omnium fidissimum speculum.*[2] Rhetoric came next, praised for its own sake and for what it gives to

---

[1] "Whoever would deprive us of letters is to be likened to him who would deprive the earth of the sun itself. Without letters all is defective; nothing abides, nothing is complete; not even the air by which we live is for us as indispensable as the use of literature."

[2] "It trumpets abroad the gallantry of heroes, of those who go on voyages, who take part in insurrections and in wars. Indeed it is the most trustworthy mirror of all things"

the State. Then follows history, *rerum gestarum imaginem,... neque ullum sit speculum vivacius in quo se quisque contempletur ad mores componendos vitamque innocenter cum lauda et dignitate transeundam.*[1] He has indeed a lofty conception of the benefits of the study of history. It was to be followed by the study of mental, moral, and natural philosophy of which, he comments, nothing too high can be said. Finally, at the pinnacle of the pyramid, is theology, the Queen of all academic disciplines. But not theology as traditionally taught. In true humanist fashion emphasis was placed on the need to understand the biblical tongues. If theology is studied without the languages it is utterly, completely blind - *quando absque linguarum cognitio pene caeca est.* There is at this point no detailed reference to the languages. Only once did he use the word *trilinguis.* As was to be expected there is no mention whatever of dialectic - the absence of which induced one conservative reader to add the marginal comment, *Proh pudor!* - For shame!

Hay concluded this little humanist gem by urging the Archbishop to avoid all further delay in erecting the College. In the name of all *studiosi*, he begged that the work be put in hand that all may drink from the purest fountain of letters, and that the everflowing rivers might scatter abroad their gold. Never has there been a work more acceptable to all good men. Nor indeed was there, he maintained, a lack of learned men able to accomplish it. He mentioned by name one of his fellow students in Paris, who would consider it no small part of happiness to see this work carried out - a man of outstanding uprightness and erudition - John Douglas, of whom more will have to be said.

The *Panegyricus* - Hay's second work on the foundation of the college - suffers from its inordinate length, but its place in Scottish humanist literature is assured. He expected David Beaton who had succeeded his uncle as Archbishop to carry through his project. In his hands he placed this sacred hope. Beaton had secured a good education; he had studied at Paris under the most erudite scholars where he had seen the

---

[1] It is the image of the past...nor is there any mirror more lively in which we may contemplate ourselves for the ordering of our ways and of a blameless, praiseworthy and honourable life".

benefit of the study of languages for some ten years. Much is therefore expected of him in the much needed reform of the Church. Beaton was reminded that only by outstanding deeds do men approach the divine nature, that only those who do not neglect to do good will sow the seed whose harvest will nourish others. Liberality and charity were shown not just in looking after the poor but also in providing for the young the opportunity to undertake literary studies, and promoting the learned to higher degrees. Further, the erecting of the College would be a cause of admiration in the years to come. The task, Hay acknowledged, would be difficult, the expense great. With humanist eyes he regarded the previous four hundred years as a period of *inimicissima barbaries*. In its place he hoped to see begun in Scotland a *regnum literarium* in which the liberal arts, without which men are unable to embrace or retain the practices of humanity (*morum humanitatem*), will be cultivated above all else, in which the highest glory will be pursued in *ornamentis virtutis*. In the immediate past Cardinals, Archbishops, and other prelates have aided the study of letters. Kings have also played their part in erecting colleges and providing for professors. In this matter none can be compared to King Francis I of France - a reference to the College of Royal Lecturers in Paris - who is, Hay maintained, entirely unique as a *parens et instaurator literarum et literatorum*. By his royal munificence Greek and Latin and the Scriptures are studied. And although these studies can be found in Paris, in the principal university of the world, Hay, nevertheless, wished for Scotland a share in them. The Cardinal alone had the power to accomplish that desire to the glory of Christ.

In these studies the place of honour was due to divine worship. Thus there would have to be in the College pious and learned priests who would win by the moral splendour of their lives the favour of good men, priests who, embued with the knowledge of the Scriptures, would, as ornaments of light, bring an end to ignorance among the clergy and the laity. He stressed the benefits to be gained from having learned doctors to comment daily on the scriptures at specified hours; as well as to expound the Divine Word on the solemn festivals. Only learned priests were to be admitted as professors of the languages for whom nothing should be more dear than the training of the minds of the young in Latin, Greek, and Hebrew. To these three languages should be added Chaldaic and Arabic because of their affinity to

Hebrew, and because much is written in them that is important for the understanding of the Scriptures. The professors of philosophy should teach only the methods of reasoning and argument, and not fly into the labyrinths of useless *quaestiones*. They should turn away from the *suppositiones, amplificationes, expositiones,* and the *ineptitudines* on which their masters (*maiores nostri* now a term of contempt with humanists) had poured forth their efforts. To instil brief moral aphorisms and the basic ideas of Christian piety and the duties of every day living would bring them a well deserved place of honour. Hay thus made it abundantly clear that he did not want to see the youth trained in scholasticism. It was not expedient to waste money and effort on the frivolous and prating discourse of the philosophers. In their place should be substituted the Divine Plato whose doctrine the most holy Jerome and Augustine not only fed upon but in many ways improved. Aristotle should be studied only for his skill in *rerum naturalium*. There was to be, of course, no place for the sophists. Canon and Civil Law were to be studied as both protect the Church. Nevertheless, he did severely criticise their professors for their obsession with endless detail in their barbarous commentaries that served only to render their disciplines obscure. Neither were those who teach and study medicine spared his criticism. Medicine he regarded as the most difficult subject of all. But as the spirit is more pre-eminent (*praestantior*) than the body so the health of the spirit is above that of the body. Men pray, he said, that there be a sound mind in a sound body in order that they may be able to contemplate more freely the divine harmony of both and give thanks to God the creator of so noble a work. Medicine is to be honoured because it is necessary, theology because of the sublimity of its subject.

Throughout, the *Panegyricus* reflects the contemporary northern Christian humanism. Emphasis is placed upon the person and work of Christ who is the *speculum* of life whom we should imitate in all his ways. Thus in peace with all men we are enabled to become partakers of eternal life. It was said by the prophet "Let not this book of the law depart from your mouth but meditate upon it day and night". The professors of sacred theology must occupy the highest places in the College and have responsibility for its entire administration. He has, however, no place for those who have merely the outward profession of theology, but only for those whose lives conform to evangelical sincerity, for those who show themselves to be theologians not just in what they teach. In all things they must show themselves performers (*praecones*) of the truth.

Hay concluded this extensive treatment of his subject by emphasising that no one was to be admitted to this *domicilium*, house of letters and of peace, who was not of the highest moral standards. And as in the earlier *Oratio* he advocated the need to have a well endowed library and a printer skilled to produce not only works in Latin but also in Greek. Finally, there is a warning against the evils of nepotism. Nevertheless he maintained that even if the best qualified person to head this new college is related to the Cardinal, he should on the account of his qualifications be preferred.

The *Oratio* and the *Panegyricus*, although little known, are among the finest treatises on academic reform of the period and entirely representative of northern Christian humanism. Yet they can only be fully appreciated when set within their continental context. It should not be forgotten that in 1538 the year of Hay's *Panegyricus*, Jean Sturm, who had been strongly influenced by what had happened at Louvain, had been instrumental in organising "La Haute Ecole de Strasbourg", and in turn influenced the protestant academies of Lausanne, Nîmes and Geneva.

But to return to St Andrews. We noted at the outset that on 12th February 1538 the papal bull granting the necessary licence and making available the initial funds for establishing the College had been issued. At the earliest the bull could not have reached St Andrews before the summer of that year, and there is every possibility that it took longer. In any event little could have happened that year in which "a great pestilence" swept through the city. The first recorded steps towards the formal legal foundation of the college were taken on 7th February 1539 in the Castle and in the chapel of St John the Evangelist three days later. Prior to those meetings a foundation charter had been drawn up and was confirmed and ratified by the Crown on 7th March. The charter has unfortunately not survived, but something of its contents can be gathered from a study of other contemporary documents.

The College of doctors, regents, masters, chaplains, and students, was to have both an academic and a religious purpose. Educational aims included instruction in the Catholic faith, the resisting of heresy, and training in the administration of justice. The religious purpose entailed, apart from the regular worship of God, the daily offering of prayers for the soul of the late King James IV and those of his successors. The royal confirmation stated that the new college was to have the same privileges and immunities that had been granted to St Salvator's College, and to St Mary's College in Aberdeen. The reference to Bishop Elphinstone's foundation in Aberdeen suggests that Beaton and his associates in St Andrews had in mind a similar foundation. Support for such an inference is supplied by our knowledge of what took place here.

The meeting in the Castle on 7th February had been hurried on by the advanced age and declining health of the Archbishop. He was in his seventies and his nephew, David Beaton, had been appointed his coadjutator. The legal formalities had in fact been rushed through during the final illness of James Beaton (He died on 14th February) in order to avoid repeating the tedious, time consuming, and expensive business of a fresh Supplication. At the ceremony in the Castle the Archbishop personally instituted Robert Bannerman as theologian and principal Master. He had been the principal regent in arts in the Pedagogy since 1526. His appointment as head of the new college was in the nature of a holding operation. He could not easily have been passed over. The other masters, a canonist and a civilist, were members of the ecclesiastical administration. Four regents in arts represented the continuing element of the pedagogy in the new *Collegium Nostre Domine*, the existence of which is first referred to in *Acta Facultatis Artium* on 26th February 1540. Six choristers or chaplains were appointed from the number of priests serving altars in the Parish Church of the Holy Trinity. With the appointment of masters, regents, and chaplains the College was formally constituted. By virtue of the licence conferred by the Papal bull the Archbishop entrusted to those whom he had appointed authority and power to meet in the *templum* of the College, the Chapel of St John the Evangelist, and after offering their first mass of the Holy Spirit to hold a chapter. At that meeting three days later - just four days before James Beaton died - the College had come into existence.

The new Archbishop lost no time in furthering the project, the parishes were annexed, land secured and building operations were started. But little else seems to have happened. No students are assigned to the College in the matriculation register and the Faculty of Arts continued to be responsible for the maintenance of the pedagogy for at least another five years.

But Archibald Hay and his proposed Trilingual College had not utterly disappeared from the scene. It was no doubt on the Cardinal's invitation that Hay returned to St Andrews and was incorporated in the University in 1545 where his scholarly reputation had preceded him. In the early spring of 1546 all must have seemed set for a significant step forward. But the political and religious events of that spring and early summer had a shattering effect on the city and the University. George Wishart was burned for heresy, the Cardinal was murdered, and the Castle seized by those involved. The very existence of the new foundation was in June 1546 denied! Yet by the end of that month the Crown presentation to the principalship of the College was secured for Archibald Hay in the event of the resignation of Bannerman. Hay took up office on 18th July. The ceremony is described in detail in contemporary documents after which he delivered his inaugural oration. It has not survived but no doubt it set out his earlier plans. The notes of Erasmian humanism must have rung out clearly and unmistakably in the College *aula* on that summer day. Had the political and religious climate been more favourable St Mary's College and St Andrews might indeed have taken decisive steps forward.

Hay was not destined to occupy the principalship for more than fourteen months. Along with many other beneficed men he joined the army to resist Somerset's invasion in July 1547. He fell on 10th September in "the rout and massascre of the Scottish army at Pinkie". One of his benefices was on 20th September given to his colleague of Paris days, whom he had, as we noted earlier, highly praised in his *Oratio*, John Douglas. Seven days later Douglas was given the Crown presentation to the Principalship in the Pedagogy and New College. The disaster at Pinkie had robbed Scotland of an outstanding young humanist whose early career gave promise that he would have gone on to make a distinctive contribution to Scottish academic and literary life. At a crucial stage St Mary's College had been deprived of the one man who for a decade at least had planned at the highest scholarly level its future. His mantle fell on John Douglas who was head of the College from 1547 to 1574. He was the effective force behind the refoundation in 1555. How far he would have gone in carrying out Hay's grandiose project, had the opportunity existed, is difficult to determine. Douglas was five years later, however, to take the protestant side. He was one of the framers of the *First Book of Discipline* where trilingual studies were again advocated for St Andrews. These plans did not materialise but they were basic to the New Foundation of the University in 1579 carried through by Andrew Melville, an outstanding representative of Scottish humanism - an alumus of St Mary's College, who had studied in France at the feet of some of the Royal Lecturers and at the Academy of Geneva.

IV. ST MARY'S COLLEGE 1547-1574
- THE SECOND FOUNDATION:

THE PRINCIPALSHIP OF JOHN DOUGLAS
- James K.Cameron

With the arrival in St Andrews of Archibald Hay from Paris and his installation as Principal of the new college of St Mary on 18th July 1546 it seemed that new life was at last to be breathed into the ancient Pedagogy and that the plan of the Beatons was now heading for development and success.

But whatever hopes their might have been were speedily dashed. The political disturbances that followed the murder of the Cardinal in May 1546 and the subsequent war with England - 'one of the most embittered and destructive in the history of Scotland and England' - had a well-nigh disastrous effect upon the infant college and the university. Hay was not to occupy the principalship for long. With other beneficed men he enlisted in the army to resist Somerset's invasion in July 1547. Undoubtedly he was amongst those who fell at the Battle of Pinkie for his benefices were quickly thereafter redistributed according to promises made to such holders should they not return.

The effects of political disaster are reflected in contemporary records. The matriculation registers record no new incorporations for 1546, 1547 or 1549. Those of the small number entered in 1548 were not assigned to any college. In 1550 students were assigned to St Leonard's but not to St Salvator's nor St Mary's. The *Acta Rectorum* and the Faculty of Arts *Bursar's Book* for the same period are ample testimony to the disruption of university life. An exhortation for the confirmation of crown privileges addressed to the Regent Arran by the Rector of the University in the interval immediately following the death of the Cardinal reflected the gravity of the situation. St Andrews, it was stated, was 'sa desolate and destitute bayth of rederries, techarris and auditouris that it is neir perist and meretis nocht to be callit ane universitie'. Particular attention was drawn to the spread 'of hereses and strangis opinionis amangis the commone pepill quhilkis will nocht be suppressit and put avay wythout universities quhair cunnying men ar'. Of the colleges St Mary's had suffered most; her ranks had been severely depleted. Of the original masters appointed in February 1539, one who alone seems to have taken part in college affairs, the learned William Manderston, was dead; and the names of the others had completely disappeared from the records. Of the regents in Arts, some continued to be active till February 1552. Some of the original chaplains continued to serve in the choir of Holy Trinity Parish Church and even lived on to accept the protestant settlement in 1560, but nothing is known of their participation in college activities.

The unsettled position in the archbishopric could not have helped. Although appointed archbishop on 28th November 1547, John Hamilton, half brother of the Regent Arran, and Bishop of Dunkeld, was not enthroned until July 1549. Only after long delay and opposition did he 'attain the high position to which he had the strongest claims, through his connection with the Governor, his experience and his ability'.

The settlement of the vacancy in the principalship of St Mary's was not so tardy. One of Archibald Hay's benefices, the Parish of Collace, was given on 20th September 1547 to a colleague of his Paris days whom had earlier highly praised as one to whom the erection of the Trilingual College was a matter of particular concern, John Douglas. Hay had then described Douglas as a man of outstanding uprightness and erudition. On 27th September 1547 Douglas was given the Crown presentation to the principalship in the Pedagogy and New College. Four days later, 1st October, he received formal collation to the office which he was to hold without a break until his death on 31st July 1574 - that is for some twenty-seven years, among the most momentous in Scottish history. The task that faced the new principal, despite his previous academic experience in Paris - he was for a time regent in Montaigu College - must indeed have appeared daunting. He would have to make the most of his own undoubted ability, reputation and family connections, but much would also depend upon the attitude to the University and the college of the new archbishop, and the emphasis he would place upon the need to improve educational standards.

That Archbishop Hamilton was at this time a staunch supporter of the
Catholic Reform movement that had been making headway in
Europe, particularly in Germany, soon became apparent. Central to
that movement and to that headed by many who were active in the
currently assembled Council of Trent was the need to secure a better
educated clergy. This theme was taken up and developed in the series
of provincial councils inaugurated in 1549. Time and time again the
statutes emphasised the urgent necessity to take seriously the lack of
education among the clergy and the religious. Of particular relevance
was the emphasis placed on the study of the Scriptures. In language
that was distinctly humanist it was resolved that in public schools and
universities there should be better provision for instruction in the
liberal arts and that lecturers in Holy Scripture and theology be
appointed to expound the Bible as accurately as possible according to
the sense of the Catholic Church. Within the universities the Councils
also wished to see a tightening of discipline and a raising of standards;
none was to be admitted who could not speak Latin grammatically or
promoted unless found fully qualified. This encouragement of high
academic standards throughout the Church must have had the
support not only of John Douglas, but also of the archbishop for it was
almost immediately reflected in his interest in reviving - or as he later
referred to it - refounding St Mary's College.

Plans were being put forward and discussed in 1550 for the continuation
of the building project that had been begun in 1539 by Cardinal
Beaton and continued till at least 1545. Extra land adjacent to the
west of the College was bought and the Archbishop with the consent
of the Abbey Chapter annexed to the College the rectory and vicarage
of the Parish of Conveth on 26th June 1550. The donation charter by
emphasising the importance of education and learning in protecting
and strengthening the Catholic faith *in his et aliis diversis mundi
partibus* made it plain that the college was intended to be one of the
instruments in fulfilling the recent council's reform programme.

The archbishop's plans for the future of the College were embodied
in a fresh supplication to Rome. As had already been pointed out the
circumstances in which action was taken in St Andrews on the basis
of the Bull of 1538 had been somewhat rushed and probably aroused
concern in some legal quarters. Hamilton, as his predecessor, David

Beaton, had done, wished to have papal confirmation of the earlier annexations of parishes and of the licence to found the college granted to Archbishop James Beaton by Pope Paul III, and in addition to have the licence extended. In his Supplication Hamilton expressed his desire to bring the unfinished work to completion, and claimed, as contemporary documents confirm, that he had already endowed the College and its Chapel with lands and goods. From the day of his promotion to the archepiscopal see, he informed the Pope, he had not delayed in seeking to procure in it a continuous educational programme including, grammar, rhetoric, poetry, music, arts, medicine, theology and laws, (note again the absence of dialectic, as in Hay's earlier humanist programme), nor had he delayed in bringing to the college *prece et pretio* (by prayer and provision) doctors, lectors, regents, and scholars from far and wide. Undoubtedly the Supplication was intended to impress the Holy Father and more was claimed than had actually been accomplished. Of the Primate's good intentions and of the validity of some of his claims there is no question. On 25th August 1552 Pope Julius III granted all that had been sought and in addition power to amend the original foundation in any way he thought fit.

Indeed a new beginning can be dated from as early as 1551. In St Andrews John Douglas was emerging as the man of the future, and was taking the leading role in the affairs of the University. The fresh start is evident in the Rector's *Album* with Douglas's election as rector on 28th February 1552, an office he was to hold for the unprecedented continuous period of twenty-two years. With an eye to the future, the entry recording the election is entitled Douglas's, first, and the university is described again in humanist terms as *florentissima respublica litteraria*. The names of those that follow include some whom Douglas had almost certainly brought to St Andrews for its reinvigoration. Among them a few inevitably did not stay long but went on to benefit other academic centres such as Alexander Anderson, Licentiate in theology and subsequently sub-principal of Aberdeen and later principal, but others such as William Cranston, a doctor of theology of Paris later became principal of St Salvator's College. The list also includes John Macquine, lecturer in Scripture at Paisley Abbey and Richard Smyth, the first Regius Professor of Divinity at Oxford who subsequently moved to Louvain and ended his colourful career as head of the College of Douai. There is ample evidence that plans to strengthen the Faculty of Divinity were uppermost. Of the recent scholars incorporated two were doctors and two were licentiates in theology, and in the previous year the Prior of the Dominican House at Newcastle, Richard Marshall, also a doctor of Divinity at Oxford, who like Smyth had fled from England, had been incorporated in the university. In the following year, 1552 John Rutherford, the distinguished philosopher from Paris and subsequently a Professor in St Mary's and Dean of the Faculty of Arts was incorporated. He ended his career as Provost of St Salvator's.

Obviously the desire for academic reform expressed in the statutes of the Provincial Councils was gaining momentum. A council held in January 1552 placed emphasis on the preaching of the Word of God and the theological education of priests and religious at the universities. It was freely admitted that the lower clergy and the prelates had not sufficient proficiency in the Scriptures rightly to instruct the people in the Catholic faith or to convert the erring. To this end it was decreed that a book be written in the common Scots, approved by the most prudent of the prelates and the most learned of the theologians and be put into the hands of rectors, vicars, and curates. This book known as *Archbishop Hamilton's Catechism*, was printed and published in St Andrews in August 1552, and was the product of the St Andrews theologians who enjoyed the patronage of the Primate. It must be held to represent the current doctrinal emphases of the theological faculty in St Andrews. There are substantial grounds, as Dr Durkan has demonstrated, for concluding that the English Dominican, Richard Marshall, by 1552 a master in St Mary's, must be regarded as its primary author, and the Catechism recognised as the first book to emanate from a master in St Mary's College.

The reforms enacted by the provincial councils, the subsequent strengthening of the Faculty of Divinity, and the publication of the Catechism, all alike acknowledging the needs of the Chuch for an educated priesthood form the background both to Hamilton's Supplication to Rome and to his subsequent charter or as it is always called, New Foundation of 1555. In the eyes of the Primate and of his academic advisers what Scotland required was not another college along the lines of the foundations earlier in the century in Aberdeen or St Andrews, nor yet the Trilingual College so eloquently proposed by Archibald Hay, although that plan, had it been put into effect, would have greatly benefited Scotland and its church. Rather what was needed was a college in which emphasis would be placed upon theological, particularly biblical, study and which would have as its primary objective the provision of more and better facilities for raising educational standards among the parish clergy. The St Mary's College of the future, it had been determined, was to be the vehicle of Catholic Reformation, as that phase is now understood by ecclesiastical historians and not one of Counter-Reformation or of Reformed Protestantism.

Archbishop Hamilton's *Nova Fundatio*, for which John Douglas must be given the credit, proposed a college of splendid dimensions, capable of supporting thirty-six founded persons as well as the vicars pensioner who were to serve the cures of the incorporated parishes, the revenues of which largely maintained the College. The emphasis on theological education was indicated by the provision that the first three masters should all engage in theological teaching, study and biblical exposition, and not as in Beaton's foundation the principal master only. In that charter, as at Aberdeen, two lawyers, a canonist and a civilist held third and fourth place. In Hamilton's the canonist alone remained, although there is evidence that he might have intended at one time a civilist. The next place in the college hierarchy, as we might call it, provided for eight students in theology, who had not only to be graduates in arts, but also to have already begun on the long mediaeval theological course. Immediately after them in order of seniority came the three regents in arts and philosophy. The individual regents were expected to take two successive groups of students through the entire traditional arts course. They would thus hold office for an eight year period at the end of which they would be replaced by new appointments. Sixteen poor students were to be appointed and be supported on the foundation. The domestic officers, the provisor, the cook and the janitor, completed the list.

The charter goes in considerable detail into all these matters including the conduct of the College's financial affairs, but of those we say nothing. Particular attention was paid to the organisation of the college worship, although there is no mention of a choir of chaplains or of the chantry nature of the foundation. It is evident that the college chapel was in a fit state to be used for the regular worship of the College, each member of which had his own individual stall. A particularly interesting feature of the charter is the detailed provision made for the oversight of the College, which was to be in the hands of a joint committee representative of the University and of the Church. Emphasis was placed upon residence and the pursuit of a rigorous routine of lectures and disputations which did permit some time for recreation, but vacations for both students and teachers were to be completely abolished (*penitus tollantur*). Jurisdiction over all founded persons was to belong to the Principal, the Archbishop and the Pope, but not to the Rector of the University or any other judge even in the second instance. The charter made it abundantly clear that in virtually every way the Archbishop intended a new beginning for the College. Of the earlier foundation all that survived were the endowments secured by James Beaton and added to by his nephew, and the buildings that had been inherited from the Pedagogy or been built or repaired by the Cardinal.

The formal promulgation of the charter was made as grand an occasion as possible. It took place in Edinburgh on 25th February 1555. The signing was witnessed by the highest in the land, the Governor of the Kingdom, James Hamilton, Duke of Châtelherault and leading members of the ecclesiastical hierarchy. The St Andrews Colleges were well represented by their heads, but in their ecclesiastical and administrative roles rather than as members of the university. There is, significantly no record of a separate royal confirmation or of registration under the Great or Secret Seals. The New Foundation was very much a Hamilton creation.

The refounding of the college on such a grand scale reflects both the confidence of the Archbishop and of John Douglas in the Church and the university that they would be able to meet and triumph over the emerging Protestantism, as seemed to be happening elsewhere in the West or perhaps even come to some sort of accommodation with some of its demands. On the Continent events were moving fast towards the conclusion of hostilities in the Empire between Catholics and Lutherans brought about by the Peace of Augsburg. In France the Protestant movement, although spreading rapidly and to a large extent underground, had not yet become a highly organised or challenging force. In England Catholicism had been restored to its place as the national religion. At Trent the Council had made only little headway and, still in its Catholic reform phase, had not yet taken up its most strident Counter-Reformation stance. In Scotland John Knox made in this very year his secret visit, which no doubt put heart in the Protestants, yet it seems to have been recognised by all of them that the time for their open emergence as a national force was not ripe. Of the urgent necessity to bring about Catholic Reform the Archbishop and those who had planned the refoundation of the College were not in doubt. They were participating in a movement that had widespread continental support. Education of the clergy had been singled out as one of the principle means of reforming it and of overcoming the spread of protestantism.

From the outbreak of Luther's Reformation in 1517 the Dominican Order had provided one of the most consistent challenges from a Lutheran and Reformed standpoint to theological change, and had at the same time been active in advocating the eradication of corruption and the development of academic reform. It is not therefore surprising that Hamilton and Douglas, part of whose Paris education had been at Montaigu College, that stronghold of catholic orthodoxy, should look to that Order to staff the new foundation. The position of Douglas, Principal since 1547 was of course secure. As second master, the English Dominican, Richard Marshall, already well established in Scotland and in St Andrews as a scholar and preacher, was chosen and seems to have served in the College until 1558. The third master, was another Dominican, John Black, who succeeded as second master when Marshall left. It is not known how active he was in the College yet he maintained his post until his death on 8th March 1566 - the night of the assasination of the much more colourful and much better known David Riccio. Dempster described Black as *praeclarus Christi miles*, one noted for his opposition to heresy and his constant profession of the faith. In 1561 he debated in public with a better known fellow Dominican of Perth, John Willock, later a leading protestant and for a time Superintendent of the West. Perhaps not surprisingly Black became on Mary Queen of Scots' return to Scotland in 1561 her confessor..[1] Of the fourth master, the Canonist,

---

[1] Lady Antonia Fraser, somewhat surprisingly for her, gets his name wrong. She calls him 'Father Adam Black'

much more is known. William Skene, older brother of Sir John Skene, a noted civil lawyer, was one of the young scholars invited to return home from abroad. He was incorporated in the College in 1556 and held office without a break until 1576. His library, of which an inventory exists, reflects a scholar of wide taste and intellectual catholicity.

The New Foundation made provision for the support of eight theological students, but lack of evidence prevents us from knowing who they were or even if any with certainty were appointed. Of the Regents in Arts there is much information. Two took an active role in the life of the Faculty of Arts and later became parish ministers. The most notable, however, was, John Rutherford, who like Douglas and Skene was to have a long and distinguished career in the university. He accepted the Reformation in 1559 and became Principal of St Salvator's in succession to Cranston who, remaining loyal to the catholic faith left St Andrews. Rutherford represented new trends in philosophical studies. Sir Thomas Malcolm Knox described him as a 'giant among pygmies'. Of his *De Arte Disserendi* (Paris 1557) Knox wrote 'it certainly succeeds in being what it professes to be, a short and direct summary of Aristotle, and the discontent with decadent Scholasticism which animated Peter Ramus, Rutherford's famous contemporary, is often displayed in its pages.' A junior colleague was Alexander Arbuthnot. He went abroad soon after the Reformation to study law and returned in 1566 and two years later was appointed Principal of King's College, Aberdeen. One other regent calls to be mentioned, Robert Hamilton. Appointed a regent in November 1557 he had an unbroken connection with the College for twenty-one years. He succeeded Douglas as Principal in 1575.

Robert Hamilton was one of the large number of Hamiltons who were to be found in St Mary's in those early years, and who owed much to the patronage of the Archbishop. During the Reformation crisis in the city Robert Hamilton took a prominent part both in the affairs of the college and the city. According to John Knox he was one of the 'zealous men' who exhorted the carrying through of the Reformation in St Andrews. In 1559 he accompanied Knox on an important mission to England on behalf of the Lords of the Congregation. He was but one of the some twenty Hamiltons who matriculated as students in St Mary's between 1552 and 1588, and not the only one subsequently to hold teaching office in the College.

From 1551 matriculations in the College steadily increased sometimes exceeding the numbers in the other two colleges. Apart from "poor scholars" several members of the nobility are to be found as students of the College, but clearly the College was attracting a number of able and promising young men. Of the students, apart from Arbuthnot already mentioned, a number taught in the College, and became parish ministers of distinction. Let me mention Patrick Adamson, later Archbishop, a more than respectable humanist, and Thomas Buchanan, minister at Ceres, brother of George Buchanan the celebrated Scots scholar. Many of the students of this brief period 1551 to 1559 seem to have become protestant ministers; one however, Robert Abercromby became a member of the Society of Jesus. Among the Hamiltons there were later two notable apostates from their earlier protestantism.

Although the New Foundation charter during the brief period 1555 to 1559 was only partially put into effect, the refounded college had considerable potential for achieving Hamilton's objective, Catholic Reform. His advocacy of Reform through Provincial Councils, the printed vernacular Catechism, and the College providing educated clergy, was in line with much continental thinking. Nevertheless other forces were at work and had begun to influence the Scottish scene, especially the growing political dissatisfaction with the policy of the Queen Regent which was linked with popular support for protestantism amongst some of the nobility, the barons and several of the burghs, particularly on the east coast. Those who supported the Archbishop's ecclesiastical policy must have begun to have grave doubts about its peaceful fulfilment. With his half-brother, Châtelerhault, tending to the Protestant side and the Hamilton family's political interests at stake, the Archbishop himself might have been tempted to consider the accomplishment of a programme of Catholic Reform, including co-operation with protestants, such as had previously been contemplated in Cologne and of which many in St Andrews were fully informed. By 1558-1559 the more staunchly Catholic such as Richard Marshall and John Black had left the College, but Douglas, Skene, and Rutherford along with the Sub-prior

John Wynram and several others in St Andrews apparently found no difficulty in supporting the Reformation in June 1559 when after a sermon by John Knox in the Parish Church a reformed congregation was with the co-operation of the Town Council established in the city. In St Mary's, Douglas and Skene had remained loyal to the Catholic Church as long as a programme of conservative Catholic Reform was being attempted. Nevertheless, when a decision was made they were there playing their part, locally in 1559 and nationally in 1560. Douglas and Wynram were members of the commission that drew up the *Scots Confession* and *The First Book of Discipline* in 1560. Reform was henceforward to take a Protestant form, yet Douglas clearly saw his college continuing in the service of the national church. In it the transition from Catholic to Protestant could hardly have been accomplished more smoothly or with less dislocation in its common life. Although ecclesiastically deprived of his office as Archbishop, Hamilton, as we shall presently see, continued to take a close interest in the college rightfully, as he claimed, as its Refounder and Patron by making appointments to the foundation in truly nepotistic fashion from among his protestant kinsmen.

The dislocation in the university brought about by the local and national events of 1559-60 were for the most part reasonably quickly resolved. Not surprisingly, however, only three students matriculated in 1560 in the university and they were in St Mary's College; but by the next year a measure of stability had returned. Among the eleven incorporated in St Mary's were Andrew Melville eventually to be principal and James Lawson, Knox's successor in the High Kirk of Edinburgh. By November 1561 regular meetings of the Faculty of Arts in St Mary's were resumed and a revision of the Faculty Statutes undertaken. As far as the actual educational programme was concerned there was in the College and university an unwillingness to take extreme measures. Its members were content with much that had come down from the immediate past, provided all that was now confessionally unacceptable was excised.

In St Mary's, Douglas brought to the education of future ministers the same devotion to scholarship as he had done under the previous dispensation. He was supported by William Skene, who now devoted his attention to teaching Civil rather than Canon Law. He had joined the local protestant congregation by 13th July 1559. Along with his work in the College he was Commissary of St Andrews until his death. Robert Hamilton's attachment to the Reformation and to Knox was at this time, as has been said, well attested. The fact that leading members, including such regents as Arbuthnot and Adamson of St Mary's College were recognised and put forward by the first General Assembly in December 1560 as qualified for the ministry raises interesting but probably unanswerable questions about what was being taught and discussed in the College prior to 1559. We note that within the first three years under the new ecclesiastical arrangements, some 41 new students matriculated in St Mary's, compared with 38 in St Leonards and 21 in St Salvator's. On completion of their studies some, like Melville and Lawson, went on to study in the higher faculties at Continental universities, while others remained to complete the normal necessary requirements as regents in Arts. In the composition of the teaching staff of the College little change had in fact been effected as a result of the religious changes in 1559-60.

When the Queen and her Court came to St Andrews in the late Spring of 1563 - almost certainly the occasion on which the date on the magnificent Royal Coat of Arms was altered from 1542 to 1563, and probably the occasion on which the thorn tree was planted - there seems to have been some concern about the way in which the St Andrews colleges were conducting their affairs. As a result we have the appointment of the first of the much dreaded Royal Commissions, and a very high-powered one at that. Its members included Moray and Maitland, both at that time in high favour with the Queen, as well as the President of the College of Justice, the Clerk Register, the Clerk Justiciary, George Buchanan and the Superintendents, John Erskine of Dun and John Wynram. The sons of some of the legal members of the committee were at this time students in St Mary's. Of the commision's deliberations we have no record. The matter of university education was raised again in 1567 in the new reign of Mary's infant son, and was pressed by the General Assembly. The idea that one of the colleges should be set apart for the study and teaching of Divinity, as proposed in the *First Book of Discipline* and again by George Buchanan in 1563, again was raised. It was eventually agreed that St Mary's College would be preferable to St Salvator's on account of its 'rents and all other commodities'. Although nothing came of the proposal at this time it is interesting to note that it had the agreement of its Re-founder and legal Patron, the former Archbishop, John Hamilton.

During the years 1564 to 1574 St Mary's continued to maintain its pre-eminent position in the university. Douglas was the unchallenged rector of the university, Robert Hamilton became second master and one of the ministers of the parish church and held both offices for the rest of his life, even after he became principal in 1594. Another Hamilton, Archibald, who had been a student and regent became in what can only he described as blatant nepotism third master in 1569, and with this appointment the four masterships were for the first time filled by teachers who owed allegiance to the reformed faith and were resident in St Andrews. This arrangement was to continue for some years to come.

With a full teaching complement the College was in a position to carry out its functions. It did not lack students. From 1564 to 1574 the number of matriculated students increased considerably. A peak was reached in 1567 when 29 new students were added to the lists. Some of them became prominent in the legal profession, an indication that legal studies were being maintained, while many others became prominent in the Church and in education. The nobility too were well represented by their sons. But the most notable feature of the matriculation lists continues to be the frequent occurrence of Hamiltons and Douglasses.

The session 1569-70 proved a troublesome one at the student level. A rebellion against a rigorous enforcement of examination regulations began in St Mary's The young men of the College were particularly insolent towards their superiors. Three students were publicly disciplined in the College and had to crave pardon of the Dean, the Faculty of Arts and the Principal. The act of defiance involving at least six St Mary's men may well have had something to do with the way in which the Hamiltons were being favoured. The discontent continued into the next session.

At all the levels of the university the evidence demonstrates that St Mary's was very much at the centre of university life and that the university was in good heart. But then as now governments do not find it possible to leave the universities to get on with the business they can best do. The Regent Morton visited St Andrews in 1574 and claimed he had good proof of negligence. But any idea that the college was in these difficult years between 1559 and 1574 sunk in decay or corruption is not supported by the records. Whatever discontent there was was political. St Mary's was very much a Hamilton preserve and could be expected to take, and indeed took the Hamilton side in the conflicts that had engulfed the country during the latter part of Mary's disastrous reign and the early years of the minority of King James VI. The events of these trouble-filled years had their repercussions in St Andrews. St Mary's College was not noted for zeal towards the 'guid cause' (i.e. the cause of Moray and the Protestant ascendancy). Accusations were made against Robert Hamilton. He had 'begun to grow cauld in his sermondis'. For health reasons he discontinued regular preaching.

Such was the situation when in 1571 John Knox, now old and ill and out of favour in Edinburgh, took up residence in apartments in the priory. The Hamiltons were in ugly mood. Political divisions in the university were fomented by Knox in the parish church where he took over the pulpit from Robert Hamilton. By his outspoken sermons Knox aroused against himself 'a deidlie hatred and envoye' especially 'of the Principals of the New College and the auld'. John Douglas, now Archbishop of St Andrews, as well as Rector and Principal attempted to calm the waters by having what Knox had said in the pulpit discussed privately, but to Knox this suggested procedure seemed too much like an attempt to censor the pulpit. Robert Hamilton went further and claimed that that which was said in the pulpit should be able to be defended before the schools in order to show whether or not it was consonant with the Word of God. It was this demand that brought forth the well known but frequently misunderstood and not fully quoted statement of Knox in his letter to the next General Assembly at Perth. He wrote "Above all things, preserve the Kirk from the bondage of the Universities. Persuade themselves to rule themselves peaceably, and order their schools in Christ: but subject never the pulpit to their judgment, neither yet exempt them from your Jurisdiction".

To those now in the political saddle the loyalty of the university to the protestant cause and the Church's unwavering support for the monarchy were primary issues. Hence the re-introduction of a form of episcopacy. Douglas was elected archbishop while retaining his other offices, but he was now old and weak and pleaded ill health. In his hands had lain the fortunes of the College for twenty-seven momentous years in Scottish political, religious and academic history. To St Mary's he had brought scholars of distinction to teach and might have been more successful had not the Hamilton hand lain so heavily upon him. He made the College the centre of the university. He had seen it initially as the instrument of Catholic Reform, but as moderate Catholic Reform was no longer a viable objective, with the closing sessions of the Council of Trent pursuing a strongly anti-Protestant policy, he and the best of his colleagues accepted the Protestant Reformation. At the same time he held his college and the university together. He continued to see it as responding to the needs of the country and of the Reformed Church. He had, however, to contend with the Hamiltons who sought to make the College their special possession and no doubt he earned in part the contemporary criticism of being 'ambitious and simple, not knowing who dealt with him'. James Melville, a student in St Leonards during Douglas's last years, referred to him as 'that honourable father of the University'. Melville also records in moving terms the humanity and kindness he had shown to the brilliant young orphaned student in the College - Andreas Melville. In his will he was generous to his colleagues and his fellow citizens. To the College he left his Library, only two volumes of which are today in the University Library. One would like to think that he left a greater legacy to the university and to the Church in the College's devotion to teaching the young to be scholars.

V. ANDREW MELVILLE IN ST ANDREWS

- James K.Cameron

In the long history of St Andrews and its University Andrew Melville occupies a prominent position. He matriculated as a student in St Mary's College in 1559, and although we have no record, he almost certainly graduated four years later. Soon thereafter he left for the continent and did not return to his *alma mater* until 1580. By then he was recognized as one of the foremost scholars of the country, who had succeeded in breathing new life and prosperity into the declining, almost extinct University of Glasgow. The man destined, on almost every count, to make a success of the most recent attempt by the State and the Church to reorganize - 'refound' is the word the Act of Parliament uses - the University of St Andrews in the best interests of the realm. More specifically he was to become the head of what had been a long considered and much delayed project - a college of theology within the University.

In the initial stages of the Reformation in 1560 the compilers of *The First Book of Discipline* had advocated that one of the St Andrews Colleges be solely concerned with the theological instruction of those who would enter the ministry of the reformed Church. It had been maintained that the work of reformation could not endure without adequate provision for such education and that this objective could best be accomplished by reorganizing the country's oldest university. The unsettled state of the nation during the unhappy reign of Queen Mary did not, however, provide the necessary conditions for academic reform, although several attempts were made to re-shape the University. Not until the Act of Parliament of November 1579 did the concerted efforts of Church and State result in practical proposals for St Andrews embodying the essential principles of the 1560 scheme.

Of this 'New Foundation' the most significant and most far reaching feature was the setting apart of the University's youngest and in many ways best endowed college for the study of theology. The 'New College', as St Mary's was almost universally called from the 16th to the 19th century, was for this purpose to undergo a radical reorganization. Since the days of Archbishop John Hamilton and his

Nova Fundatio of 1555, the theological element had been dominant, and he himself had in 1569 agreed that the College, of which he was still acting as Founder and Patron, was the best suited to become the home of the Faculty of Divinity. The Act of 1579 proposed that there be five masters whose responsibilities would be entirely restricted to the teaching of the four year course in theology. Each master was to have his own specialised area. In addition, the foundation was to support eight bursars, (graduates in Arts), and the usual domestic officers, economus, cook, janitor. In many ways this was intended to be a princely foundation (Hamilton had originally proposed that its income should support thirty-six founded persons) and should have been able to provide for the masters and bursars in considerable comfort. It might be added that the buildings were comparatively new, presumably reasonably comfortable, and able to accommodate an additional number of self-financing students.

The radical nature of these proposals must be stressed, and being radical they were not popular in St Andrews. The King had given instructions on 13th December, 1579, immediately after the Parliament, that they be carried out, and his instructions were renewed one month later (January 14th, 1580). The royal commissioners were to brook no opposition. The old, unpopular and protesting Provost of St Mary's, Robert Hamilton, was deprived and two of the other masters removed to St Salvator's. Only one of the early founded members was to remain, John Robertson, whom James Melville later described as 'a guid-weill-conditionet man, but of small literature and gifts', along with the janitor. Those who had been under the old constitution regents in Arts were, if found competent, to be placed as bursars in theology. From January 1580 until the new staff were appointed and had taken up residence the College was to be closed. These instructions make it abundantly clear that the Government was determined to carry through the reorganization, but not only that; it was determined to pay very close attention to all that was taking place. The Crown regarded itself as having succeeded the mediaeval church in the oversight of the University in the interests of the country and the Protestant religion, and was, it seemed, determined to spare no effort in preventing further delapidation. For too long had the Universities been left on their own. St Andrews was now to know the strength of the arm of 'Government' control as never before.

Melville, as I said earlier, was in many ways the obvious choice to head the new college of theology, but not the only one. Glasgow naturally did not want to lose him and there were others furth of Scotland with the necessary educational and theological qualifications and outlook, but attempts to bring them failed. Eventually Melville was appointed. Towards the end of November 1580 - almost exactly one year after the Act had been passsed by Parliament - he left Glasgow, accompanied by his young nephew James, and with undisguised regret passed to Edinburgh to receive more details from the King's commisioners, among who was his college contemporary, now Knox's successor in Edinburgh, James Lawson, one who in all probability had a considerable part is shaping the 1579 Act. They arrived in St Andrews towards the end of the year.

No doubts about the difficulties that would confront them existed in the minds of the Melvilles. Their task would not be easy. They would be among 'malcontents and mislykers'. The College was initially poorly staffed. The bulk of the work was to be carried out by the new Principal, with Robertson and James Melville, his nephew, as 4th and 5th masters, for the first year and indeed until the plan to have 'strangers' as 2nd and 3rd masters had been realized. In addition, the King's commmissioners recommended that a commission of twenty-six members drawn from both Government and Church should be appointed overseers of the Universities. The powers of this body (of whom seven formed a quorum) were extensive, taking in virtually every aspect of academic life. Further, the royal control of the University was emphasized by the explicit statement that there was to be no formal admission by the local aurthorities of any of the new masters. The royal warrant was in itself deemed sufficient and the taking of an oath of allegiance to the University was regarded as unnecessary.

One of those of whom Melville must have entertained some doubts was the bishop, Patrick Adamson, whom he had known from his student days and who had at one time taught in the College and had been proposed as the Provost of St Leonard's College in succession to George Buchanan. Adamson was, in regard to the controversy over episcopal and presbyterian systems of government, something of a chameleon, and one whom it must have been difficult to trust.

Nevertheless, he warmly welcomed the newcomers, attended the public divinity lectures given by Melville, and held out to him high hopes that he would go far, if only he played his cards in the right way. But Andrew Melville, whatever else he was, was not one to give priority to self-interest.

We look first at his work in the College. His public lectures were attended by many in the University, particularly by the regents in Arts and in the other colleges who intended to enter the ministry, among whom was Robert Rollock, subsequently the distinguished theologian and first Principal of Edinburgh University. Rollock does not seem to have studied abroad at any time; consequently the high reputation which his books later enjoyed on the continent, and on which Beza favourably commented, bear testimony to the the good grounding which he must have received at the hands of Melville. But not all were as appreciative as Rollock. The regents of St Leonard's noted with disapproval Melville's Ramist rejection of Aristotle and rallied in defence of the traditional philosophic basis of their theology in its Roman and Lutheran forms. Much research has still to be done on this topic and unfortunatley we have so little from Melville's pen that it is difficult to say to what extent he was a convinced Ramist. His nephew credits him with converting his chief oppponents in St Andrews as he had earlier done at Glasgow, but probably too much is claimed when the Diarist stated that those who taught theology in the time of the Hamiltons, because of their 'ignorance and negligence', had made the regents and scholars care nothing for divinity, and that Andrew Melville within a year or two, brought a great transformation by encouraging the study of the languages and the reading of Aristotle in Greek. However, we may judge his achievement at this date, there is no doubt that there was much 'feghting and fasherie', and that peace was only restored on the intervention of the General Assembly.

As well as his detractors in the University, who did not take easily to the new brand of learning, Melville had his opponents in the town. As a doctor of the Church, he could be expected to take an active part in the life of the local congregation which lacked a pastor, and as the bishop was often absent, Melville occupied the pulpit on Sundays until he discovered that by so doing he was preventing a regular settlement in the vacancy. He then worked to secure first Robert Pont (a man

61

well known in St Andrews) as minister, then Thomas Smeaton from Glasgow, and Alexander Arbuthnot from Aberdeen, but with no success. Had he been able to secure for St Andrews any one of these highly qualified scholars and churchmen his own position would have been considerably strengthened. Nothing but the best in Melville's mind was good enough for St Andrews. What the Church needed was a highly respected pastor who would set about making St Andrews the Geneva of Scotland; in the time of the Hamilton's discipline had become lax and much ground had to be regained. Melville is undoubtedly behind the effort at this time to strengthen the kirk session discipline. Not even the provost and baillies were spared. On one occasion the opposition to the new discipline reached such heights that placards were attached to the College gates - an incident that recalls a similar incident in Geneva, when Calvin was publicly warned not to go too far.

Although occupying a full-time post in the University, Melville was a diligent attender at meetings of Synods and General Assemblies, which must of necessity have often drawn him away from his teaching. Adamson no doubt had hoped to keep him out of the courts of the Church where he was his outspoken rival, but had failed. Having taken the court side after the King had escaped from the hands of the Ruthven Raiders, Adamson went in the royal interest to London. Was one of his errands to secure professors for St Mary's? Was he now anxious to have someone of high academic standing but more favourable to episcopacy in St Andrews, where Melville had in fact succeeded in bringing a process against him? He was certainly active in discrediting Melville both in England and on the Continent. And his opposition fitted well into the King's wish to have more control over the Church. The story of Melville's summons to appear before the King early in February 1584, and his subsequent flight to London, is well known. Of the wisdom of his action it is not easy to judge. Would the King have risked putting him to death? Melville's closest friends believed that that was most likely.

Melville had undoubtedly raised about himself much opposition. He was a hyper-activist with a finger in every pie. Yet he seems by the Spring of 1584 to have gained considerable respect and support in the

University and in the town, if we can judge by the testimonials which were given to him but not heeded by King and Council.

With Melville on the run would the College now founder, bereft of its helmsman? James Melville, with some help from Thomas Buchanan and Robert Bruce - another of Melville's distinguished pupils - attempted to keep alive 'anie spark of life in the College', until he too was forced to flee. Adamson, now back in Scotland and armed with one of the Black Acts passed at Edinburgh in May, procured yet another parliamentary commission to reform the Colleges. For Melville in London it must have been a bitter blow. He wrote to his friends in Switzerland that Adamson had 'destroyed the College' which had been consecrated 'to holy erudition and virtue', the only one of its kind in Scotland dedicated to the knowledge of the sacred tongues and theology. The professors and students had been cast out, the College library plundered, and the light of heavenly knowledge extinguished. This may be an overstatement of the case, and things were in the end to turn out better than appeared possible to Melville in London in 1584. Nevertheless, it all seemed to him to spell the end of the bold experiment of a college of theology in St Andrews.

The Act of 1579 had never been popular in the University. Melville's role was crucial. He had turned out to be far from popular with those in power. He had, of course, his supporters and his admirers, but he also had his detractors. Adamson and those who hankered after a less exacting ecclesiastical discipline had become his sworn enemies. Adamson found it particularly galling to be continually overshadowed in the University, in the pulpit, and in the wider life of the church by the young, vigorous champion of Geneva discipline, who gave every indication that he would not be content with an academic life separated from the wider work of the Church and who was, now that so many of the older generation of 1560 reformers had been removed by death, emerging as a leader in both Church and University. It is difficult to assess Melville's academic success over scarcely four years. But perhaps the strength of the royal and episcopal determination to silence him and remove him from a position from which he could exercise a profound influence may be taken as a measure, if not of his success, then of his potential.

Adamson was not long to remain in sole control of the University. The Church petitioned for the repeal of the Black Acts. The King relented, but the request to have 'masters of schools and colleges' restored was not quickly taken up. By the spring of 1586 the Melvilles were back in St Andrews on the crest of the wave and well to the fore in seeking the excommunication of Adamson, who was now reaping the harvest of his activities of 1584 and 1585. Melville seemed determined to have his revenge, only to be driven out yet again by the King. James Melville without much delay returned to the College, and by August 1587 was joined by his uncle. There were, however, strict conditions laid down by the King who had not abandoned Adamson. Melville was to confine himself solely to his teaching. Obviously, the King was anxious that he be bridled. The conflict between Melville and Adamson was to continue - a microcosm of the much larger conflict between the Kirk and the Crown - Melville, the rigid academic, with no ability as a diplomat in trying to get what he wanted; Adamson the courtier, who believed he could get what he wanted by pleasing the King. The King, by allowing Melville to return, was perhaps bowing to pressure and providing one more opportunity for the upbuilding of a college of theology, in which the Crown was eager and willing to take a direct interest.

Royal Commissioners visited the University on 16th April and, with a thoroughness that would do credit to any University Grants Committee today, proceeded to business. Among the visitors were some of those who had been directly concerned with the reorganization in 1579; to their number was added by Mr John Lindsay, parson of Menmuir, 'a man of greatest learning and solid natural wit' and probably the most effective member. The record of the examination of Melville and others shows that despite difficulty he was doing virtually single-handed as much as he could, assisted by John Robertson and the former bursar John Caldcleuch, whom Adamson had elevated during Melville's absence. By this time James Melville had left to become minister at Anstruther. Considerable attention was being given to the study of the Old Testament in Hebrew. Andrew Melville taught the Psalms in Hebrew from 5.00 to 6.00 each morning; Caldcleuch, Hebrew Grammar and the Prophets from 7.00 to 8.00; and on 3 days in the week Andrew Melville gave public lectures on the Common Places of Divinity. Robertson continued to teach the

New Testament in Greek. There was, however, one additional member of staff who was on probation, Patrick Melville; he taught Hebrew and the Book of Ecclesiastes. On Saturday a student commented on part of the Scriptures at 7.00 a.m. and there were public theological disputations on prescribed theses at 10.00 a.m. On Sundays the masters taught from the Epistle to the Hebrews or some other parts of the Bible. At table each day the old pre-reformation practice of reading and expounding a chapter of the Scriptures in English by one of the students continued. This interesting glimpse into the life of the College indicates a well-ordered society, one in which by careful teaching much could be accomplished. Student numbers were around twenty. In 1588 there were eight bursars supported by the foundation and fourteen others.

Doubts had, nevertheless, been raised many times about the possible misappropriation of College funds. Quite naturally Melville and his colleagues were not over-anxious to open their account books. Indeed they claimed that since 1580 there had been much confusion - the economus had at one point left and then returned - and they tried to get away with saying that no accounts existed for the past decade. In the face of the resistance of all three Colleges, which clearly resented close Government inspection, the Commissioners were insistent, and the masters had in the end to produce their accounts. The result of this Government pressure led to a reorganization of many of the Universities' recording practices, which, I am told by the University Archivist, is most notable after 1588.

One significant result for our purpose is that we know with reasonable accuracy the names of the bursars and other students in St Mary's from 1588 to well into the 17th century. From 1588 to 1599 the College was regularly receiving its income, supporting at least three founded masters, seldom fewer than ten bursars and housing on average fifteen other students. All the bursars were graduates as were most of the other students, although frequently the College provided accommodation for about two non-graduates, almost always sons of the nobility or landed gentry, probably accompanied by their tutor who would be supported as a student in divinity by his pupil's father or patron.

Around 1590 the King's attitude to the Church and to Melville mellowed somewhat. Adamson died in 1591, and in the following year Parliament passed the 'Golden Charter' that embodied some of the aspirations of the Presbyterians. In St Andrews Melville was probably at the height of his personal popularity. He became Rector of the University, championed the civil jurisdiction of the University and its members against that of the local magistrate; succeeded in securing David Black, a fervent reformer, for the parish church, and it is just possible that he had something to do with the rejection by the guildsmen of their traditional provost in 1593. He certainly led a spirited defence of the burgesses and, armed, he put himself at the head of those prepared to defend their civic liberties against the family of the virtually hereditary provosts.

The College had since 1580 been struggling without adequate staff, and was sorely in need of new academic blood. St Andrews in the recent past, had not looked far afield for its teaching staff. Melville had employed successively two members of his own family, and with the translation of John Robertson to the parish church of Dundee in 1592 he was faced with the possibility of having to advance John Caldcleuch, who, as we have already said, had at one time been a regent and then a bursar in theology. He had given Melville some trouble in the past and owed his promotion to a mastership to Adamson in 1585. Melville, in the interests of the College, resisted on this occasion internal promotion. Two young scholars, both graduates of Aberdeen and educated in the humanist tradition of his old friend Arbuthnott, had recently distinguished themselves at several of the great Protestant universities on the continent, and had sent to Melville copies of theses that they had defended, and some of their other publications - one was Robert Howie, the other John Johnston. Why it was that Johnston came to St Andrews and that Howie went to New Aberdeen to be the third minister in the Parish Church and then first Principal of the newly founded Marischal College, will probably never be known. Howie was an out and out Ramist, and a strong exponent of the Covenant Theology of Herborn, whereas Johnston was a little more open in his theological outlook, and had been deeply influenced both by the moderate form of Calvinism taught by David Paraeus of Heidelberg and embodied in the Heidelberg Confession, and by the irenic outlook of Franciscus

Junius the Elder at Leyden. Both young men were humanists, and Johnston had already shown himself a talented neo-Latin poet. St Mary's would no doubt have been equally well served at this stage by either man. In Johnston, St Mary's now had as one of its teachers one well known on the Continent who, if we were to judge from his correspondence and the books he left to the College, had considerable scholarly interests and was able to carry on a regular communication with some of the *literati* of the day - a fact that was to bring credit to the College and from 1595 onwards an ever increasing number of overseas students. Men from the Low Countries, Germany, France, Scandinavia and Poland at first, then from further afield, came to study, some for more than one year, and there were others who were on the grand tour and who took in St Andrews, and although they did not spend so long here they were anxious to have their presence here recorded in their album.

The last decade of the century began well for Melville and for St Mary's College. Melville was undoubtedly at the height of his popularity and in amity with the King whom he accompanied on his expedition to put down the Catholic earls. But a consistent open hostility to the forces of Catholicism operating amongst the Scottish nobility, which was Melville's price for his support of the King, was not in the royal reckoning. Consequently, the more tolerant policy of the King towards the Catholic earls enraged the Church. David Black from his pulpit in St Andrews, and Andrew Melville and others in the courts of the Church, by 'exceeding the bounds of their texts' convinced the King that he had earlier been right in seeking to confine Melville within his College and to his academic teaching. The King's eyes were now set upon his succession to the English throne. Melville, although an advocate of the union of the two countries, convinced that it was in the European Protestant interest, viewed any attempt to bring the Church into closer line with the Church of England as hostile to the Reformed churches' interests and one that would lead to closer control by the King.

Melville's attendance at General Assemblies and his attacks upon the royal political policy form the background to yet another series of royal visitations of the University. By 1596 King James had determined to curb his opponents who in their over-confident, overbearing conduct had exceeded the mark. The visitation planned in August 1596 took place in July 1597, with the King present in person determined to seek out 'all he could get or find out against Melville'. James Melville records that he saw 'a quire of paper of accusations' that had been given in to the King, and some of the points that were made possibly survive in documents preserved in the Balcarres Papers, but he summarily dismissed what must have been a most exacting occasion, by merely recording that the King and his commissioners called Andrew Melville, 'diverse times, levied things to his charge, heard all his mislikers, evil willers, and such as had any complaint against him ... but they could do nothing to him, but make him give up the office of Rector, and in turn had to revive the office of Dean of Divinity'.

This naturally sympathetic account glosses over what must have been a traumatic experience. The King was determined to assert his authority. The minute of the proceeding shows that Melville was able to give assurance on many points of the investigation. But there were serious omissions. The College had no economus, registers of those who attended lectures were not kept, the accounts were not subscribed by the masters every year. Assurances were given that the full course of teaching was followed, but there were doubts about that. On the second day of the examination the commissioners again returned to the subject of the College accounts. There was the now normal resistance, but the King was determined to grasp the nettle. The masters were instructed to produce their accounts over the weekend. The royal pressure was enough. Melville produced them the very next day. On July 11th Melville was, after the taking of a vote among the commissioners, found guilty of failing to perform the office of Rector to the benefit of the University and of not governing his college according to the Act of Parliament. In the Balcarres Papers in the National Library, there is a draft report of the visitation drawn up on 12th October for presentation to Parliament. It contains a number of serious accusations against Melville. How far they are reliable is difficult to say. Obviously some are false: for example, the accusation that 'not a course of theology has been taught there nineteen years bypast'; unless by that is meant that the full prescription outlined in the Act of 1579 had not been implemented. How could it have been? The College had never more than three of the five masters required for such a programme. Nevertheless, Melville's frequent absences at General Assemblies and Synods, and those occasioned by requests to appear before the Sovereign or to accompany him, must have severely eroded the time available for the instruction of his students. There were undoubtedly grounds for concern and complaint.

For too long in the King's eyes the University and its Colleges had been independent institutions. Had their leading members confined themselves to their books, they might have been allowed to continue as they were. But that freedom, that independence, was to be taken from them. The King and his commissioners decreed the setting up of a new Council of the University to oversee its affairs. Chosen by the King and made up of those not teaching in the College, it was headed by John Lindsay. In this way there was to be brought into existence the machinery for keeping a close eye on all that was taking place. The Council was to choose the economus for every College, to inspect the accounts regularly. In future no University teacher was to have a seat on Kirk Session, Presbytery, Synod or General Assembly, although the University was to be represented in the General Assembly by one man chosen by the King from a leet of three nominated by the University. This particular provision was directed against Melville who was now effectively excluded from the Courts of the Church. He was also deprived of the rectorship and a regulation made that in future the office could not be held by the same person for more than three years. The only concession to the College was the recommendation that the fourth master be appointed but not the fifth. It is a little surprising to find in the records detailed courses being prescribed for the masters. They required that much of the Bible be studied in the original tongues over the four years and the Common Places of Divinity.

This new 'agreement' was not immediately embodied in an Act of Parliament and it is doubtful if it was brought into effect in 1597 or 1598, but the King acted as if it had the force of law and debarred Melville from attending the General Assemblies at which James was persistently seeking a means of greater control over the Church by a re-introduction of some form of the episcopal office. Melville's continued hostility and his refusal to be confined to his academic duties brought the King and his commissioners to St Andrews again in July 1599. As all the members of the Council appointed in 1579 had died, a new Council was selected. Once again, but this time in greater detail, the theological course was laid down. There was, however, to be no addition to the staff. Examinations in theology were to be held on the 15th December each year, and an impressive board of examiners was nominated, the Vice-Chancellor, the Rector, the two Deans, and the heads of colleges. All those regulationms were immediately embodied in an Act of Parliament passed on the last day of July 1599, which also ratified the decision of the visitors in July 1597. Instructions were sent off the very next day from the King to the new Council of the University to have the promises of the Act implemented immediately, and to report back to the King and Privy Council. A little over a decade had passed since Melville's re-establishment in St Andrews. In the King's eyes he had as Rector and Principal failed in his responsibilities, and the University was in need of closer royal attention in the future. No doubt he would have liked to have silenced Melville altogether, but he could not. Melville had his own body of support.

These ten years in St Andrews could not have been academically as unprofitable as the King and his commissioners believed. The attempt to deprive the University of its independence was a political move intended to serve political ends for the University had become through Melville a centre of opposition to the royal support for episcopacy. James Melville claimed that the King could not get it all his own way because of the rising reputation of the College which had been attracting students from all over Europe. There is a little exaggeration here, but records do show that the numbers of students continued to be about twenty and sometimes as high as thirty, and that surplus funds intended to support the fourth and fifth masters were being used to support additional bursars, undoubtedly an indication of success.

What, if anything, can be said of Melville as a teacher of theology during these years? Unfortunately we have little from his pen to help us here. But we do have in the small group of seven printed sets of theological theses for the years 1595 to 1602 proof that theological instruction was being given. Bibliographical details of these publications are provided by Dr Cant in his learned article in the

Transactions of the Edinburgh Bibliographical Society in 1941. In six of the set the respondents or student defenders are named. They form a most interesting group. One is a Dane, one is French, three are Scots who later became ministers, one, John Scharp, became Professor of Theology at the French Protestant academy at Die and was from 1630 to 1648 Prorfessor of Divinity at Edinburgh. One of the sets of theses is defined by Dr Cant as 'Class theses', that is theses based on a course of lectures but to which no particular students were assigned as respondents. It is worth noting that this set, on general theological topics, was to be defended on 26th and 27th July, 1599, the year and month of that severe royal visitation. Were they in fact printed to show to the royal commissioners that the regular work of instruction was being carried out? Drawn up by Melville, who was to act as *Praeses* or *Moderator*, they were based on his lectures on the Common Heads of Theology. The subjects cover Predestination in 1595, Free Will in 1597, general topics in 1599, Justification and the Doctrine of Sin in 1600; and in 1602 the Doctrine of the Sacraments and the Mass, and the only 'non-controversial' one at the time, 'Whether the Bishop of Rome is the Anti-Christ or not'.

In addition to the theses we have only one other theological work ascribed to Melville. It was not known to McCrie and was first printed in 1849. It is a short commentary on Romans, derived from Melville's own manuscript copied by one of his students, Daniel Demetrius of Heidelberg. The little work is not strictly speaking a commentary but rather an analysis intended to form the basis of the lecture course - the 16th century counterpart of the modern 'handout'. It starts with an outline of the Argument which clearly illustrates how closely Melville followed Ramist method. The epistle is divided into prografh, grafh and epigrafh, or *praescriptio, scriptio,* and *postscriptio,* and then each section is divided and sub-divided as far as was considered necessary. For example, the grafh is divided into two parts, *doctrina* and *adhortatio,* i.e. the part explaining the doctrine, in which the salvation conferred by Christ in the gospel is treated, and this leads to a discussion of the cause of salvation - which is *vera justitia* and so on. Then there is the *adhortatio ad vitam sanctum* as set out in chapters xii to xv v.14. That is to say, Melville begins with an overall and in some ways oversimplified 'diagrammatic' analysis. There follows a philological section in which he discusses some of the key words. I take an example from the very beginning, Paul's description of himself as *doulos*. Melville is careful to point out that this word defines Paul's apostleship as the '*munus publicum*' which he exercised in the Church. And that this office is to be distinguished from the parallel public offices in the civil society. The two are not to be confounded.

During the years 1588 to 1606 Melville continued to participate in the life of the burgh and its church. Strangely enough he was not elected to the Kirk Session until 1591 and took an active part only until 1597, the year King James forbade doctors to sit on Church Courts. St Andrews, even before the King's decision became an Act of Parliament, came into line and did not elect him to serve on the local Church court. This was a radical departure. From the outset of the Reformation the Principal of St Mary's served on the Session. It is perhaps noteworthy that at the privy censures in the Kirk Session nothing was ever raised against him. On one occasion it is recorded that 'the haill bretherin thanks God for him'.

The King prevented Melville taking his place in the courts of the Church. He could not, however, prevent him from attending the Exercise - or Presbytery as it became. At its meetings he took an active part in the regular exposition of scripture and in the discussion of the *Theological Theses* which became so important a part of the Exercise. He also used the Exercise to gain for himself a commission to General Assemblies as a doctor of the Church. In this way he continued to pursue his opposition to the royal ecclesiastical policy which was in the end to provide the King with the pretext for summoning him to London, and for depriving St Andrews and in particular St Mary's of its most notable Principal.

VI. 'THE VOICE OF REPROACH AND OUTRAGE':

THE IMPACT OF ROBERT HALDANE ON FRENCH-SPEAKING PROTESTANTISM.

- Deryck W. Lovegrove

'Geneva is no longer Christian! is the cry which resounds in the city itself, and, reiterated by malevolence, is heard in England, in Holland, in Germany, in France; and has even reached the astonished ears of the inhabitants of the new world. Why this outcry? Why this tumult?'[1]

So asked Monsieur Chenevière, pastor and Professor of Divinity at Geneva in 1823 in an article published in the London Unitarian journal, the *Monthly Repository*. Geneva, in common with Reformed Protestant communities throughout the French-speaking area of Europe, was experiencing the effects of a century of rationalist philosophy: the impact of the anti-supernatural thrust of the Philosophes, and especially in the Swiss city's case the close attention paid by Voltaire and by her own Deist son, Jean-Jacques Rousseau. Nor was this phenomenon limited to French-speaking territories, for as Poland points out, 'The departure from a strict Calvinist orthodoxy was an experience common to the greater part of the Protestant world during the eighteenth century'.[2]

British evangelical concern for France and its environs had first appeared in the late 1790s as an offshoot of the wider interest in overseas missions which marked that period. Stimulated by a domestic ministry to French prisoners-of-war, and fuelled by apocalyptic hopes, the London Missionary Society under the influence of David Bogue had used the return of peace in 1802 to launch a missionary venture based on Paris, but the return of hostilities the following year did not allow the distribution of Bibles and religious tracts printed in French to get under way.

---

[1] **The Monthly Repository** 19 (1824), 1-2.

[2] B.C. Poland, **French Protestantism and the French Revolution. A Study in Church and State, Thought and Religion 1685-1815** (Princeton, 1957), p.242.

Not until the post-Napoleonic period was the British evangelical initiative revived, and then not in organizational form, but as a private venture by a remarkable and wealthy Scot, Robert Haldane of Auchingray near Airdrie. Haldane arrived in Geneva with his wife at the beginning of January 1817 during a short Continental tour, in the course of which he hoped, without having any specific plan of action, to do 'something to promote the Knowledge of the Gospel'.[1] He was on the point of leaving the city for Montauban in southern France when he came into contact with one of the Genevan theological students, a man who spoke English. Within the space of a few days he discovered the opportunity he had been seeking, establishing evening expositions of Paul's Epistle to the Romans at which very soon the majority of the *proposants* from the theological academy (*auditoire*) were present. The tenor of the unofficial theological education offered by the visitor resembled in many ways the emphases found in the Pietist programme in Germany a century earlier.

Inevitably the presence of this new theological attraction aroused the wrath of the city's clerical leadership. The Register of the Venerable Company of Pastors betrays the general sense of concern: 'The former Moderator reports... that at the request of an elder the Consistory has attended to complaints relating to the Scotsman Haldane who is attracting many of the students in Theology to private lessons, and has given its committee on the state of Protestantism at Geneva the responsibility of making enquiries and reporting'.[2] Particular offence was taken by the Professor of Divinity at the academy, for he not only warned the students not to attend the unauthorized lessons, keeping watch from the Promenade on those who disobeyed, but set in motion with his colleagues disciplinary measures designed to check the promulgation of the new doctrines from the city's pulpits.

---

[1] R. Haldane, **Revival of Religion on the Continent. A Letter from Robert Haldane Esq., to the Rev. Edward Bickersteth** (1839), p.2.

[2] Registre de la Compagnie des Pasteurs de Genève 1816-26, minutes 8 May 1817, Archives d'Etat de Genève MS R 37, p.71.

In spite of this opposition and the brief duration of Haldane's stay in Geneva, his exposition of Pauline theology made a deep impression on the young men who gathered at his house between February and June that year. By the time he departed for Montauban at the beginning of the summer, there existed among the *proposants* a nucleus of individuals who were no longer willing to accept standard eighteenth-century theological views.

It is necessary to consider not only the effect of Haldane's visit upon Geneva but also its wider significance for the nineteenth-century Continental *réveil*. As a nephew of Robert Haldane and a disciple of militant evangelicalism Alexander Haldane as biographer had every reason to emphasize the influence of his uncle. But was that influence as fundamental as he believed?[1]

At an earlier stage Robert Haldane had created a similiar stir in Scotland by a series of steps he had taken during the 1790s. Firstly there had been the notorious political speech delivered at Stirling in which he had seemed to welcome the early revolutionary developments in France. That had been followed by a scheme for leading a missionary group to Bengal. When the latter had proved abortive his financial power had been channelled into the contentious area of popular domestic evangelism. He had been one of the architects of the programme of lay preaching which had provoked the 1799 General Assembly to circulate a Pastoral Admonition to all parish churches in Scotland, accompanied by a Declaratory Act which denied their pulpits to unauthorized preachers. Subsequently he had embraced openly the very sectarianism of which the Pastoral Admonition had warned. Was he not, therefore, a restless troublemaker who was able to exploit the tensions within the strategic and cosmopolitan community of Geneva for the purposes of institutional subversion?

Much of the detailed knowledge of events at Geneva in 1817 comes in the form of Haldane's published defence against the charges made

---

[1] A. Haldane, **The Lives of Robert Haldane of Airthrey, and of his brother, James Alexander Haldane**, 3rd edn. (London, 1853), pp.414, 461-2.

by Chenevière.[1] The professor's accusations were that the Scotsman focused the students' attention on the mysterious aspects of the Christian religion, inoculating them with his own intolerant spirit, pouring contempt on reason and waging war against good works. In his long and closely argued response Haldane explored each of these allegations in turn, and in doing so revealed many of his own theological and religious presuppositions.

The Scottish layman insisted that he had begun teaching the Genevan students when he became aware of their ignorance of the Bible and of orthodox Christian doctrine. In his reply he advanced a range of evidence attesting the almost universal Arianism of the city's clergy at the time of his arrival. He recalled the earlier approval of D'Alembert who, writing in the *Encyclopaedia*, had said 'To say all, in one word, many of the pastors of Geneva have no other religion but a perfect Socinianism, rejecting all that they call mysteries.'[2] Haldane used his exegesis of Romans as a basis on which to construct a coherent theological framework and from which to establish the essential principles of Christian philosophy. In this process he regarded the more mysterious aspects of the faith, such as the relationship between Jesus and God and the operation of divine grace, not as irrelevant metaphysical probings, but as essential constituents of vital religion and commitment: the very ingredients he believed were lacking in the degenerate Genevan church.

Predictably Haldane rejected the charge that he imbued his disciples with an intolerant spirit. Having admitted the exclusive character of the claims made by Christianity, he argued that the true Christian is bound by scriptural precept to be tolerant in his treatment of others. By contrast it was the Arian pastors of contemporary Geneva who were intolerant, seeking to induce the civil authorities to banish those

---

[1] R. Haldane, **Letter to M.J.J. Chenevière, Pastor and Professor of Divinity at Geneva: occasioned by his "Summary of the theological controversies which of late years have agitated the city of Geneva", published in the Monthly Repository of Theology and General Literature** (Edinburgh, 1824). The following paragraphs relate to this publication.

[2] R. Haldane, **Letter to Chenevière**, p.135.

who showed any inclination to revive the old orthodoxy. Religious intolerance was by no means the prerogative of the older confessional era: eighteenth-century Geneva had demonstrated a tradition of intolerance towards unwelcome views associated with the political struggles of the city, while in neighbouring France the rejection of supernaturalism had led ultimately during the Terror to a vigorous campaign of dechristianization.

In accusing the unauthorized teacher of pouring contempt on reason, Chenevière had selected an argument that was difficult to sustain. The logical ideas of orthodox Calvinism would have been awkward at any time to dismiss as lacking in reasoned content, but their new exponent was an able thinker who had received a good education at the High School and University of Edinburgh. As Haldane's early work on Christian evidences shows, he stood at the confluence of two important streams of eighteenth-century Scottish thought: on the one hand the traditional influence of Calvinist theology and on the other the philosophical ideas stemming from the Enlightenment. His works, though no more exciting than his person, were solid and well-reasoned. His Genevan audience was amazed, moreover, at the extent of his biblical knowledge and at the facility with which he was able to compare diverse scriptural passages.[1]

The fourth charge contained both negative and positive elements. There was, on the negative side, in the allegation that Haldane waged war on good works, a resort to the common smear that Calvinism implied antinomianism which in turn opened the way to licence. On the basis of his exposition of Romans that allegation was easy to refute. On the other hand there was also the positive belief of the enlightened pastors of Geneva that religion could be equated with humanity and good works. While never subordinating grace, Haldane argued that true faith issued in good works, whether the latter were construed in behavioural terms or as specific acts of charity. Pointing to the practice of his opponents, by contrast, he noted with disapproval the widespread disregard for the sabbath revealed by the leisure

---

[1] A. Haldane, **Robert Haldane**, p.430 quoting a letter from Frederic Monod.

pursuits of the Genevan clergy on Sunday evenings, and the equally common violation of the fourth commandment by pastors and laity alike.

In reviewing Haldane's success in attracting and influencing at a formative stage the future leaders of Protestant expansion - a circle which included the names of César Malan, Henri Pyt, Charles Rieu, Merle d'Aubigné, Gaussen, Gonthier and James - it is necessary to ask whether the Scotsman should be seen as the architect of the subsequent religious revival, or whether he was merely a contributor to a wider movement springing from other sources whose roots drew upon a pervasive mood of dissatisfaction with French-speaking Protestantism. In France during the earlier period of dechristianization the future dean of the yet to be established theological faculty at Montauban had reacted bitterly against the craven disappearance of his church. 'I see with grief', wrote Daniel Encontre in 1794, 'that we live absolutely without worship'[1]. Similarly in 1817 there remained in Geneva a small remnant which clung to the old orthodoxy, a group composed of the elderly pastors Cellerier and Moulinié and the professor Antoine Demellayer.

Not only are there these signs of continuity with an earlier orthodoxy, but there is other indisputable evidence that whatever part Robert Haldane may have had in reviving interest in Reformed orthodoxy in southern France, he did not initiate the process in Switzerland. There seems in the Swiss city to have been a chain of influences, beginning with contacts with the surviving members of a Moravian community established by Zinzendorf in 1741, and extending through the medium of a *Société des Amis* founded by a group of likeminded young men in 1810, to the visit in 1816 of a Welsh Calvinistic Methodist named Richard Wilcox. Ami Bost, who was part of the Genevan *réveil*, yet who never came into contact with Haldane while he was in the city, makes it clear that the movement in these early stages was characteristic of Pietism[2] : an emotional religion centred upon the person of Christ,

---

[1] Poland, **French Protestantism**, p.207.

[2] A. Bost, **Mémoires pouvant servir à l'Histoire du Réveil Religieux des Eglises Protestantes de la Suisse et de la France** (3 vols.,Paris, 1854-5), vol.1, p.84.

laying considerable emphasis upon personal devotion, and exhibiting a typical doctrinal imprecision.

Haldane's contribution to the developing taste for religious revival took a number of forms, though Ami Bost considered his theological rigour to be the most important ingredient. He offered those already involved in the religious quest a period of systematic training in Christian ideas, thereby laying a foundation capable of giving substance to the earlier Pietist leanings.

His approach, moreover, endowed the new movement with a strongly biblical character. The new evangelicalism which Haldane represented was not opposed to confessions or catechisms (indeed the 1802 body established by the London Missionary Society to evangelize France had ordered the printing of several thousand of the latter), yet doctrinal statements did not occupy a primary position in its strategy. Much greater emphasis was laid upon the primacy of the Bible, imparting to the movement a wide-ranging appeal that narrow confessionalism would never have allowed.

The third and most significant element centred upon Haldane's view of society as something essentially unchristian and at variance with the Church at large. For Geneva, if not for France, given its protracted persecution of Protestantism, this marked a change in thinking. Gone was the old notion of the godly community, its rejection marked by the departure from the established church between 1817 and 1832 of the majority of Haldane's students, each in turn following the example of his teacher.

To some extent the term 'departure' is a euphemism in the Genevan context. In almost every case pressure was applied to those who had the temerity to preach the new evangelical doctrines from the city's pulpits. By contrast Haldane's own earlier move into Independency in Scotland was at least in some measure a voluntary development. In the Swiss context the enforced move into separatism, while it may have given those involved a greater freedom of movement and merely constituted de facto recognition of the secularization of society, led, at least initially, to individualism and a certain excess, extending from César Malan's autocratic high Calvinism to the Irvingite tendencies of the Bourg-de-Four congregational church, especially in the person of Pierre Mejanel, one of its pastors. Not until 1831 and the founding of a *Société évangélique* did the Genevan revival achieve a more stable and secure footing.[1]

Chenevière regarded Haldane as an interferer bent on reviving discredited theological beliefs.[2] Other commentators, while not necessarily sympathizing with the Genevan professor's strictures, have concurred with his assessment of the Scotsman's rigid Calvinism.[3] But is this correct? In the strict seventeenth and eighteenth-century sense, Haldane does not stand out as a marked exponent of the full, logical Calvinist system. In his theological response to Chenevière, which is grounded in his interpretation of Pauline theology, Haldane emphasizes the gospel as being for everyone,[4] upholds the use of 'means' for its propagation,[5] and pays little attention to the doctrines of predestination and election. Election is treated for its positive value only. Nowhere does he show any regard for the notion of predestined reprobation.[6] In his theology he appears to exemplify the pragmatic form of Calvinism which characterized the early nineteenth-century evangelical movement. Yet a degree of caution is necessary, for at a later stage in his life he showed himself equally prepared to dismiss the 'moderate Calvinism' of contemporaries as unscriptural and faulty.[7]

---

[1] E. Léonard, **Histoire Générale du Protestantisme Tome III. Déclin et Renouveau (XVIIIᵉ - XXᵉ siècle)** (Paris, 1964), pp.193-6; T.Stunt, 'Geneva and British Evangelicals in the early nineteenth century', **Journal of Ecclesiastical History** 32 (1981), pp.36-46

[2] **Monthly Repository** 19 (1824), 4; R. Haldane, **Letter to Chenevière**, p.3.

[3] Bost, **Mémoires**, p.81; Léonard, **Histoire Générale**, p.182.

[4] R. Haldane, **Letter to Chenevière**, p.37.

[5] R. Haldane, **Letter to Chenevière**, pp. 110-11.

[6] R. Haldane, **Letter to Chenevière**, pp. 93-5, 109-12.

[7] R. Haldane, **For the Consideration of the Ministers of the Church of Scotland. Remarks on Dr Tholuck's Exposition of St Paul's Epistle to the Romans, translated by one of themselves** (Edinburgh, 1837), p.18.

How should the Continental response to Haldane be evaluated? Much of the situation at Geneva is beyond dispute. The visitor's sessions with the theological students and their effect caused a considerable stir. Bost noted that 'at the end of a few weeks the whole of Geneva was in commotion. For or against, willingly or unwillingly, everyone was occupied with religious questions; and even the pulpits soon resounded with opposing preaching.'[1] Henry Drummond, another wealthy British evangelical in search of a cause, heard of the furore while in the port of Genoa and made haste to reach Switzerland.

In the eyes of the Venerable Company Haldane had poisoned the minds of a generation of theological students by reviving long dead religious superstitions. Even before he terminated his visit to the city the Company sought to stifle pulpit discussion of his ideas by publishing the regulation of 3 May which forbade preaching concerning the person of Christ, original sin, the operation of grace or predestination.[2]

If the universal hostility of the pastors was all too obvious, the warm affection in which the Scottish layman was held by his student hearers provided a contrasting theme for accounts of the Genevan awakening. Yet even in positive reports a few reservations were expressed, most notably in the autobiography of Ami Bost. Having gone to considerable pains to emphasize the diversity of causes behind the *réveil*, Bost added the comment that even had he not been resident at Moutiers-Grand-Val in the canton of Berne, 'it [was] probable that, even after having come under [Haldane's] influence, [he] would have shaken it off later where it was too narrow'.[3]

From both the reference to the self-appointed teacher found in the records of the Venerable Company, and the state of ecclesiastical unrest which Haldane left behind him in June 1817, it is evident that his presence exerted a significant force within the canton. Yet the situation at Montauban is much less certain. Alexander Haldane

---

[1] Bost, **Mémoires**, p.82.

[2] A. Haldane, **Robert Haldane**, p.434.

[3] Bost, **Mémoires**, p.81.

portrayed a similar scene of successful influence, but he admitted that it was less striking than Geneva, and that the situation confronting the Scottish evangelist in France was different from that which obtained in Switzerland. Despite the Arian sympathies of Professor Pradel, the dean, in company with the Professor of Hebrew and at least one senior member of the local Montauban consistory, showed himself receptive to Haldane's concern for the revival of classical Reformed doctrine.[1]

Yet there is no record of Haldane's presence in two years of closely minuted details of faculty life; not even a mention of his gift to the dean of copies of Luther's *Letter to Erasmus, on Justification by Faith* which he had privately printed for distribution among the students.[2] Only in the consistory records is there the briefest acknowledgement of a sum of money received from Haldane for charitable use.[3]

At first sight this silence in the Montauban records appears to support Bost's view that whatever success was experienced at Geneva had in part to be attributed to the particular conjunction between an influential teacher and conditions of local receptivity. He insisted that by comparison Haldane enjoyed little success in France.[4] Yet neither the Scotsman nor his biographer-nephew regarded the stay at Montauban as unprofitable. The young French faculty, which had opened in 1810, lacked the urbane environment of the Swiss academy. It did not possess the undoubted talent of the twenty or so Genevois who had listened so attentively a few months earlier. But it was part of an institution which was still only beginning to recover from a process of deliberate and systematic dechristianization; an experience in

---

[1] In 1817 the Dean was Daniel Encontre, while Francois Bonnard held the chair of Hebrew. The sympathetic member of consistory was M. Marzials.

[2] A. Haldane, **Robert Haldane**, p.479.

[3] 'Mr le Pasteur Marzials, apprend à l'assemblée le don généreux et charitable, que fait Mr haldane anglais, de Cent francs pour le soulagement des pauvres: La Compagnie, prie Mr le pasteur Marzials, d'exprimer, à Mr haldane, toute sa reconnaisance, pour un don si pieux'. Registre de Délibérations du Consistoire de Montauban, minutes 3 March 1819, Archives de Tarn-et-Garonne MS 15 A.

[4] Bost, **Mémoires**, pp. 82-4.

which a long persecuted religious minority had lost its books, pastors, buildings and many of its followers, and had even ceased for a while to make any attempt at holding public worship.

Whatever can be said regarding Haldane's influence on the French Reformed community, the impact of his teaching and presence owed little to the kind of preparatory circumstance witnessed in Geneva. Yet the effects of his two year residence at Montauban were felt by the French Protestant Church. In a letter written in 1842 the elderly M. Marzials suggested that the result of his evangelical impetus was to be seen in the doctrinal orthodoxy of the majority of French pastors.[1]

It is fitting to leave the final assessment of Robert Haldane's Continental impact to Ami Bost, for in his measured words the observer comes as close as possible to an impartial contemporary appraisal of the man and his contribution to French-speaking Protestantism:

'But, after all, the influence of Mr Haldane upon Geneva was fundamental; firstly because Mr Haldane was a man of weight, but without doubt also because his influence fell on perfectly prepared soil, and which had the advantage of contrast with an unbelievably lowered state of affairs. The evidence that these circumstances entered greatly into the success of Mr Haldane at Geneva is that he did not have later any comparable success at Montauban. But as for [the situation] at Geneva, I repeat, the effect was fundamental... A score of students or of young ministers went to hear him twice weekly, then employed their other evenings in undertaking, in little gatherings, the apprenticeship for their future functions as pastors or as missionaries'[2]

---

[1] A. Haldane, **Robert Haldane**, p.493.

[2] Bost, **Mémoires**, p.82.

VII. THE BAILLIES AND SCOTTISH THEOLOGY: THEIR INHERITANCE AND THEIR LEGACY.

- A.C. Cheyne

"The ideal required for our theological schools is that we, the teachers, should be the kind of men who, without knowing how, and whatever be the subject of our discourse, inspire and awaken and change men. The greatest chapters in the history of education are those that tell of individual magnetic personalities, of men whose power lay as much in the inherent transmissive quality of their own consecration as in any counsels they gave".

JOHN BAILLIE, "The Fundamental Task of the Theological Seminary", **Reformed Church Review**, No. 3, July 1922, p.261.

I am only too aware of how ill-qualified I am to deal with this fascinating but daunting subject, and in my less exalted moments I have amused myself with speculation as to how many competent theologians and historians of theology were unsuccessfully invited to give these lectures before the lot fell on me. There is no point, however, in bewailing what must now be endured with Christian humility on my part and Christian charity on yours. I'd like, therefore, to introduce my superficial and ill-ordered remarks by indicating very briefly why I found Professor Whyte's invitation to take part in this Summer School so attractive, and why (in a moment of lunacy) I decided to accept it.

As a son of the manse, I was familiar with the names of John and Donald Baillie from my childhood onwards. My uncle, J.Y. Campbell, had been a schoolfellow of theirs at Inverness Royal Academy, and remained a close friend of them both - Donald in particular - to the end of their lives. I still vividly recall a visit which Uncle Jack and 'Donnie' Baillie paid to my family while we were holidaying in the Black Isle one August in the 'thirties - during which visit a small boy of seven played hide-and-seek with the future Professor of Systematic Theology. (At the end of these lectures some of you will probably say that I am still doing so.) Perhaps it was on the strength of that episode that, some 15 years later, Donald sent me a card of congratulation - I still have it - when the results of my Final Examinations in History were published, a typically thoughtful and generous gesture. Then in 1939 came one of the more significant experiences of my life, when as a teenager on holiday with my parents in Willie Rogan's beautiful Helensburgh manse, I chanced upon John Baillie's *And the Life Everlasting* and read it with a kind of bemused fascination - delighting in the wide culture it displayed (here was someone who was equally at home with poets and philosophers), feeling very superior as I intoned such phrases as *soma sema* to those who were prepared to listen, and rejoicing (even when I didn't fully understand the argument) at the author's demonstration of the intellectual respectability of Christian belief.

And so to what, in the kindness of your hearts, you may care to call my years of discretion. It was, I think, during my very first General Assembly - I was still an undergraduate in Arts - that I witnessed from the public gallery a memorable clash between John Baillie and John White of the Barony (the occasion, a report by the "God's Will" Commission which John White considered too left-wing for any churchman to accept) and gloried in the little professor's victory. By that time, I seemed to be heading for the ministry; and when, after several years of evasive tactics, I finally reached the point where a decision for or against simply had to be made, I was sensible enough to consult the man for whom among theologians I had the greatest respect.

We met for tea in the New Club on Princes Street, and his advice is with me still. "Two thoughts: first, if the considerations on either side are so evenly balanced in your mind you can be pretty sure that whichever choice you make will not be wrong; and second, once the decision has been taken you'll realise that this was what, deep down, you always knew would happen". That, and an encouraging word of dismissal, was all; but a few months later I had enrolled at the College of which John Baillie was Principal. It was the great teacher's last triennium there, and few things give me acuter pleasure than to recall that I was commissioned to make the students' presentation to him on the last day of the summer term in 1956.

All my relations with him - even when I had shamefacedly to confess my failure to complete an assignment of work - were pleasant ones; and I have not a single memory of him which does not do him credit - not least his dignity and graciousness at our last meeting within a month or two of his death. John and Donald: they were both not only great but good men, whose equals we are unlikely to encounter more than once or twice in a life-time. It is an awesome privilege to be asked to speak about them, and I apologise to them even more than to you for the inadequacy of what I have to say.

INTRODUCTION

A few short biographical details to begin with, as a kind of framework for what I have to say.

John Baillie was born in the Free Church manse of Gairloch, Ross-shire in 1886. On his father's death in 1890 the family moved to Inverness: John and his two younger brothers, Donald and Peter, were educated at the Academy there. In 1904 he entered the Arts Faculty of Edinburgh University, graduating four years later with a First in Philosophy (and an assistantship to the Professor). He studied at New College, Edinburgh, then one of the seminaries of the United Free Church of Scotland, and spent summer vacations in Germany at the universities of Jena and Marburg. There followed two years as assistant minister of Broughton Place Church in the capital; and the War years were spent with the Y.M.C.A., chiefly in France. From 1919 (when he got married) to 1927 he held the Chair of Christian Theology at Auburn Theological Seminary, New York State; from 1927 to 1930 the Chair of Systematic Theology at Emmanuel College, Toronto; and from 1930 to 1934 the Roosevelt Chair of Systematic Theology at Union Theological Seminary, New York. In 1934 he returned to Scotland on being appointed to the Chair of Divinity at Edinburgh, which he held until his retirement in 1956 (though there was a break, for Y.M.C.A. service again, in 1940). In 1943 he was elected to the Moderatorship of the General Assembly of the Church of Scotland, and in 1950 he became Principal of New College and Dean of the Faculty of Divinity. He was named one of the six Presidents of the World Council of Churches at Evanston in

1954, was appointed a Companion of Honour in 1957, and served on the joint Committee of Anglicans and Presbyterians which produced the so-called "Bishops Report" in 1958. He died in Edinburgh on the 29th September, 1960.

In the life-story of *Donald Macpherson Baillie* the first third and the last (roughly speaking) are remarkably similar to his older brother's: only in the middle period was there a striking divergence. He was born, also in Gairloch, in November 1887, underwent his schooling at Inverness Royal Academy, and had an equally distinguished career in Philosophy at Edinburgh from 1905 to 1909. Like John, he did his stint as Assistant to the Professor of Philosophy, Pringle-Pattison. From 1909 to 1913 he studied theology at New College, serving thereafter as assistant minister in North Morningside. During the war, after a short period with the Y.M.C.A. in France, he ministered as *locum* at St Boswells in the Borders; and in 1919 he was called to be minister of the United Free Church congregation at Inverbervie in Kincardineshire. For the next sixteen years he held pastoral charges - first at Bervie (until 1923), then in St John's, Cupar (from 1923 to 1930, by which time the congregation had entered the re-united Church of Scotland), and finally in St Columba, Kilmacolm (from 1930 to 1934). His increasing reputation as a theologian - his first, and for long his only book, *Faith in God*, had been delivered as the Kerr Lectures at Glasgow in 1926 - led to his appointment in 1934 to the Chair of Systematic Theology at St Mary's College, St Andrews. Here he taught until his death in 1954, by which time he had achieved international fame as the author of *God was in Christ: An Essay on Incarnation and Atonement* (1948) and as one of the leading figures on the Faith and Order Commission of the World Council of Churches.

So much by way of introduction. In the remainder of these lectures it is my plan first to look at what might be called the Baillies' inheritance (dividing it, rather arbitrarily as you may think, into The Highland Inheritance, and The Liberal-Evangelical Inheritance), and then to consider certain aspects of their achievement, the legacy which they bequeathed to theology and the Church. Throughout, my intention is as much as possible to let them speak for themselves, allowing you to judge, in the light of my fairly extensive quotations from their writings, whether or not I have been as fair as a mere historian can hope to be in the circumstances.

THE BAILLIES' INHERITANCE

a) The Highland Inheritance

There is probably no better way of introducing this part of our study than to quote a sentence from John Baillie's *Our Knowledge of God*, the first major work which he published after his return to Scotland in 1934. "I was born", he wrote, "into a Christian home, and God's earliest disclosure of His reality to my infant soul was mediated to me by the words and deeds of my Christian parents." The home referred to was the Free Church manse at Gairloch in Wester Ross, and it is worth remembering that the minister, the Revd. John Baillie, and his wife Annie Macpherson were Christians of a very special kind:

> Celts by race and (like nearly all Highlanders
> outside Arisaig and Moidart and the southernmost
> islands of the Outer Hebrides) Calvinists
> by conviction.

The influence of both these facts was clearly evident not only in their lives but in the lives of their children, and consequently deserves some further attention.

In the charming 'Lyrical Appraisal' of Edinburgh's recently retired Professor of Divinity which John A. Mackay of Princeton (another Gael!) contributed to the Scottish Journal of Theology in 1956, notice was taken of "the curious circumstance" that the first Scottish President of the World Council of Churches should belong to an area which the Romans, because they failed to conquer it, did not regard as within the Oikoumene. But of course there was - and is - a Celtic culture in spite of what the Romans (and later the Sassenach) may have thought; and Mackay was surely right when he opined that the Celtic inheritance helped to account both for the beautiful and imaginative prose in which the Baillies' books were written and for their life-long commitment to learning *and* piety in indissoluble union. "The fact", Mackay observed, "that to a greater extent than any (other) professional theologian of our time John Baillie's work") we should include Donald's name here too) "combined the finest scholarship with a deep devotional spirit harks back to Highland religion at its best." According to the same writer, it was this Highland background which helped to produce the *Diary of Private Prayer* (with which should be coupled the earlier *Daybook of Prayer* for which Donald was largely responsible), as well as accounting, at least in part, for the brothers' interest in religious experience. In Mackay's phrase, "It was the glory of religion in the Scottish Highlands in those days" - he is referring to Victorian period - "that theological orthodoxy and personal piety were an equal concern."

But if the Celtic influence is clearly perceptible in various aspects of the Baillies' lives and work, it was the orthodoxy of Calvinism and the Evangelical fervour of the Late-Victorian Free Church which played the most prominent part in their religious upbringing. The father of the family, who arrived in Gairloch from a charge at Moy and Tomatin in 1875, has been described (by John) as "a Calvinist divine of strong character and courtly bearing"; the mother, though perhaps less severe and more flexible in outlook, shared her husband's loyalties to the full and was "not only conversant" with the intricacies of the Westminster standards but "well able to answer any objections that might be brought against them." The atmosphere which, together, they created, and the teaching which they gave made an indelible impression on their three sons: John, Donald and Peter (who was drowned in 1914, only months after arriving in India as a medical missionary). Perhaps the earliest testimony to their influence which I have come across is to be found in an article contributed by John to an American compilation, *Contemporary American Theology : Theological Autobiographies*, which was edited by Vergilius Ferm of Wooster, Ohio and appeared in 1933.

Entitled 'Confessions of a Transplanted Scot', this essay draws attention, in the author's characteristically lucid and stylish way, to what we might call the doctrinal and devotional ingredients in the Highland version of orthodox Calvinism. On the doctrinal side, John declares that "I have never, since those days, had the good fortune to live in a community that was, generally speaking, so well acquainted with the contents of the Bible or so well able to explain and defend what it professed to believe", and adds that "Not many systems of thought have been devised which (once certain initial premises are granted) hang together in so coherent a whole, or in which the vulnerable Achilles heel is so hard to find."

(Incidentally, *And the Life Everlasting*, which came out in the following year, 1934, contains a complementary passage which fills out these remarks in a particularly attractive, if slightly off-taking way. "Among the very earliest picture my memory provides", John writes, "is one which, though I see it but dimly, has come back to me again and again during the preparation of the following pages. I am sitting on my father's knee in the day-nursery of a manse in the Scottish Highlands, contentedly gazing into the fire which burns brightly on the hearth. My father asks me what is the chief end of man and I reply, with perfect readiness, that man's chief end is to glorify God and to enjoy Him for ever. This is, of course, the first question and answer of the Shorter Catechism which, having been agreed upon by a notable body of divines assembled at Westminster, was prescribed by the General Assembly of the Kirk of Scotland at its meeting in Edinburgh in July 1648, as a 'Directory for catechising such as are of weaker capacity'. My own infant capacity must have been very weak indeed, for 'chiefend' was to me a single word, and a word whose precise meaning was beyond my imagining. But I did grasp, I think, even then, something of the general teaching that was meant to be conveyed, and I grew up understanding and believing that only in the everlasting enjoyment of God's presence could my life ever reach its proper and divinely appointed fulfilment." That the influence of this teaching persisted to the end of life is demonstrated (among other things) by the fact that John Baillie's last book, *The Sense of the Presence of God*, contains no fewer than half a dozen quotations from, or references to, the Westminster Confession and the Catechism.)

As for the devotional side of Highland orthodoxy, John's 'Confessions of a Transplanted Scot' waxes even more eloquent thereon. The official symbols, he maintains, should be set alongside "as deep and sincere a development of personal religion as could, perhaps, anywhere be pointed to in the Christian world." And he continues, in a paragraph or two whose importance is such that I propose to quote them virtually in their entirety: "The practice of prayer, private, domestic and public, was given a primary place in the daily and weekly round and was a deep reality for men's thoughts. There was a strong evangelical note, so that one's mind was constantly being turned upon the necessity of regeneration, and yet any kind of sensational or over-emotional 'evangelistic' movement was looked at askance. For never in any type of religion was there a greater sense of solemnity than in this one. Nowhere else, however imposing and fitting may have been the ritual, have I ever been so aware of the *mysterium tremendum* as in those rare celebrations of the Lord's Supper. Here, if ever, *das Numinose*, 'the sense of the holy', was found prevailing; the comparative rarity of the occasion giving to the sacramental feast that very same acuteness of emphasis which in another tradition (that which I have since learned to prefer) is fostered rather by the opposite rule of frequency. In recent days and in certain other parts of the world to which Scottish influence has penetrated, Presbyterianism has on occasion become a markedly unsacramental religion, the 'coming to the Lord's Table' being sometimes regarded as not very much more than a pleasant piece of old fashioned sentiment and therefore an optional addition to one's central religious duties. Nothing, however, could be a greater departure from original Scottish religion as I knew it in my youth. The whole year's religion then seemed to me to revolve round the two half-yearly celebrations, together with their attendant special services stretching from the 'Fast Day' on Thursday...until the following Monday evening. The Scottish sacramental doctrine is a very 'high' one, though not in the sense of conformity to the too crude theory that developed within the Latin countries..."

Out of this rich soil, as John Mackay, John Dow, Isobel Forrester and others have shown, flowered the subtle theology of *Our Knowledge of God* and *God was in Christ*, the restrained but fervent piety of the *Diary of Private Prayer*, and Donald's last lectures on the Sacraments. It has often been argued that Scottish religion during the last two centuries or so has ever and again been re-vitalised by blood transfusions from the Gaelic-speaking North-West. I am sure that this is true; and no better example can be found of the vivifying power still present in the religious tradition of the Highland area than the contribution made to twentieth-century life and thought by those sons of a Ross-shire manse, John and Donald Macpherson Baillie.

b) The Humanist Inheritance

While the Baillies owed their initial training in theology to the tradition we have just examined, neither would have become the leader he ultimately was had it not been for the co-existence in his mind, alongside the insights supplied by Highland Calvinism, of the very different (and at times frankly inimical) inheritance of humanist culture. We must, therefore, now consider the influence exerted upon them by school and university, and the transformation wrought in their thinking when the Calvinist world-view met with another approach to the problems of human nature and destiny.

(i) At school

A memorable glimpse of the encounter just referred to is provided by John Baillie in the biographical sketch of his brother with which he introduced the latter's posthumously-published volume on *The Theology of the Sacraments*. After referring to the sharpening of mind which was brought about by their "home training in theological dialectic", he remarks: "The sharpening, however, would have been much less had it not been for our growing doubts about some of the premises on which the (Calvinist) system rested. These, as I can now see, were first generated in our minds by the considerably different climate of thought to which we were introduced by what we learned at school."

The school in question was Inverness Royal Academy, then passing through one of the greatest phases in its long and distinguished history; and the climate of thought to which John alludes was that which has increasingly dominated the Western world ever since the Renaissance. "Our minds were awakened", he writes, "and our imaginations stirred by what we heard there, and we were given the keys of what to us, brought up as we had been, was something of a new intellectual kingdom - even if our independent reading and our eager discussions with some of our fellow scholars had as much to do with the actual unlocking of the doors as what our masters (several of whom were very remarkable men) had to tell us...Together we explored the riches of European literature. Together also we served our own apprenticeship in the literary art, especially in the making of what we thought was poetry." But along with the enrichment and the exhilaration came problems and perplexities, for it was exceedingly difficult - indeed, wellnigh impossible - to reconcile the Calvinist *Weltanschauung* with that to which they had now been admitted. Just how difficult is made plain by one of the most arresting paragraphs in John's reminiscences of that time. "I have often reflected", he observes, "that parents who dutifully bring up their children in a traditional orthodoxy which has never subjected itself to the challenge of Renaissance and Aufklärung, and who then send them to a school whose whole ethos is of humanist inspiration, seldom realise the extent of the spiritual stress and strain to which they are then subjecting them. Our minds, for example, were soon set afire by the reading of Shakespeare, but there was no room at all for Shakespeare within the Puritanism of our early upbringing; no room for theatre of any kind; but no room especially for Shakespeare's large and generous and delicately discriminating appreciation of the human scene. Again, we were trained at school to develop a fastidious sense for the weighing of historical evidence, and for distinguishing fact from legend; but our training at home did not allow us to practise this skill on the Bible stories. Or once more, we were abruptly introduced to the world-view of modern science, and we could not make it square with the up-and-down, three-storey, geocentric universe of the Biblical writers and of our Catechism, or with their assumptions about the natural history of the human race."

We will concern ourselves later with some of the details of the reconciliation which the Baillies effected between traditional theology and humanistic culture. Suffice it for the moment to say that neither of them was in any doubt that such a reconciliation was called for; and that if they subsequently attained an eminent place among the Christian thinkers of their time they were also without any equivocation men of the modern world - men whose understanding of the Faith was deeply affected by the intellectual revolution which we associate with the Renaissance and the Age of Reason and the scientific advances of the Victorian era. And it is probably of considerable significance that when the Baillie family moved south to Edinburgh in 1905 they attended, not the local Free Church (as apparently they had done in Inverness, even after the split of 1900), but South Morningside United Free Church, - and that when John and Donald embarked in due course upon the study of Divinity it was to New College (one of the seminaries of the liberal United Free Church), and not the Free Church College next door to it, that they gravitated. The great divide (so far as theology is concerned) had been crossed.

(ii) At university

During the Baillies' time as students of philosophy at Edinburgh no change quite so basic as that which we have just considered took place in their over-all outlook. The tensions already alluded to were, however, by no means entirely resolved. Indeed, it was in the years between, say, 1905 and 1910 that the brothers were forced as never before to come to grips with the most negative aspects of modern thought (so far as Christian faith was concerned): the mechanistic materialism which seemed to be carrying all before it at the beginning of this century; the exuberant belief in evolutionary progress; the Comtian system of atheistic humanism. Looking back on the pre-War period from the vantage point of the nineteen-thirties, John recalled that "he must indeed have been a bold man, and must have risked the sneers of all the emancipated and knowing ones, who dared to speak a word against the principle of universal causation or the invariability of natural laws or the conservation of energy or the conservation of matter or the non-inheritance of acquired characteristics or the point-for-point correspondence of mind with brain." Yet in all their struggle with the difficulties created for traditional orthodoxy by recent developments in European thought the Baillies never allowed themselves to draw a sharply divisive line between faith and culture. What they did, rather, was to counter unbelieving humanism with the weapons of the mainstream humanist tradition of the West; and in that battle three influences above all seem to have enabled them to keep their footing - the remarkably healthy atmosphere (as they saw it) of church life in Edwardian Edinburgh, the steadying effect of their new-found delights in literature and the arts and their continued sensitivity to the beauties of the natural world, and the middle-of-the-road attitude of their honoured mentor in philosophy, Professor Pringle-Pattison. Describing the prevalent temper of Edinburgh's religious life in his student days, John remembered how "Robert Rainy and Marcus Dods were then well known and venerable figures in its streets. Alexander Whyte and John Kelman...were at the height of their powers. During several winters I was a keenly interested member of Alexander Whyte's famous Bible class...And who that ever heard or saw John Kelman can forget the fine manliness of his spirituality or the breeze of fresh air that he carried with him wherever he went?" He then went on to say - I'm quoting once again from his 'Confessions of a Transplanted Scot' - that "Moreover, one was of an age to become deeply interested in the various arts, and to begin to entertain dreams of travel such as might give those interests greater opportunity of development. And one's exploration of general literature was as eager as ever, and one's own scribblings as frequent. Thus there was not likely to be any entirely sharp cleft between one's general spiritual life and the philosophical conclusions that were gradually taking shape in one's mind." Finally, what John called his "progress towards a more secure mental outlook" was greatly aided, not only by "the two great philosophers of ancient and modern times respectively, Plato and Kant" but by the teaching of Professor Pringle-Pattison, that stalwart opponent of the extreme Hegelian Idealism represented by F.H. Bradley and Bernard Bosanquet. "I was more and more becoming convinced", he tells us, "of the essential wisdom of my honoured teacher (and later my very dear friend), Pringle-Pattison. These were the days of high (and now almost historic) debate between Pringle-Pattison and Bosanquet. I wonder if there are many who now doubt that the former, whether or not his own position be ultimately acceptable, at least carried off the honours." So fortified by their professor's contention that "our experience does not reveal itself on one plane, but on a variety of planes, and that it is the business of a comprehensive philosophy to assign to each level of experience its true place and measure of importance, according to the degree of value and ultimacy which it finds it to possess", the Baillies took from the Old College to the New three basic principles or convictions which they never really abandoned: (i) "interpret by the highest", (ii) religious faith is "a way of knowledge which is at least equal to any other in point of reliability and which leads us into the presence of a Reality that is not discoverable by any other means", and (iii) there is an organic connection between faith and morals (a point to be developed later). They had, I suggest, travelled quite a long way along the road which would lead them to a reconciliation of the two principal strands - Highland orthodoxy and cultural humanism - in their spiritual and intellectual inheritance.

c) The Liberal-Evangelical Inheritance

The two brothers came up to New College in immediately successive years, John in 1908 and Donald in 1909. So far as I can judge, their theological stance and their over-all religious attitude deviated in no important respect from that which characterised the United Free Church in general and New College in particular during that halycon period before the First World War. Their teachers - still well-known names today - included Principal Alexander Whyte (to whom John paid tribute in words already quoted), Alexander Martin in Apologetics and Pastoral Theology, H.R. Mackintosh in Systematic Theology, and H.A.A. Kennedy in New Testament. Each of them may be taken as epitomising, to a greater or lesser extent, the revolution in Scottish religion which had taken place between 1860 and 1910 approximately: the revolution which transported our national Presbyterianism out of the Conservative-Evangelical into the Liberal-Evangelical camp.

The new orthodoxy to which John and Donald fell heir was marked, I suggest, by three outstanding characteristics: deference to the methods and findings of natural science, wariness of all credal and confessional statements, and commitment to the use of literary and historical criticism in the study of the Bible. On the first it should perhaps be said that in the early decades of this century Scotland's leading theologians were more sceptical about the extreme claims then made for science, and more aware of the dangers attendant upon exclusive absorption in its pursuits, than their conservative critics were - and are - willing to admit. But it is also true that they seldom tired of affirming their belief that the discoveries of biology, chemistry and physics, if properly understood, would only reinforce the Christian interpretation of the universe; and few if any of them were inclined to repudiate the main principles of evolutionary theory. With this attitude the Baillies in their maturity indicated fairly general agreement - though they tended to express it with greater caution than their teachers had done. John, for example, after devoting a good deal of his attention in the early nineteen-fifties to the relations between science and religion, came to the conclusion that science, though of inestimable value (not least to religion) could nevertheless be dangerously misused. Arguing that it had a three-fold service to render to "the things that matter absolutely" - (i) by exposing the manner of nature's operations and so enabling us to harness these operations for the attainment of ends which we spiritually discern to be worth seeking; (ii) by revealing to us the instrumentality by which God works out His purposes; and (iii) by helping to provide "that element of otherness and conflict which is so necessary a part of our spiritual discipline" -, he averred that "it is to our Christian advantage to pursue our scientific researches with unabated vigour. No good will ever come of setting any limit to the advance of scientific knowledge. The relations of science and faith are not such that faith comes in where science stops, or comes in to fill up the gaps and supply the missing links. God is not a stop-gap. He is not to be discerned through the cracks of our experience but as giving meaning to the whole. Or, to put it more abstractly, purpose is not to be called in where mechanism fails, or primary causes where no secondary causes can be discovered. Rather is mechanism everywhere, and is everywhere the servant of purpose. The two conceptions are not alternatives but complementary." At the same time, he warned against an even more fatal error than "curtailing scientific enquiry to make room for faith" - namely, "to allow our faith to be stifled by our science." And his final observation on the subject was this: "When the two kinds of knowledge appear to conflict, or when we have most difficulty is seeing how they dovetail into each other, it is quite unreasonable, and in the end it is as unscientific as it is faithless, to cut the Gordian knot by abandoning either in order to abide by the other, by abating either to give the other greater room, or by whittling down both so that they may be more easily mortised. What we must rather do is to accept this strain as inherent in our human situation, resolutely resisting the temptation to resolve it in a premature way, living with it humbly as befits us, and profiting by the discipline it imposes, until such time as a maturer wisdom brings its own better solution."

(I have been quoting here from an article entitled, 'Relating Science to Faith', which John wrote for a little volume on *Science and Faith Today* that was published by the Lutherworth Press in 1953; but the same message is conveyed in his *Natural Science and the Spiritual Life*,

the Philosophical Discourse he delivered two years previously at
Edinburgh before the British Association for the Advancement of
Science.)

The second distinguishing mark of pre-War Liberal Evangelicalism,
I have suggested, was wariness of all credal and confessional statements:
a wariness which had served to bring about the great Declaratory Acts
of 1879 and 1892 and the Church of Scotland's Act on the Formula
of Subscription in 1910. In 1903 Professor W.A. Curtis's inaugural
lecture at Aberdeen asserted that the doctrinal details of the
Westminster Confession could "no longer be claimed to represent the
spontaneous beliefs of the great majority of our preachers and
teachers", and four years later (the year before John Baillie went up
to New College) that view found support in an important compilation
which had as its title, *Creed Revision in Scotland: its Necessity and
Scope*. None of the authors (who included James Moffatt, E.F. Scott,
R.H. Strachan and John Herkless) was a teacher at New College; but
J.H. Leckie became one of Donald's close friends, and I doubt whether
either of the brothers would have quarrelled with his analysis of the
contemporary situation. "The fact of dominant force today", wrote
Leckie, "is that the professed creed of the Church does not any longer,
as a system, have any particular relation to its religious life. The
Westminster Confession is not expounded in our theological colleges.
You may search the libraries of many divines and find no copy of it
there. It was read for the first time by many official Presbyterians
when the decision of the House of Lords in the Church case gave it
a new and painful interest. No man writes his sermons with conscious
regard to its venerable propositions, nor does any theological professor
compose his books in the light of its authority. The central thoughts,
also, of the Confession are no longer the central thoughts of living
faith. The doctrine of Predestination, which is the keystone of the
Westminster arch, holds no vital place in the belief of modern men;
while, on the other hand, the idea of the Divine Fatherhood, though
it is the centre of real faith today, finds no adequate expression
whatever in the ancient creed of the Presbyterian Church."

Leckie was no doubt a rather shrill expositor of the view then
prevailing; but even the briefest scrutiny of John Baillie's earlier
works would seem to suggest that he was not devoid of sympathy with

it. *The Roots of Religion* (1926) contains a reference to "the many who have lost their way in (Christianity's) maze of doctrines and of sects", and declares: "We must make re-discovery, and help others to make re-discovery, of the true centre of gravity in this accumulated mass of tradition." And in *The Place of Jesus Christ in Modern Christianity* (1929), while admitting that "the Christian epic" (Santayana's phrase) "reflects and embodies the most profoundly important truth that has ever presented itself to the mind of man", Baillie also asserts that "to a large number of men and women of our day this great drama reads, not like a history, nor yet like a philosophy, but...like a chapter from the world's mythology...And you and I understand these feelings of theirs well enough, and even share them ourselves in no small measure. The fault, we feel, is at least not all on one side. We cannot think that all this modern estrangement from the traditional epic of salvation" - the epic to which Westminster bore witness - "is *wholly* due to spiritual obtuseness and corruption of heart on the part of our eagerly-seeking contemporaries. We are ready to acknowledge that in part at least it is due to some serious defect in the epic itself." In so writing, John was not untypical of the mood which dominated Scottish theology for some time both before and after the years when he and Donald were students at New College - though it is interesting to find that even in such a relatively late work as *Our Knowledge of God* (1939) he was concerned to point out that "the members of that Assembly (he means Westminster) were too intellectualistic in their interpretation of Christian faith, too ready to understand revelation as consisting in communicated information."

The third characteristic of Scotland's Liberal Evangelicalism in the years before the First World War was, I have suggested, commitment to the use of literary and historical criticism in the study of the Bible. John tells us (in the 'Confessions' of 1939) that "the historical study of the New Testament" was one new world which opened up to him at New College, and continues: "During my first year as a student of theology a small group of us - most of whom were 'philosophers' - made a habit of meeting together once a week for the study of the Greek text of Mark. The following year we received much stimulus from the lectures of the very distinguished scholar (Harry Kennedy) who then occupied the chair of New Testament in our college. And in the summers I listened to the lectures of two equally distinguished

New Testament scholars in Germany. I have never since lost my interest in these studies." So far as Biblical studies as a whole were concerned, what the Baillies found at New College - as also in Germany - was a fairly general consensus on the "assured results" (so called) of the literary and historical criticism of the sacred books. Theories concerning the non-Mosaic authorship of the Pentateuch, the non-Davidic authorship of many of the Psalms, and the non-apostolic authorship of the Gospels (theories canonised by Peake's Commentary, which was first published in 1919 and found on most ministers' shelves in the nineteen-twenties) were widely accepted; an evolutionary account of Israel's religion was probably the rule rather than the exception; the literal interpretation of many a Biblical narrative was being abandoned and open acknowledgment of a diversity of attitudes among the New Testament writers frequently made. While the more exciting and radical implications of the new approach did not find such enthusiastic advocacy at New College as they did in the Glasgow College of the United Free Church, it should not be forgotten that Marcus Dods, whose brief principalship ended in the year when Donald Baillie became a divinity student, had in his inaugural lecture of 1890 asserted that the doctrine of verbal inspiration was "a theory...which has made the Bible an offence to many honest men; which is dishonouring to God, and which has turned inquirers into sceptics by the thousand - a theory which should be branded as heretical in every Christian Church." Dods survived the uproar occasioned by these remarks to become an honoured figure in the Church, earning praise from none other than Alexander Whyte for his "noble catholicity of mind and heart." And of course Whyte himself (who was Principal of New College throughout the Baillies' student days there) had at Dod's induction as Professor of New Testament declared that "The historical, exegetical and theological problems connected with New Testament study in our day are not the ephemeral heresies of restless and irreverent minds; they are the providential result of that great awakening of serious thought, and of scholarly and devout enquiry, which began at the Reformation and has been in steady progress in the best schools of Christendom ever since." I think it would be true to say that Whyte, more than anyone else, set the tone of New College in the period of which we are thinking - and it was he who, at the height of the Robertson Smith case a generation earlier, had dared to tell the Free Church General Assembly: "You cannot arrest the movement of minds in Christendom of which these inculpated writings are an outcome. Had this movement of the theological mind been confined to Professor Smith and a handful of German or Germanised scholars like himself, you might have ignored it or arrested its progress in your Church. But the movement is not of them; they are rather of it. They are its children, and they cannot but be its servants. Fathers and brethren, the mind of the world does not stand still. And the theological mind will stand still at its peril."

Although the Baillies' dominant interest was always in theology (strictly defined) rather than in Biblical studies, there can be no doubt that the attitude of men like Kennedy, Dods and Whyte became their own, and that their Evangelicalism was always much more of the liberal than the conservative brand. As late as 1956, for example, John wrote as follows in *The Idea of Revelation in Recent Thought*: "The intelligent reading of the Bible - 'in the spirit, but with the mind also' - and the reading of it so as to understand how it *Christum treibt,* depends entirely on our ability to distinguish what is central from what is peripheral; to distinguish its unchanging truth from its clothing in the particular cultural and cosmological preconceptions of the times and places in which it was written; to distinguish also between its essential message and its numerous imperfections - historical inaccuracies, inaccurate or conflicting reports, misquotations or misapplied quotations from the Old Testament in the New, and such like; and withal to distinguish the successive levels of understanding both within the Old Testament and in the transition from that to the New. We must be as frank in our acknowledgement of this as is, for example, Dr {C.H.} Dodd when, having quoted some passages from Isaiah, he goes on: 'Any theory of the Bible which suggests that we should recognise such utterances as authoritative for us stands self-condemned. They are relative to their age. But I think we should say more. They are false and they are wrong. If they were inevitable in that age - and this is a theory which can neither be proved nor disproved - then in so far that age was astray from God. In any case the men who spoke so were imperfectly harmonised with the will of God.'" And in perhaps the very last autobiographical statement which we have from him - 'Some Reflections on the Changing Theological Scene', which appeared in the *Union Seminary Quarterly Review* in 1957 - John recalled how in the battle of the nineteen-twenties between fundamentalists and modernists he was very ill at ease with the latter, who "seemed to me to be using their new-found freedom in order to read their own very nineteenth-century predilections and philosophy of life into the Biblical teaching, and thus to be corrupting the true and original Christian message." Yet he had "scant enough sympathy" with the fundamentalists. They, he tells us, "thought of themselves as defending the tradition of their Puritan forefathers, and so in a sense they were, but their defence was inevitably tempered very differently from the original formation of that tradition. The Puritans might be said to have been naive fundamentalists because up to that time the plenary inspiration of Holy Scripture and the reliability of Biblical history had never been challenged. But in endeavouring to occupy the self-same position the fundamentalists of 1919 were belligerently repudiating the whole development of modern documentary criticism and scientific historiography which had grown up in the intervening period, and I had no doubt at all in my mind that in doing this they were defending a lost cause."

That fundamentalism must be looked upon as a lost cause was a conviction which (so far as I can see) neither of the Baillies was ever persuaded to abandon. Thus to the very end of their lives they remained true to the Liberal Evangelicalism which they had embraced at New College nearly half a century before.

THE IMPACT OF THE WAR

For most people who took part in it, the first World War (the "Great War") was by far the most memorable experience of their entire lives. Even for intellectuals, who sometimes march to a different drum from other people, it was deeply influential - and the Baillies were no exception. John, in particular, found his whole way of life transformed and his range of experiences immeasurably broadened, as he tells us in his 'Confessions of a Transplanted Scot' of 1933. "The years - not much less than four - which I spent in France during the War", he writes, "were fallow years for me, as for so many others. I hardly read a page either of divinity or of metaphysics, and I had little time or opportunity for consecutive thinking. Yet the period brought with it a very great broadening of experience and, above all, such an understanding of the mind and temper, the spiritual needs and capacities, of average (perhaps I should rather say of *normal*) humanity as I at least had not before possessed." He refers to a remark made in E.M. Forster's *The Longest Journey* about a character who was "only used to Cambridge, and to a very small corner of that" : "He was more skilled than (his companions) were in the principles of human existence, but he was not so indecently familiar with the examples". And then he adds this revealing sentence: "When I turned again to my old pursuits after the War was over, the khaki figures still seemed to keep their place in the background of my mind, and in much of what I have written since these days a clairvoyant reader may find them haunting the margins of the page."

I think it could be said without fear of contradiction that - more than anything else - John Baillie's experience during the War strengthened his already very considerable desire not only to grasp but also to communicate what is *real* in religion. His first book, *The Roots of Religion*, bears ample testimony to that. You may recall how he discusses at its outset "the main features of the situation that is at present confronting the Christian Church", and calls to his help "the very considerable number of books and articles which were written during, or immediately after, the Great War about the religion of the men who were engaged in it." And he reports a two-fold conclusion. First, the soldier's concern for *reality*, not least in matters of faith. "Not only...was the army's religion the religion of the nation's prime manhood, but it was the religion of that manhood when face to face with most searching and testing experience that had come to it for long centuries. In their own vernacular, these men were 'up against it' as they had never been before. They were thrown back upon the roots of their being, and there was in consequence among them - as one can testify not only from the literature but from one's own long experience among them - a most remarkable and hardly-to-be-exaggerated sense for reality and for the difference between reality and shame. No word indeed appears more commonly in the literature of which I am speaking then just this word *reality*." Second, and much more disturbingly, Baillie had to report the Churches' failure to satisfy this passion for reality. "If we put all the evidence together", he told his readers, "one main charge stands out in the very boldest relief, and that is that there is a lack of reality about the religion of the Christian Church, and a conspicuous unrelatedness to the real problems of human life."

The Roots of Religion was a preliminary attempt to uncover the reality of the Christian faith and to demonstrate its relevance to the problems of life - but one could say without too much exaggeration that the remainder of John's career, and Donald's also, was devoted to the same endeavour.

THE BAILLIES' LEGACY

a) Sensitivity in the Treatment of Doubt and Unbelief

There are some arresting sentences in John Baillie's *Invitation to Pilgrimage* where he advises the Christian apologist always to remember that "the debate between belief and unbelief is by no means a debate between himself who believes and another who disbelieves. It is also in large part a debate within himself, who both believes and disbelieves, and who must ever continue to pray humbly, 'Lord, I believe; help Thou mine unbelief'." And he continues: "When we who are within the visible Church of Christ reason with those who are without, we are never in the position of feeling that there is in our interlocutors no disposition to believe, and in ourselves no disposition to doubt...We still do not find faith easy, and hence our *apologia* is always in some sort addressed to ourselves as well as to our neighbours...The most moving and persuasive arguments are always those in which the arguer is felt to be holding high debate with himself...When one looks back over the road oneself has travelled, anything like dogmatism appears very much out of place; anything also like a fencing method or a parade of dialectical skill or the desire to score merely a plausible victory over the opponent." Elsewhere in the same volume, indeed, he is even prepared to say of believers and unbelievers that "in our outlook on *everything*, in our response to *all* life's alarms, there is something that we have in common and again something that divides us. And I am sure that the bit of the road that most requires to be illuminated is the point where it forks. If we could only discover why it is that, when a certain stage is reached, we take different turnings and begin to walk apart, we should perhaps be doing all that we can humanly do. The rest is not in our hands, but the hands of Something or Someone not ourselves; for faith is not an achievement but a gift." (A similar view, incidentally, can be found in Donald's work - as when, speaking in his British Association sermon at Edinburgh in 1951 of the difficulties which "sincere and honest souls" have with belief, he commented parenthetically: "far be it from me to speak of these difficulties with anything but respect and sympathy".)

It is clear that the sympathy thus expressed and the sensitivity thus shown had their origins - at least in part - in a history of personally-experienced anguish and scepticism. Donald, in particular, was haunted from an early age by doubts which his brother later diagnosed as due to the conflict then raging in his mind between traditional orthodoxy and the humanist ethos. The distress they caused him was great even during his schooldays; but at university, where they extended to more fundamental issues, their effect was still greater. As John tells us in the biographical essay which introduces *The Theology of the Sacraments*, "Donald was afterwards to be a valiant defender of the faith...but he had to pass through a long struggle from which only slowly was he able to emerge. It brought with it nervous strain of an acute kind. He could not coerce himself to the methodical reading of the texts required for the approaching examinations, but would rather concentrate his thought for hours at a stretch on a single page, or even sentence, in one of them which seemed to promise some possible relief of his problem. And how often did I see him sit for a whole evening, staring at a book but not seeing it, and turning no page of it, while his mind kept reverting in spite of himself to a spiritual predicament concerning which the book had no real enlightenment to offer!" By the time he got to New College, Donald's struggle for faith had "measurably eased"; but it was by no means altogether a thing of the past, and his brother's memoir suggests that perhaps the shadow never entirely lifted. "Even in his latest years", we read, "he had periods of depression, in which life seemed to be emptied of its divine meaning. He was in the poorest possible health then, a martyr to a long-standing asthmatic condition, and the depression was physical as well as mental. He would put to himself and to me the question as to whether the extreme bodily lassitude was the cause or the result, or merely the accompaniment, of the darkness of the soul.

But one thing was always clear to him - that without God and Christ human life was without significance of any kind, devoid of all interest. He would say, 'When the darkness is on me, I walk down the street, and see people walking aimlessly about, and shops and cars and a few dogs, and it all seems to mean nothing and to matter not at all'! It was Pascal's misère de l'homme sans Dieu."

Nor was John exempt from the same *Anfechtungen*. In *The Idea of Revelation* he recalls a conversation he once had with a lawyer in the States whose expression of elemental doubt brought back the memory of his own youthful agonisings. "'You speak', he said, 'of trusting God, of praying to Him and doing His will. But it's all so one-sided. We speak to God, we bow down before Him and lift up our hearts to Him. But He never speaks to us. He makes no sign. It's all so one-sided.' Nor was it without real understanding and fellow-feeling that I heard him speak thus, for there had been a time when I used to say the same things to myself...I can remember, during my student years in Edinburgh, walking home one frosty midnight from a philosophical discussion on the existence of God, and stopping in my walk to gaze up at the starry sky. Into those deep immensities of space I hurled my despairing question, but it seemed to hit nothing, and no answer came back...The stars that night did not seem to say to me, 'The hand that made us is divine.'"

Against the background of experiences like those, the Baillies spent a great deal of time and energy in tackling the religious difficulties of their contemporaries and in suggesting how - despite such difficulties - a return to faith might be made. As an example of their approach, I don't think I can do better than quote *in extenso* an illuminating (and very typical) passage from Donald's first book, *Faith in God and its Christian Consummation*, published in 1927. "What counsel", he asks, "would the wise counsellor give to a man in the modern world who professed himself perplexed by universal doubt regarding the truth of religion?" His answer is as follows: "Instead of simply arguing with the doubter and endeavouring to prove religion, or telling him to make up his mind to believe, by an effort of will, or even advising 'religious practice'" (references, these, to notions first published by William James at the end of the nineteenth century), "*the wise counsellor would probably say something like this. 'Underneath your* doubt, don't you feel at least a basal kind of certainty about the meaning of your life in the universe? You may feel uncertain about all the dogmas of religion as you have been accustomed to conceive them. But, to go down to something much more simple and elemental, can't you find in the bottom of your heart an ineradicable conviction that the universe is not without a purpose of good, which makes it worthwhile for you even to face your doubts and play the man; that all is not blind chance, but that there is a meaning and principle of good at the heart of all things?" Then, commenting on the answer just given, he adds: "Now it is very important to note that in saying all this to your doubter, in such a persuasive and practical way, you are not appealing to his will, his choice, his voluntary agency, or to his wants and wishes as to what he shall believe. Nor are you practising suggestion in the proper sense. You are appealing to a conviction which you think he has even underneath his doubts. And if you are successful, and he confesses to such a conviction, then you will tell him that he is not so entirely devoid of belief as he had miserably supposed; that this is already the beginning of faith, though it looks so different from the dogmas he had been doubting; and that this faith is enough to begin with, enough to live on for the time, until, through faithfulness to it, he gradually finds it growing into something more explicit. It may be no more than what R.L. Stevenson calls

'The half of a broken hope for a pillow at night

That somehow the light is the right

And the smooth shall bloom from the rough.'

Stevenson cries out, 'Lord, if that were enough?' and again, 'God, if this were faith?' Well, you would tell your doubter that it *is* enough to begin with; it *is* faith, though he does not realise it. And it is to this deep, fundamental, unrealised faith, and not merely to his will, that you make your appeal. Thus, when the doubter valiantly makes up his mind to believe, as James would have him do, he is not really so much *making up* his mind as *discovering* his deeper mind, falling back upon a basal conviction which had been obscured by doubts and difficulties, but which was really there all the time in an elemental form. If he *chooses*, he does so because of a fundamental conviction that the side of faith is the right side... The venture of faith does not mean the determination to accept a belief without any grounds, nor the adoption of the 'religious hypothesis' with a view to verification, nor the resolve to act as if this 'hypothesis' were true, nor the courage which lives nobly without any sure beliefs at all. It means rather the advantage of living nobly in a world which can never give us direct proof of the triumph of good, living nobly in the light of a conviction which is not, indeed, uncertain so far as it goes, but which may be hard to grasp and articulate, which leaves us uncertain on many points, and which in any case is not demonstrable in the ordinary way. It is really the living and acting that can be called a venture, not the faith itself. And this venture of faith can be called a venture, not because it acts without any assurance, on a mere chance, but because its assurance is a faith in the ultimate reality and triumph of good, and cannot give any guarantee as to the immediate outcome of any particular endeavour in this world. That is the sense in which every man of faith has 'gone out, not knowing whither he went', to 'look for a city which hath foundations, whose builder and maker is God', not sure of where it is to be found or what it is like, or perhaps of anything else about it that can be put into words, and yet sure at least in a dim and desperate way of its existence."

There is a not dissimilar passage in John's first book, *The Roots of Religion*, published just a year previously, where in a chapter addressed to "the needs of those who have difficulty about the acceptance of religious belief", he writes: "I may be in the direst uncertainty about the nature of this 'scheme of things entire', about its constitution and construction, about its origin and destined end; but I *know* that love is better than hurt, that courage is better than cowardice and honour than treachery, and that it is right to help one's fellow traveller out of the ditch and to pour oil and wine into his wounds. There may be little to know, and little assurance in the knowing of it, but there is always plenty to do, and for the man who looks it straight in the face, plenty of assurance that it is worth doing." And so, by way of a quotation from Carlyle's *Sartor Resartus* ("Do the duty which is nearest to thee") to the Baillies' early favourite, F.W. Robertson ("It must be right to do right") and this conclusion: the argument with doubt "should consist simply in the attempt to bring to clear consciousness, and to express in precise language, the nature of the compulsion which in every age had led earnest seekers after righteousness to trust in an Eternal Righteousness, and has inspired devoted workers to believe that they are working for a more-than-human Cause.... It is agreed that there is nothing of which I am more certain than that an absolute obligation is laid upon me to do the right and eschew the wrong, but what is it that thus obliges me, if it be not some larger order of things to which I stand related? How can values like truthfulness and unselfishness and courage have any claim upon me, if they are not grounded in the all-enclosing system to which I belong? How can the Ultimate Reality demand Righteousness in me, if Itself be not righteous?"

Most of us are probably very conscious, in listening to all that, of its Ritschlian flavour and its rather dated argumentation. My concern is by no means to defend it *à l'outrance*, but simply to note (as an indication of what the passage of time did, both positively and negatively, to the line then taken) "some simple bits of encouragement and counsel for those times when (like Elijah) you are under the shadow of the juniper tree" - advice which Donald gave in a sermon broadcast, more than a quarter of a century later, on Low Sunday, 1954: " (1) Remember that *what really matters in the Christian life is not our feelings, our emotions, our moods, but how we live*, with dedicated wills, in faith and love ..... (3) In your bad hours, remember *the fellowship of your fellow Christians*, and lean upon it " (this last point being driven home by a beautifully apposite quotation from Bunyan's *Pilgrim's Progress*).

More importantly, perhaps, before leaving this whole subject I should like to look for a moment or two at what John has to say in *Our Knowlege of God* concerning discreditable and creditable doubts and the origins of the latter. "Part of the reason why I could not find God", he tells us, "was that there is that in God which I did not wish to find. Part of the reason why I could not (or thought I could not) hear Him speak was that He was saying some things which I did not wish to hear. There was a side of the divine reality which was unwelcome to me, and some divine commandments the obligatoriness of which I was most loath to acknowledge. And the reason why I was loath to acknowledge them was that I found them too disquieting, involving for their proper obedience a degree of courage and self-denial and a resolute reorientation of outlook and revision of program such as I was not altogether prepared to face ...... For some of what God would say to me I had a very ready ear, and I was therefore greatly disquieted by my doubts as to whether He was really addressing me at all. But because there were other of His words to which I turned a deaf ear, my deafness seemed to extend even to that for which I was most eagerly listening. It seems to me that this is very commonly the case..... We seek God 'carefully with tears'. But because we are so loath to find Him as He is, sometimes we cannot find Him at all. We have conceived our own idea of God, but it is an idea in the formation of which our sloth and selfishness have played their part; and because there is no God corresponding to our idea, and because we are looking for none other, we fail to find the God who is really there.....We cannot be assured of His care if we reject His claim. Before religion can be known as a sweet communion, it must first be known as an answered summons."

There is another side to the matter, however, and a few lines further on the writer seeks to deal with it. "But is *all* our doubt of God", he asks, "to be explained in this way? Or is part of it of quite another kind? Are we sometimes led to doubt God's reality by thinking which, however, mistaken, is nevertheless quite honest, and which, though crooked intellectually, is straightforward enough morally?" There is no hesitation about Baillie's reply here. "Plato would answer this latter questions in the affirmative .....Doubt may sometimes spring, not from the corruption of sin, but from the limitations of finitude" - and if there is no recognition of this in Paul we must simply bear in mind that while "honest doubt" may have been absent from the apostle's society it is undeniably present in ours, as it was in ancient Athens.

And so we come to the final query in this connection, and to Baillie's response: "How then are we to account for such honest doubt and denial of God's reality? The answer is perhaps two-fold. First, there is the circumstance that our conviction of God first forms itself in our minds in close association with a wide context of other beliefs. In the course of our later intellectual development, however, many of those other beliefs are seen by us to be false and are quite rightly surrendered. The effort of dissociation that is then required to separate our deep-seated belief in God from that part of its original context which we have now been forced to reject, is an effort to which our mental powers are not always equal, so that we are faced with the difficult alternative of either keeping our belief in God and keeping with it certain other beliefs the falsity of which seems quite obvious to us, or else surrendering these false beliefs and surrendering with them our belief in God also. Secondly, however, we must consider the appeal of arguments that are directed, not against the original context of our belief in God, but against that belief itself. In ancient Greece, and again in Western Europe since the Renaissance, but especially in the nineteenth century, there have been current a number of philosophical outlooks which found their starting-point elsewhere than in belief in God - that is to say either in external nature or in man...Not having set out from the reality of God, not only have they (as indeed we should have expected) failed to arrive at any conviction of His reality, but they have conducted us towards a conception of universal being from which God seems to be definitely excluded. Many men of our time are therefore in the position that, while they do (as I should contend) believe in God in the bottom of their hearts, they cannot think how to answer the arguments which certain prevailing philosophies direct against his reality, and are thus led to doubt Him 'with the top of their minds'."

b) The Linking of Faith and Morality

Those who are familiar with the whole range of the Baillies' published work will need no convincing that one of their most constant and characteristic emphases - particularly in the earlier years, but not only then - was upon the intimate and deeply significant connection between religion and ethics. Perhaps the classic statement of their views on this subject is to be found in the fifth chapter of Donald's *Faith in God*, the chapter which bears the title 'Faith and Moral Conviction'. It merits closer examination than can be given here, but in summary form it runs as follows (and I rely on Baillie's own synopsis of the argument): "When we take our moral convictions seriously, they are found to carry with them a religious conviction that goodness is at the heart of the universe, or that our ideals are laid upon us by One in whom they are somehow realised. This is the germ of faith in God, the 'grain of mustard-seed' out of which all true religious belief grows." We must, of course, be quite clear that "it is not a matter of arguing from the existence in man of a unique faculty called Conscience to the existence of a supernatural Author who could have implanted it....but rather a matter of hearkening to the *utterances* of Conscience...and so coming to detect in it the voice of God." How,

111

precisely? "Not simply (as Kant held) by a moral postulate, but in a much more direct way, as part of the very *meaning* of the moral consciousness. Either our moral values tell us something about the nature and purpose of reality, i.e. give us the germ of religious belief, or they tell us nothing at all. Thus 'mere morality' is an abortion: if morality means anything, it ultimately means - God."

Some twenty years later, Donald's unpublished lectures, *Beyond Morality*, vigorously reaffirmed the intimate and indeed intrinsic connection between morality and religion. It is true that in the nineteen-forties he was particularly anxious to stress what he called "the paradox of moralism", and to argue that "the quest of goodness defeats itself"; yet he was still prepared to speak of morality as bankrupt without religion and of religion as utterly corrupt without morality - which, in the late Professor Norman Robinson's words, does indeed represent a "manifest and impressive continuity of thought" with his earlier writings.

All the way through from *The Roots of Religion* (1926) to *The Sense of the Presence of God* (1962), Donald's brother John took a remarkably similar view. In *The Roots of Religion* he speaks of religious faith as "a consciousness which comes to the dutiful...,to those who reach after the highest values they know, that in being thus dutiful and loyal to their values, they are doing what they were meant and appointed to do, and are putting themselves in line with the Eternal and having his backing behind them." *In The Interpretation of Religion*, he declares: "What faith, when squarely interrogated, seems centrally to insist upon, is that in our consciousness of duty, or of ultimate values, there is contained an authentic intimation of the nature of the system to which we belong; and hence the only proper apologetic for religion is that which sets out the logic of this insistence. Perhaps there is no better way of setting it out than the very simple one of asking what else it can mean to say that I 'must' do this or this, except that the nature of things demands that I do it... If I am right in feeling that it is absolutely demanded of me that I be pure in heart, and just and honourable in all my dealings, then can this mean less that that reality demands these things of me? And if reality demands these things of me, then reality must be interested in moral value; it must have a stake in the moral issue; it must be on the side of the good and against the unworthy and the evil. But that is to say that it is a moral Being itself, not indifferent to moral distinctions but, on the contrary, supremely sensitive to them, and really and deeply caring whether good or evil prevails. The ultimate reality must thus be One who loves the good." In *Our Knowledge of God*, after remarking that "If a man ask himself, 'What things must I rather die than betray?' then he will know what things for him are holy", the writer goes on to argue that "the recognition of such an unconditional obligation does in fact contain in itself the recognition of a holy God who is its source" - contending that "no obligation can be absolute which does not derive from the absolute", and that "since morality is essentially a function of personality we can feel no moral obligation to an Absolute who is not apprehended by us as a personal being." And it has been pointed out (by Dr James Brown, in a valuable little study originally contributed to the *Expository Times*) that in John Baillie's last major work "The 'sense' of the presence of God...is an intuitive knowledge of divine reality given in and with the consciousness of moral obligation. Nothing can exceed the certainty of the rightness of goodness, and this contains an immediate and *a priori* acquaintance with a transcendent perfection which is God: immediate yet mediated with a certitude which 'pulses through all our thinking'."

The most interesting discussion of this typically Baillian emphasis which I have come across occurs in Professor John McIntyre's introduction to the 1964 re-issue of Donald's *Faith in God*. The verdict he passes on it can hardly be described as enthusiastic. "It is doubtful", he remarks, "whether many contemporary theologians would be prepared to agree that knowledge of one's duty is *ipso facto* knowledge of God, even of a very embryonic kind"; and he actually goes so far as to say that the passage of the years has "wrought havoc" (his words) upon such a view. "Neo-Conservative suspicion of natural reason and natural law, combined with its fear of the revival of a doctrine of justification by works" has had something to do with this; but he believes that two additional circumstances have reinforced the unfriendly attitude of the present generation. "The first is the revival of the humanism which insisted that morality was not the sole property of religion, and that it was perfectly possible to adopt moral attitudes without accepting any alleged presuppositions or consequences of morality and even to deny the necessity of religious

sanctions for the enforcement of morality. The second...is the sharp
attack levelled by positivist and linguistic philosophers upon supposedly
religious or metaphysical implications of morality." Between them,
these circumstances have "reduced the confidence of religious
philosophers in the moral argument for divine existence and generally
made them reluctant to draw any deductions from morality that might
be of significance for theology. In fact, what has tended to happen has
been that Christian ethics has been made into a discipline dependent
on Christian dogmatics, and a question-mark placed against anything
that might claim to be ethics *simpliciter.*" At the same time, Professor
McIntyre has other, somewhat more approving things to say. In one
intriguing aside he suggests that what we might call the ethical strand
in the Baillies' thinking has an interesting affinity with "popular"
existentialism. Again, when dealing with the criticisms that have
been directed against the moral argument for faith he lets fall the
provokingly enigmatic remark that he "in no way" acknowledges
their validity. And on yet another occasion he asks whether Donald
Baillie, by his insistence upon a close internal relation between faith
and morality, has not "something of tremendous relevance to say to
present-day theology." I'm not quite sure where all this leaves us; and
in any case only a foolishly brash church historian would venture to
swim in the shark-infested waters of modern theological debate. But
as I recall the deep impression which the central argument of John
Baillie's earliest writings (the argument also contained in Donald's
Kerr Lectures) made upon my own youthful religious development,
I cannot help feeling - or wishing - that in the whirligig of time the
worth of what the brothers had to say on this matter may yet be given
more unstinting recognition than it presently receives.

c) An Apologetic Concern

The Reasonableness of the Christian Faith: the attractive, if controversial,
title of a little book which David Cairns, senior, published in 1918,
might well serve as a kind of motto for much if not all of what John
and Donald Baillie stood for, and strove to demonstrate, in the years
between 1926 (when *the Roots of Religion* made its appearance) and
1963 (when *A Reasoned Faith*, a posthumous collection of John's
addresses and sermons, closed the long list of their publications).
Whatever else may be said about them, the brothers were pre-

eminently apologists for the Faith; and their life's work, from beginning to end, was dominated by an apologetic concern. Much, therefore could obviously be said under this heading. In the time available I cannot do much more than refer you, as a valuable starting-point, to the remarks made by Professor McIntyre at the conference held in New College some four years ago to celebrate the University of Edinburgh's Quater-Centenary - remarks which can be found in the September 1983 number of *New College Bulletin*. Let me mention just a few of the things he says.

(i) Professor McIntyre suggests that it was what he calls "Theology's compresence in the University with other disciplines" which challenged John Baillie - whose whole life was spent either in a university or in theological colleges closely associated with their university neighbours - to explore the relationship of theology to other branches of study. (ii) He highlights one of the key phrases in *Our Knowldge of God* - "a mediated immediacy" - as especially characteristic of John Baillie's understanding of that relationship. The concept, according to Professor McIntyre, is "a rejection of the idea that we know God directly and intuitively, by means of some sixth sense, which some have and some do not have. It is awareness of God which occurs, as [John Baillie] sometimes said, borrowing Lutheran language, 'in, with and under' other entities, such as other selves, the world, human history. The university setting is not irrelevant; for God is thought to be known in those fields in which other disciplines operate. In fact, a religious awareness is often presented as an alternative interpretation of phenomena already within the range of those other disciplines." It is not difficult to see how such a concept enabled John Baillie to relate sympathetically to the world of culture around him and to pursue the task of persuading his colleagues in Arts and Science that the theological quest was less alien from them than they had been inclined to consider it.

(iii) Professor McIntyre contends that the apologetic enterprise (as we might call it) spanned John Baillie's whole career, but that its underlying presuppositions changed quite markedly in course of time: "In the earlier years, he had worked on the assumption that any apologetic that is to be relevant and effective today has to be directed at people who are thought of as sharing the Christian heritage, and whose awareness of other traditions is only second-hand. That assumption informed his *Invitation to Pilgrimage* which though published in 1942 summed up his attitude for some time previously. My impression is that by the time of his writing *The Sense of the Presence* of God he had widened the target of apologetic thrust, directing it as much at those who actively rejected the Christian tradition, or had never at any time stood within it, as at those who lived on its dividends without declaring their capital."

(iv) Finally, Professor McIntyre draws attention to the fact that "One special feature of the kind of apologetic which John Baillie practised was that he not only endeavoured strenuously to understand those who objected to the Christian faith or some aspect of it, but set himself to state the faith or aspects of it as lucidly as he could. Faithful statement is worth more than many refutations. A good example of this purpose is to be seen in the way in which he dealt with variant forms of the interpretation of history across the centuries in his *The Belief in Progress*. He did so in a manner which dealt with the problem in hand, which also however anticipated the intense discussion of the nature of hope which was to come some twenty years after that book was written." - All this, in Professor McIntyre's estimation, made John Baillie "one of the most distinguished practitioners of the discipline of theology as it occurs in and is affected by the situation within a university"; and of course the same could indubitably be said about his brother Donald, as anyone will agree who has read the tributes paid to him by Principal Knox of this university and Principal Taylor of Aberdeen, or Rudolf Bultmann's description of *God was in Christ* as "a model of versatile and understanding dialogue with other theological and religious outlooks."

Before leaving this important topic I should like to take a brief look at what I consider one of John Baillie's most interesting pronouncements: the lecture entitled 'The Fundamental Task of the Theological Seminary', which he delivered at the Conference of Theological Seminaries of the United States and Canada held in Toronto on June 27th 1922. He was then in his earliest professorial appointment (at Auburn) and at the very outset of his long teaching career; but I venture to think that the convictions he then expressed were never departed from, and indeed continued to motivate him

116

throughout the remainder of his life. At the heart of the lecture is a careful consideration of the ever-recurrent question, what kind of training do our future ministers require, vocational and practical or scholarly and intellectual? Baillie's answer begins with the contention that the modern theological school had its origin in two very different but confluent sources: Jesus' teaching of the Twelve, and the education provided in the philosophical schools of Athens. While historians like Harnack have believed that the fusion of rational criticism (derived from Greece) with the allegedly simple Galilean gospel was a retrograde step, Baillie does not agree: "One of the things that mark off Christianity from all other religions", he avers, "is precisely this - that though having had its rise, like nearly every other great religious force, in an entirely popular movement among a primitive and backward people in a half-forgotten corner of the world, it yet had had the spiritual vitality to graft into itself the best fruits of the most advanced culture that the race has known, and to develop in the process into being the greatest spiritual force in the modern world." In the light of this fact of history, Baillie is moved to remark that the question with which he began is really a superficial one. "Priests or scholars? Of course, if we must choose, we will say priests. But if history has taught us anything, it has taught us that within Western civilisation the priest is not likely to be effective if he is not a scholar too. And is not contemporary experience teaching us the same thing?"

But the young professor has it in mind to be yet more provocative. Observing that "*the* great problem facing the Christian Church at the present moment is the defection or alienation, to a very serious extent, of two classes in the community - of the intellectual class and the masses", he asserts that it is in large measure a problem of the Church's making. "It seems to me clear that *one* reason why the intellectuals in our midst sit on the whole so very loosely to the Church is that the Church itself is not, as it once was, at the forefront of intellectual attainment, nor are its ministers, as they lately were, the intellectual leaders of their communities. I can testify with personal experience to cases in which it is very generally assumed by even the leading business and professional men of a city that the ministers who represent the Church in their city are second-rate men with second-rate minds. And I know also that an even more extreme view is constantly taken by students and teachers of other subjects of the student body of certain theological seminaries." As for the average working man, bearing in mind the reports brought back from the Western front of the soldiers' prevailing attitude to religion, Baillie is inclined to suspect that "*at last* the mass of men have begun to do their own thinking, instead of letting the priest think for them", and that "a far greater proportion of the disloyalty of the masses than is commonly allowed is due to intellectual dissent or doubts or puzzlement." "What we have to explain", he adds, "is why so many...were and are entirely sceptical as to the ability of the accredited representatives of the Christian Church to help them, and so ready to assume that the chaplain's philosophy was a ready-made affair, or, in their own vernacular, a 'put-up job'"; and his conclusion is that "there has never been an age in which it is more necessary than it is now for the Christian minister to be alert mentally and well-equipped intellectually. The minister who fulfils the priestly function only, and is neither prophet nor thinker, may succeed in ministering effectually to the small circle in his community who are already completely loyal to the Church; and one cannot help remarking a certain tendency among us to rest content with that as the main part of the minister's work. Surely, however, the minister's effectiveness can be measured in one way only - by his success in meeting the religious needs of the whole community. In a modern community he can have no such success unless he be able, among other things, to inspire general confidence in himself as a keen-minded, fearless and well-equipped seeker of the truth about God and Man and Life and Destiny."

The general thrust of Baillie's arguments is therefore clear. It is the seminary's task to equip men who can provide the leadership he has described. "Here is something which we teachers of divinity *can* do - we can (according to the measure of our native ability and theirs) teach the young men to *think* - to think fairly, to think deeply, to think boldly, to think humbly. I believe that there are no questions that should be more in our minds about the students we graduate each year than these: Do they clearly know exactly what they are recommending when they recommend Christianity? And do they clearly know, and profoundly feel, why it is more worthy to be recommended than any other solution of the great riddle of life?...The problem of Christianity in the coming years will not be solved by turning out men who (in addition to being devoted servants of their race, for that must go without saying) are good-speakers, experts in homiletic form and illustration, able organisers and administrators, diligent pastors, and the like. It can be resolved only if it is represented in our communities by men who can answer, in such a way as to inspire trust, the often very independent questionings of the modern mind. I believe that what the men of today are looking to the Church to provide is above all things *guidance* - not comfort, not good fellowship, not even religious exaltation and inspiration, and certainly not either oratorical thrills or social evenings, but light on the great puzzle of life. And I believe that if the Church will but realise in a really enterprising way her role as teacher, she has a magnificent future before her in our generation."

Imbued with such convictions as these, and calling upon his contemporaries (if I may quote him once more) to "reflect...whether it is likely that Christianity can continue her influence undiminished if our ministers cease to be looked up to as leaders of thought as well as of worship", John Baillie strove as few of his generation did to present a clear and cogent case for Christian faith, to strengthen the ties which traditionally have bound Church and University together in Scotland, and to raise the standards of theological education not only here but throughout the English-speaking world.

d) Resistance to the Barthian Onslaught

As the nineteen-twenties gave way to the 'thirties, and the storm-clouds of another international conflict began to gather, new influences from the Continent of Europe gradually transformed the theological scene. In particular, churchmen became acquainted with the names of Karl Barth and Emil Brunner, and with what has at different times been called "the Theology of Crisis", "the Dialectical Theology" and "the Theology of the Word of God." They were thereby introduced to a temper and attitude very far removed from that which had prevailed among them for something like half a century. Dogmatic rather than apologetic, it started not from man - his predicament, his virtues, his self-consciousness - but from God and the divine Word of judgment and salvation. It asserted a complete discontinuity between the Christian revelation and human life even at its best. Supernaturalistic, authoritarian, strongly church-centred, it was given to paradox and contemptuous of the unredeemed intellect; stressed the transcendence rather than the immanence of God; and violently opposed a number of modern 'isms' , including psychologism, historicism, and subjectivism. In short, it was bent upon questioning, if not reversing the dominant tendencies of Christian thought as they had developed in the West throughout the nineteenth century.

Scotland, like other Protestant countries, was very deeply divided in its reaction to the new movement. I have suggested elsewhere that our theologians fell, roughly speaking, into four main groups: those who were only superficially influenced and in consequence continued the liberal tradition without much change (the first group); those whose entire outlook was affected but in the end withheld their whole-hearted approval (the second); those who may be described as real if cautious admirers (the third); and those in whom we can discern the unqualified zeal of out-and-out converts. To the first group I would assign David Cairns the elder of Aberdeen; to the third, H.R. Mackintosh; and to the fourth, G.S. Hendry, later of Princeton. The Baillies belong fairly obviously in the second group, and there is much about Barth and Barthianism in the writings of each of them - John in particular.

Though he had responded with considerable enthusiasm to the ebullient pre-War Liberalism of New College, John had his reservations about it; and on going to the chair of Systematic Theology at Auburn seminary, New York, he seems to have decided to act as mediator between two extremes, what a contemporary called "a conservative biblicism which is suspicious of all modern scientific conclusions" and "a liberal modernism which is equally eager to assimilate every new scientific suggestion as the messianic deliverer of religion from its bondage to custom and tradition." The consequence was that while in America he appeared a conservative among liberals; in Scotland, some years he later, he was a liberal among conservatives. Yet the general movement of his thought - at least after the publication of his first three volumes, *The Roots of Religion, The Interpretation of Religion,* and *The Place of Jesus Christ in Modern Christianity* - was pretty steadily towards a greater traditionalism. Of the years around 1930 he wrote later: "I remember being vaguely haunted by the feeling that, exhilarating as the thought of this period had been, it was now approaching something like a dead end. It seemed as if there were nowhere much further to go along the paths we were then pursuing. As things fell out, however, we had not long to wait before we found ourselves being headed off in a totally different direction... The turning-point is most conveniently marked by the publication of Karl Barth's *Epistle to the Romans* in 1918." By 1931 (influenced by Kierkegaard, Buber, Brunner and Tillich, among others) Baillie could publish an article with the revealing title, "The Predicament of Humanism."

Despite all this, however, it is clear (as one of his students at Union Seminary, the young Dietrich Bonhoeffer, noted with regret) that he never yielded completely to the new Swiss and German fashions. As he told the readers of his "Confessions of a Transplanted Scot" in 1933, "the so-called Theology of Crisis seems to me, as regards one side of its teaching, to have grown out of precisely those aspects of Ritschlianism which I found myself from the first rejecting" (he means, particularly, their "narrow Lutheran Christocentrism", their "inhospitable attitude toward whatever religious insight stands outside of the Christian tradition" and their "extreme opposition to mysticism") "and this in spite of the fact that the Ritschlian system is in other respects the object of its direct and very bitter attack. Professor Barth listened to Herrmann's lectures at Marburg very nearly at the same time as I was listening to them, but we must have been attracted and repelled by very different sides of our teacher's thought." In that same article, therefore, Baillie spelled out in some detail his agreements and disagreements with the new theology. On the positive side: "Its protests against our over-weaning humanism, our cheap evolutionism, our smug immanentism and our childish utopianism have been most challenging; and in what it has to say about our human insignificance as over against God and about our utter dependence on Him for our salvation it is difficult to do anything but rejoice. In debate with my theological friends in this country (America), I have, more often than otherwise, found myself defending the Barthian positions against the very opposite principles which are professed by perhaps the majority of them." On the negative side: "Yet even here I am unwilling to follow Professor Barth all the way. There are indeed many things which he might have been the first to teach me, and in which I might be ready to follow him more unsuspectingly, had I not learned them first from Von Hügel - and learned at the same time to beware against understanding them in too one-sided a fashion. Barth and Von Hügel have very much the same medicine to administer to our caring modernism, but only Von Hügel is careful to provide also a suitable antidote against an overdose." So, bearing in mind Justin Martyr's assertion that "whatever things have been rightly said by anyone belong to us Christians", as well as Von Hügel's aphorism that "'In my flesh abideth no good thing' will somehow have to be integrated with 'the spirit indeed is willing but the flesh is weak'", Baillie kept his balance even in the headiest days of the Barthian challenge; and although practically all his references to Barth in *And The Life Everlasting* (1934) were favourable, this was not the case in what may be his most important work, *Our Knowledge of God* (1939).

Nor did the further passage of time remove his misgivings. In the years immediately after the second World War he began (as one commentator has said) "to move beyond his earlier neo-orthodoxy on the basis of a renewed confidence in reason." The closing pages of the posthumously-published *The Sense of the Presence of God* (his Gifford Lectures) therefore contained not only the last but also perhaps the strongest expression of his resistance to Barthian teaching. "That it provides a much-needed corrective to certain errors into which we had been lately inclined to fall", he writes, "I cannot doubt; but it administers this medicine in so brusque and defiant a way, and in such merciless over-doses, that in the end I find myself not only refusing to swallow it but at the same time suspecting that something is wrong with the prescription." And after quoting from Gustav Wingren's "cogent and indeed merciless refutation of Dr Barth", in which the Swedish theologian had remarked that "Barth has the ability to a very large degree of being able to employ the language of Scripture in a system that is totally foreign to the Bible" he comments: "I should probably not myself have been quite so outspoken as Dr Wingren, but I am in full agreement with him none the less". Despite all his indebtedness to the great Swiss master, Baillie was never really a member of the Barthian school; and his most memorable utterances seem always to have been of a mediating kind. "I believe", he declared in the late fifties, "any effective and significant post-Barthian movement must go *through* Barthianism, not repudiating the remarkable contribution it has made to all our thinking but entering fully into its heritage, while at the same time correcting its deficiencies and also recovering for us much that was of value in those early ways of thought that were too brashly jettisoned."

As one whose formal introduction to theology took place at New College in the nineteen-fifties, I cannot pass from this subject without affirming my own deeply-felt belief that the attitude of critical reserve which the Baillies adopted towards Barthianism and its apostles was among their very greatest services to the Churches of their day.

e) Social Concern

An interesting and portentous phenomenon of the nineteen-forties was the emergence into leadership in Britain's two most influential non-Roman Churches, the Church of England and the Church of Scotland, of a pair of able theologians who had both elected to turn their attention to social issues. Between 1942 and 1944 the occupant of the See of Canterbury was William Temple, author *inter alia* of an immensely popular Penguin book, *Christianity and the Social Order,* a man who (in the words of a recent historian of the period) "was able to hold in synthesis theology, philosophy, politics and economics" and thus to grasp the nature of the social principles which ought to guide the Church. "He persuaded many Christians", it has been said, "that faith demanded a concern with the affairs of the world. He appeared to be the ideal leader for the Church at a time when many of the principles which he saw as leading to action in the fields of housing, health, education and social welfare seemed to be on the verge of being put into practical operation as the war drew to its close."

Almost simultaneously, John Baillie was elevated - in 1943 - to the Moderatorship of the General Assembly of the Church of Scotland. Though he was a relative newcomer to the Scottish ecclesiastical scene (having returned from America to Edinburgh's Chair of Divinity as recently as 1934), Baillie had been chosen in May 1940, that month of supreme crisis, as convener of a special "Commission for the Interpretation of God's Will in the Present Crisis" whose task was defined as follows: "to seek reverently to guide the Church in the interpretation of the Holy Will and Purpose of God in present-day events, and to examine how the testimony of the Church to the Gospel may become more effective in our own land, overseas, and in the international order." Baillie proved to be an exceptionally gifted chairman, and all the tributes paid to Temple as one possessing special gifts for leadership in a time of change and opportunity could be applied to him also. The Commission over which he presided had to handle a vast array of complicated and controversial topics, but thanks to a skilful division of labour among its members it succeeded over the next five years in producing an impressive body of material for the guidance - and also the inspiration - of the Church. Sub-Commissions were appointed to deal with Church Life and Organisation, Education, Marriage and the Family, and Social and Industrial Life (their handiwork in every case being discussed and licked into shape by the parent Commission before submission to the Assembly), while the Commission itself in plenary sessions considered the more fundamental theological problems arising out of its remit, as well as matters concerned with the task of International Reconstruction. Five annual reports were made to the General Assemblies of 1941 to 1945 inclusive. Of these, three were published by the S.C.M. Press under the titles *God's Will in our Time*, *The Church faces the Future*, and *Home, Community and Church*, while in 1946 (after the Commission's discharge) a composite volume, containing whatever in the reports was likeliest to be of more permanent interest, came out under the title *God's Will for Church and Nation*. Excluded from this compilation was a good deal of material relating to the internal life and organisation of the Church of Scotland, as well as sectional reports on such topics as the Feeding of Europe, the Treatment of the Vanquished Nations, our Duty to the Jewish People, Religious Freedom, and so on, which had inevitably been "left behind by the march of events". But what remained nevertheless constituted a remarkably comprehensive epitome of responsible and forward-looking thought in the Kirk during an epoch-making quinquennium, and in course of time it may come to be seen as a kind of high-water mark in twentieth-century Christian social thought.

If a good deal of the credit for the unusually fine quality of the Commission's reports is laid (as I'm sure it ought to be) at John Baillie's door, it is at the same time worth observing that their prevailing temper was very much an inheritance from the revolution in social attitudes that took place within the Scottish Churches in the period just before, during and just after the First World War - the very period when John and Donald Baillie were passing through Arts and Divinity and receiving the imprint of that Liberal Evangelicalism which was, in greater or lesser degree, to characterise all their subsequent ministry. It was in the eighteen-eighties and eighteen-nineties that churchmen in Scotland really became aware of the gravity of the social situation confronting them and manifested a willingness to abandon time-honoured prejudices in order to cope with it. Men like Marshall Lang and Donald McLeod and David Watson (all, be it noted, at work in the Auld Kirk's presbytery of Glasgow) came to believe, in one historian's phrase, that "environmental factors and not personal sinfulness lay behind immoral, irreligious, unsocial behaviour of all kinds, and the Churches must remove or help to remove the environmental problems before evangelisation had any hope of success." At the same time, parallel developments of equal importance were taking place in the theological realm. There was a rediscovery, particularly by Professor George Adam Smith in the Free Church, of the Hebrew prophets' distinctive emphasis on communal as well as individual righteousness; there was also a concentration (one thinks particularly of Professor A.B. Bruce, Smith's colleague in Glasgow) upon the so-called "historical Jesus" and His teaching about the Kingdom of God. The traditional churchman's animosity against Socialism in any shape or form weakened dramatically; much more sympathy was shown towards the activities of the Trade Unions than ever before; and the Free Church gave considerable support, both locally and centrally, to the agitation carried on in the Highlands against the oppressive land laws - an agitation which eventually resulted in the Crofters' Holdings Act of 1886 (the very year in which John Baillie was born in the Free Manse of Gairloch). Between 1900 and 1914 the new spirit at work within the Churches became even more evident. 1901 saw the formation of the Scottish Christian Social Union, 1909 the creation in the United Free Church of a Special Committee on Social Problems - soon to become Scotland's first standing Church committee on social questions. In the words of Professor Donald Smith, "This period preceding the first World War is of great importance in that it witnessed in the Scottish Church the first significant break from traditional nineteenth-century Christian social concern based on an acceptance of the existing order, and which expressed itself in charitable and reclamation work, and a new Christian social concern based on a suspicion or rejection of the existing order, and which expressed itself in charitable and reclamation work, and a new Christian social concern based on a suspicion or rejection of the existing order, and which expressed itself in social criticism and in more dynamic and radical forms of social action."

It was, incidentally, in this transitional period that the Baillies reached adult life, and I find it interesting to read what John had to say about Donald's settled attitude to the matters just touched upon. "A concern for social justice", we are told, "lay very near to the core of his understanding of the Christian faith." (Was it this, perhaps, which helped to fuel his enthusiastic support for the Iona Community from its early days?) "He was zealous not only for religious but for political and especially *economic* freedom; zealous also for equality, not in a doctrinaire understanding of it, but in the sense of the removal of the many unjustified inequalities with which he felt our society to have traditionally been burdened. He was thus inclined rather strongly to the left in his political convictions, about which he was always outspoken, though refusing to sell out to any single system of economic doctrine and hesitating to attach any label to his view. He would say, 'I don't know whether I'm a socialist or not, but I do certainly think, etc...'"

That by the way. The process of deepening social concern and intensifying social criticism which marked the Late-Victorian and Edwardian periods continued without much slackening into a new age, The first World War, indeed, that shatterer of nineteenth-century complacency, may have served to stimulate even more strenuous thought and action. (We remember the opening chapter of John Baillie's *The Roots of Religion*, and its assertion that among all the accusations levelled by service-men against the Christian church one main charge stood out in the very boldest relief", namely: "a lack of reality..., and a conspicuous unrelatedness to the real problems of human life.") In 1916, the Auld Kirk set up a commission to examine the moral and spiritual issues raised by the conflict, and its researches inevitably highlighted areas of disharmony and injustice in the life of the nation. By 1920, that *ad hoc* commision had grown into a permanent Church and Nation Committe. Meanwhile, the United

Free Church's much older Church and State Committee, which had at one time been almost exclusively concerned with the issue of establishment, began to widen its remit, adding its insights to those of the already-existing Social Problems Committee. The confluence of all these streams took place when the union of the Churches in 1929 brought about the creation of a much enlarged and even more active Church and Nation Committee. Nearly every year thereafter seemed to mark an enhancement of that body's importance as new topics (not all of them peculiarly Scottish) came within its constantly expanding field of interest, while even greater publicity was given by press and radio to its annual reports and to the debates in the Assembly which these reports occasioned. Gone indeed were the days when only "spiritual" matters were conceived of as having a claim upon the attention of Christians, and when a critical scrutiny of the social order was likely to be denounced as subversive or even atheistical!

And so - with the second World War precipitating another tremendous surge of questioning and heart-searching in the Scottish Churches - the stage was set for the work of the "Baillie Commission". A detailed analysis of its assumptions and findings would be out of place on this occasion; but a clear idea of its general attitude, and its message on social matters in particular, can be gleaned from some sentences which occur in the report on "The Nature and Extent of the Church's Concern in the Civil Order". "Christians have often failed", we read in a passage whose lucid and balanced style reveals Baillie's influence, "to distinguish adequately between the religious and political spheres, and have thus misled the Church into making pronouncements on questions which it only imperfectly understood. But we hold it as certain that the greater harm has come about through the opposite error - through the indifference of Christians to the maladjustments of that civil ordering of society in which they like others have a part, and the consequent failure of the Church to bring its own light to bear upon the problems so created. If it were merely that Christians were so exclusively absorbed in heavenly things as to be indifferent to the earthly ills of themselves and their neighbours, that alone would spell a serious falsification of the true Christian temper; but it is to be feared that many of us must plead guilty to the even more damaging charge of complacently accepting the amenities, and availing ourselves of the privileges, of a social order which happened to offer these things to ourselves while denying them to others. It cannot be denied that during a period when the crying injustices of the social order were being brought prominently into the light, the Church as a whole seemd content to leave this task to those outside its fellowship or to isolated voices within, instead of itself providing the necessary volume of righteous and enlightened zeal. Arriving only as a latecomer in this most necessary field, it largely failed to bring its Gospel to bear at the right time upon a situation that continued to develop at such tragic speed...There can be little doubt that it is to the failure of Christians to realise and act upon these social implications of the Gospel that the present weakness of the spiritual life in our land must in no small part attributed. We long for a revival of spiritual religion, but there are many who suspect this spirituality to which we call them of making too ready a compliance with a social order that for them means only hunger, slum conditions, unemployment, or sweated labour...Selfishness is of the very essence of the sin from which, in any revival of religion, men need to be redeemed; but what if there be no particular form of this sin from which we more need to be redeemed today than a complacent indifference to the social evils that surround our comfortable lives?"

In their wisely historical perspective and their careful avoidance of extremes - not to speak of their quiet but warmly evangelical undertones - these sentences may be taken as not untypical of the Baillies' entire approach. And if we remind ourselves that the Report played a quite considerable part in bringing about the massive and portentous swing in British opinion which acclaimed the Beveridge Plan in 1944 and ushered in the welfare state with the inauguration of the National Health Service some four years later, it is hard to resist the thought that the brothers' influence almost certainly extended far beyond the purely theological sphere to affect the social *mores* and political outlook of a whole generation. There cannot be many modern divines of whom so much could be said.

Committed Churchmanship

Whatever may or must be said of other theologians, there can be no doubt that the Baillies carried on all their thinking within the context of the Church and - if I may put the matter so - for its sake. Their contention was, always, for what we might call realised Christianity. That is true even of their earliest work. At the climax of the argument in *The Roots of Religion*, John reminds his readers that "To be a Christian is not merely to think this and the other, nor is it merely to do this and leave the other undone; it is rather to have living and personal experience of the fellowship of Christian love....It is to know, with all the saints of all the ages, something of the breadth and length and depth and height of the love that was in the heart of Christ and, illuminated and strengthened by that knowledge, to place all our reliance upon the love of God and be filled with His fullness." And in the very closing pages of the same volume he reiterates his concern that "the common man's values" (as he puts it) should not keep him away from the Christian Church. Similarly, in Donald's *Faith in God*, the final paragraph (referring to the paradox which seems to be inherent in all our speech about God and His purposes) includes these words: "it is not altogether by thinking the matter out, but rather by living it out in daily Christian faith and love, that we shall arrive at a deeper insight. And a book about faith cannot end better than upon this note of hope and expectation."

But it is in two of their later, and most influential, writings that the ecclesiastical dimension of the Baillies' thought becomes supremely evident. The Epilogue to *God was in Christ* bears the revealing title, "The Body of Christ" and (as the author puts it) views the whole landscape that has so far been traversed "from the vantage-point of the Church of Christ, since it is the Church that has to tell the story." The book's concluding pages, indeed, might be described as a kind of rhapsody on the theme of the Church: "the new People of God, the new Israel, the Ecclesia, the Body of Christ... the nucleus of a new humanity... God's instrument of reconciliation through the ages." Even more impressive, to my mind, is the chapter on this same subject with which John concludes his *Invitation to Pilgrimage*. Arguing that "It is only in Christ that we can enjoy full community with one another, and it is only in our togetherness with one another that we can enjoy full communion with Christ", he offers the following eloquent meditation on Christian community (which I make no apology for quoting at length): "God has apparently done everything He possibly could, short of exercising actual compulsion upon our wills, to prevent us from making our religion a private luxury... For what more could

129

He have done than so to order things that men can find salvation only by betaking themselves to one place, where they are bound to meet one another - to the hill called Calvary; by encountering there a single historical figure - the figure of Jesus; by listening to the selfsame story; by reading in the same book; by praying the same prayers in the same Name; by being baptised into the same fellowship and partaking of the same sacred meal - 'all made to drink into one Spirit'; by drawing in fact their whole spiritual sustenance from the same unbroken tradition handed down from age to age?...You and I owe all the knowledge of God that we have to our upbringing in the one tradition and our reception into the one fellowship of the Church of Christ, and the only way that is open to us whereby we should bring to others the blessings of that knowlege is by initiating them into the same tradition and receiving them into the same Church." Against the exclusive individualism of the humanist ideal or the forceful appeal of totalitarianism, he argues that "our only hope lies in finding a nobler form of community which will unite us in a stronger solidarity, and call forth a more deep-seated and passionate devotion than even our [wartime] foes can claim to possess" - the universal, and more-than-human, community of the Church.

So the book (the Baillies' finest work of popular apologetics) moves persuasively to its close, taking us, as it were, to the very door of the Church in the beautifully appropriate quotation from the greatest poem of the greatest Christian poet of the last two centuries: "I hope, then, that I have provided sufficient reason why we should all seek the fellowship of the Church of Christ, there to rekindle our ideals and rehabilitate them in a solidarity that is stronger than all the solidarities of earth. There may be many more that have lately been saying of themselves, with Coleridge's Ancient Mariner,

> this soul hath been
> Alone on a wide, wide sea
> So lonely 'twas that God himself
> Scarce seemed there to be.

But I hope I have given good reason why they should now decide, again with the Mariner,

To walk together to the Kirk
And all together pray
While each to his great Father bends
Old men, and babes, and loving friends.
And youths, and maidens gay."

The practical outworking of these convictions was never in any doubt so far as either of the brothers was concerned; and if time permitted it would be easy to adduce numerous instances of their deep, life-long commitment to the Church, both local and world-wide, and of the faithful service they rendered it in a host of public and private ways. What I propose to do, however, is simply to look at three aspects of their churchmanship which are likely to be of special interest to us who are here today: their preaching, their ecumenical involvement, and their piety.

(i) **Preaching**

In the field of preaching, Donald's reputation is perhaps higher than John's (at least on this side of the Atlantic), partly because of the very considerable impression made by two volumes of his sermons which were posthumously published in the nineteen-fifties, *To Whom Shall We Go?* and *Out of Nazareth*. Scotland has had a great number of fine preachers over the generations - though not, I suspect, too many in recent years - but among those of the twentieth century Donald Baillie undoubtedly occupies a very special place. Three reasons for this (three among many) spring instantly to mind: his uncanny knack of addressing the central topics of the faith without subjecting his hearers to either a dogmatics *précis* or an exegetical exercise; the beautiful simplicity of structure and language which characterises all his sermons; and the memorable appropriateness of his illustrative material.

On the first of these I propose to say nothing - it is evident on virtually every page he wrote - save to draw your attention to his sermons on 'The Glory of the Cross' in his earlier volume, and on 'The Mystery of the Trinity' in the later. On the second reason for his eminence (what I've called the beautiful simplicity of structure and language by which all his sermon were distinguished), John Dow's Memoir

131

provides a valuable introduction. "Donald Baillie", he says, "knew from the beginning what a sermon should be. I can recall his first student 'outline'. We wondered what this brilliant philosophy student would produce. A magnificently articulated structure with four heads and many subsections like a class essay? No, we saw on the blackboard a model outline of attractive simplicity and directness. And so his sermons continued all along." Let me point to just a few examples of the structural simplicity - a simplicity bordering on elegance - to which John Dow refers, three from *To Whom Shall We Go?* and four from *Out of Nazareth.* The sermon for Palm Sunday on Matthew's quotation from Zechariah 9:9 ("Thy King cometh unto thee, meek, and sitting upon an ass") subdivides as follows: "(1) What did it mean for the man who first wrote it? (2) What did it mean to the people who thought of it that day, hundreds of years later, as Jesus rode into Jerusalem? (3) What did it mean to Jesus? (4) What does it mean for us, after 1900 years?" The sermon for Easter Day on I Corinthians 15:57, "Thanks be to God, who giveth us the victory through our Lord Jesus Christ", is a meditation on three victories: "(1) Victory over sin. (2) Victory over death. (3) Victory over the world." The sermon on Election from Matthew 4:18-20 (the call of Simon and Andrew) makes four basic assertions "(1) God always chooses us before we choose Him. (2) God does not choose us because we deserve it. (3) God does not choose us to be His favourites, but to be His servants. (4) When God chooses and calls us, we also have to make our choice." (An eminently suitable message, you may think, to be delivered in an English cathedral by a Scottish Presbyterian!). The sermon entitled "The Weeping Kings" (David and Jesus on the Mount of Olives) has three subdivisions: " (1) Jesus wept, not for Himself but for Jerusalem. (2) Jesus wept, but He went on. (3) He wept, but He trusted in God"; that on "The Fulness of the Gospel" (Romans 15:29) contains three adjurations: "(1) Don't forget His teaching. (2) Don't leave out His Cross. (3) Don't forget His victory"; the New Year sermon on Jeremiah 9:23,24 takes each clause of its text in turn: "(1) Let not the wise man glory in His might. (3) Let not the rich man glory in his riches. (4) But he that glorieth, let him glory in this, that he understandeth and knoweth Me, saith the Lord"; that on "Thy Father which is in secret" (Matthew 6.6) expounds what it calls "three simple truths about the spiritual life": "(1) Every man's soul is his own secret. (2) There is One who knows all our secrets. (3) There is one who can lead us into the secret of God." How simple, and yet how inevitable, these outlines are - and how striking the fact that the simple structure of the sermons is paralleled and enhanced by an equal simplicity and directness of language!

Let us pass to the other especial strength of these masterpieces of homiletic artistry: the memorable, moving appropriateness of the illustrative material which enriches them. Three instances should suffice to make my point. The first comes from the title-sermon of the earlier collection, *Out of Nazareth*, and tells how the preacher once visited a little place, on the borders of Shropshire and Worcestershire, which had been brought to his attention by a rather derogatory reference in a contemporary poem. First impressions were hardly favourable, it seems. "Mamble wasn't the sort of place one would choose to live in; it was a poor, unpromising kind of village." But then a chance encounter with a woman in the churchyard put a new complexion on things. "She was a farmer's wife. They were simple folk, but they had sent their son to Oxford - the only son they had, as their other child had died young. This one was a six-foot youth of brilliant parts and evidently a heart of gold. He was their hope and pride. After three years at St John's College, Oxford, he had won a travelling scholarship in the interests of international friendship, and had spent a year in France and Germany. Then, just as they were expecting word as to when he would arrive home, they received a telegram to say that he had been accidentally drowned. This was the second anniversary - it had happened just two years ago that Sunday...His gifts must have been outstanding. But now that dream was over, and his father and mother had a grave to tend and a golden memory to keep." So to the "application". "Perhaps you think that probably a mother's love somewhat glorified and gilded the picture. That may be. But when I think of Mamble now, it is not just of the lazy name in Drinkwater's poem, and the poor little village and the noisy little inn, but of that little church and churchyard, and that Sunday afternoon, and that story. What a wonder it opens! Mamble was an unlikely place for anything to happen - lazy Mamble, a mere name on a finger-post, a mean little village. But Mamble had its story to tell of the great simple human things: home, and hopes, and love, and death, and grief, and memory; yes, and its story to tell of a keen young life that was given to noble aims and dreams, until it was cut off, or rather (shouldn't we say?) called to higher opportunities in realms unknown. Its training ground for all that was the little village of Mamble. That was where the boy learnt to love the home to which he always remained loyal; that was where he first went to school; that was where he thought the 'long, long thoughts' of youth. All that had been going on in Mamble. 'Can any good thing come out of Mamble?' Of course it can, and there it was. ...Out of Nazareth came Jesus Christ, the Son of God. And it was always His way to go here and there to the most unlikely places, and seek out all sorts and conditions of men and women to make them kings and priests to God. It might be Nazareth, or Bethsaida, or Jerusalem. And a little later it might be Ephesus or Corinth or Rome. And in our time it might be London, or Mamble, or Glasgow or St Andrews, or any other place where your lot is cast or mine."

My second example of Donald's felicitous sermon illustrations comes from what was possibly a Whitsunday sermon on Joel 2:28: "Your sons and your daughters shall be prophets." Towards its close, the preacher remarks "That [the story of Pentecost] is a very old story. Can we translate it into the language and interests of our own modern world? Let us try, with the aid of a little imagination. (1) You take your seat in a railway compartment. In the opposite corner sits a labouring man, reading his newspaper. You look at him and try to picture the life he leads. A rough, bare life, you think; hard work all day, a quiet pipe in the evening, a football match to watch on a Saturday afternoon; and if he is a particularly decent man, he goes to church once in a while on a Sunday morning. So you sum up his life. Is that all? I wonder. When the man puts down his paper and leans back and shuts his eyes, what is he thinking of? Perhaps he is thinking of GOD. Perhaps he is bringing the light of his faith in God to bear upon the great issues he has been reading about in his newspaper - labour troubles, party politics, war and peace among the nations. Perhaps he is connecting all those things with the God he believes in. Why not? He is a working man. So was Jesus. And you don't know what depths of Christian faith there may be in the heart and life of that man. (2) Or you go into a shop in the city. A girl at the counter serves you. What does she care for, except to get on as well as she can in her own line, and meanwhile get as much fun as she can out of her wages when working hours are over, a round of rather selfish and empty pleasures filling up her evenings and weekends. And that is all. Is it? It may be. But it may also be that the girl has visions and dreams that would go straight to the heart of Christ Himself. It may be that behind the scenes of what seems a very commonplace existence there is a brave unselfish life of burden-bearing for other people, sustained by perhaps the fellowship of the Church of Christ and by a living faith in God."

A final illustration, even more down-to-earth than those already referred to. A communion sermon on "Christ washing the disciples' feet" contains this single but searching paragraph: "Through many of the days of our lives, we Christian men and women are pretty unaspiring. We haven't much of the heavenly vision, we let it fall away and come to be content with a very mediocre Christian life. The world has its claims, and we become preoccupied with them; and our neighbours may be difficult, and we become loveless towards them; and our devotions sometimes seem a waste of time, and we become slack about them. And so the days run on, and we are living on a pretty commonplace level, though perhaps we hardly know it, with only half our hearts in the service of Christ. And suddenly perhaps (it sometimes happens at a communion season) we get a glimpse of the poor lives we are leading, and we also get a glimpse of the beauty of holiness, the glory of a real genuine whole-hearted Christian life. Yes, and lest we should be discouraged, we at the same time get a glimpse of the wonderful, infinite love of God in Jesus Christ, and His power to help us, and His high purpose for us, that we should be perfect as He is perfect. Then we are fired with holy enthusiasm and aspiration. We resolve in our hearts that henceforth we will not go back nor turn from God at all. Our hearts leap out in faith to God, cast themselves upon his grace, consecrate themselves to His will, dedicate themselves to His service. Our whole hearts go out to Christ our Master. They were indeed His already, but we remember it now in a fresh moment of self-dedication: 'Lord, not my feet only, but also my hands and my head.'"

Although John's sermons are not so readily accessible at his brother's, a few of them appear in the little collection of his addresses edited by John McIntyre and published under the title, *Christian Devotion* in 1962, while others are to be found in the Baillie Papers at New

College, Edinburgh. In their own way, they are as impressive as Donald's: more academic certainly in form and language but also perhaps more original and thought-provoking. I'd like to introduce you (or re-introduce you) to three of them now, and in so doing to convey a little of the flavour of John's preaching as a whole. All seem to have been first delivered in the nineteen-forties, although like some of us he apparently believed that what is worth saying once is worth saying again. In 1949, the year before he became Principal of New College, John Baillie preached at Fisherwick Church, Belfast on the occasion of the Queen's University centenary celebrations. Taking as his text the words from Luke 12:48, "For unto whomsoever much is given, of him shall much be required", he offered his hearers a meditation on University education under three heads: its responsibilities, its temptations, and its limitations. What he had to say in connection with the last of these sounds a note which we can recognise as distinctively his own. "The special responsibilities", he observed, "all presuppose, and do not in the least degree replace or mitigate the one fundamental responsibility which we share before God with every member of the human race. You and I are men and women first, and students only afterwards, and therefore in the first instance it is exactly the same demands that God makes on us all. Surely our Puritan fathers were right when they said that on the Day of Judgment we shall stand before God, stripped not only of our earthly possessions and dignities, but stripped also of our accumulated learning. They were right, because that is how we stand before God *now*. There is one demand God makes on us all. And we all know what it is. It is to do justly and to love mercy and to walk humbly before Him all the days of our life. It is to give our souls without reserve to His keeping. It is to put our whole trust in the merits of His blessed Son. Nothing else matters until that has been settled. All our high culture, all our specialist knowledge, is so much useless lumber and rubble, except as it is built upon that foundation and used for its further upbuilding." A little further on, there occur these typically Baillian phrases: "the grim truth is that we have all of us more knowledge than we are willing to use, or to use for the right ends. There may be much that we do not know, but we all know enough to be better than we are, and to make our society an altogether better thing than it now is." And the sermon concludes as follows: "I believe that we shall stand firm only if, in cultivating our intellects, we take heed not to lose our souls; only if, while becoming ever more complex in knowledge, we remain simple at heart; only if, as sinful men and women, whose lives stand naked in His sight, we first put ourselves right with God, and then bring every thought, all our knowledge and all our learning, into captivity to the obedience of His Christ."

The Pauline verse quoted at the end there seems to have exerted a peculiar fascination for John Baillie, and it furnished the text for a remarkable sermon about "the conversion of the mind" which he preached in Great St Mary's, Cambridge on Sunday 26th November 1944. "Bringing into captivity every thought": the emphasis was laid upon that word *every* - little thoughts and great ones, fleeting fancies and ruling ideas ; and the sermon was neatly divided into two sections, one dealing with our little thoughts, the other with our great ones. On the little thoughts he has this (so psychologically wise, so spiritually discerning) to say: "if anybody were to ask you what you have been thinking about today, only one or two things would at first occur to you. They would be what I should call your officially acknowledged thoughts; they would be no doubt concern matters of public or professional or family importance, and though not always very weighty they would at least be eminently respectable. These are the thoughts that pass what the psychologists call the 'Censor'. But we know that our minds are also at all times giving hospitality to all sorts of unofficial contents. What was in my mind as I waited for the bus at the corner? What visions did I see in the clouds of my tobacco smoke, as I leaned back in my chair to enjoy my after-dinner pipe? What were my thoughts as I lay awake in bed last night? What were my dreams when at last I went to sleep? And what my day-dreams during my idlest waking hours? - If the soul is really dyed the colour of its leisure thoughts [the reference is to an aphorism of Marcus Aurelius] then it is clear that a man is not really converted until his leisure thoughts are converted. I may have given my full assent to all the doctrines of the Creed and have no doubts concerning any of them; I may have so re-ordered my life in accordance with Christ's commands as to fill my whole day with blameless and charitable deeds; but what Christ wants of me is something much deeper than intellectual assent and moral conformity. He wants a radical transformation of the sub-soil of my mind, so that there is no longer any hidden poison at the roots of my overt thoughts and actions ready to work its ravages at the first favourable opportunity. He is therefore as interested in my idle moments as my busy ones, as much in my reveries as my resolutions, as much in my castles in the air as in the more solid edifices of my public and professional life. No man is really Christ's until his day-dreams are Christ's - aye and his night-dreams too, if they are any wise subject to his control...Something like this is what is meant by bringing into captivity every *little* thought to the obedience of Christ."

The preacher then turns to the other part of his argument, and deals with what he has designated our "big" thoughts. "When a man seeks to submit himself to Christ", he continues, there is a danger that not only his very little thoughts but also his very big thoughts may escape the process of submission. The former are so trivial, but the latter are so general, that both may escape our Christian vigilance. And yet no man is really Christ's until his very biggest thoughts are Christ's... He is concerned with my daily habit of life and my daily habit of worship, but He is no less concerned with my philosophy. He knows that I am not fully and securely His until my philosophy is His as well. Therefore He wants my philosophy also to be transformed by the power of the Cross, and to be born again, and to repent in dust and ashes. Nor will He be satisfied until this has happened to all my reasonings and to every high thing that exalts itself in my mind." And so the second part of the sermon - a part peculiarly suited, you may think, to a university audience - moves to its conclusion: "Instead of viewing all things in the light of Christ and His Cross, Christian thinkers still tend to view Christ and His Cross in the light of other things. Instead of allowing our Lord to determine the whole of our philosophy, we too often allow our philosophies to determine Him. We try to find room for Him within a world-view that we have constructed without His help, and to understand Him by means of such ruling ideas as were in our minds before He came to us, or before we came to Him. There are men whose deeds are done beneath the shadow of the cross, but who when they begin to think, prefer to walk some distance away from it - sometimes a very great distance - in order, as they explain, to get the Cross itself in better perspective. But the experiment is a difficult one. The Cross has always seemed a queer object when seen from afar. It refuses to soften into the background of any picture. Either it is out of perspective itself, or else it puts everything else out. 'Unto the Greeks foolishness', wrote St Paul...Let us therefore consecrate not only our most trivial fancies to the Lordship of Christ, but also the master-thoughts that guide us in our studies. If I may so express it, let us not leave our station of Calvary either when we don our carpet-slippers or when we don our thinking caps. Only thus can we cast down all reasonings, and every high thing that exalteth itself against the knowledge of God, and bring into captivity not only our very smallest, but also our very biggest thoughts to the obedience of Christ".

Just one further - quite brief - quotation may serve to remind us yet again of what seems to have been the main thrust of John Baillie's preaching: the ultimate inadequacy of all knowledge save the knowledge of God. It comes from a sermon on Martha and Mary, entitled "Only one thing is necessary", which he preached in October 1946 at a University service in the Great Hall of Birmingham University. The following sentences sum up his message on that occasion, as on many others: "the one thing needful, then, is not money or power or fame or a successful career. And... I hope I may assume that it is not what we call culture - a cultivated mind... We should be fully prepared for the discovery that the one thing needful is *the same for everybody* - the same for peasant and plutocrat, the same for household drudge and high-born student, and (incidentally) the same also for students and professors. Further, we should be prepared to learn that it is something of an entirely non-competitive character, and in no sense a limited commodity of which somebody else must have less because I have more. What is it then? What is this pearl of great price? What is the one thing needful, the good part which Mary chose? The story puts it quite simply: she 'sat at Jesus' feet and heard His Word.' And that is what it is."

(ii) **Ecumenical commitment and involvement.**

This is a large subject, and one which I feel myself particularly ill-qualified to speak. The essentials, however, are clear enough, and require no deep insight for their enumeration. It would seem that for both John and Donald the earliest stimulus to interest in the world church came from "Edinburgh, 1910", the great World Missionary Conference of which John R. Mott was the chairman and J.H. Oldham (a Scot) the general secretary. But it was not until they were in middle life that their standing in the theological realm as well as their enthusiasm for Christian unity brought them to leadership in the Movement. From the early 'thirties, however, John was an active worker in Faith and Order; he was a member of the British Council of Churches almost from its creation in 1942; he was elected a member of the Central Committee of the World Council of Churches at its first Assembly in Amsterdam in 1948; and at the second Assembly, held at Evanston in 1954, he was appointed - a signal honour - one of the six World Presidents. On the home front, he was a member of the Church of Scotland's team in the conversations which produced the famous "Bishops Report" in the late nineteen-fifties - the Report whose rejection by the General Assembly caused him much disappointment towards the end of his life. But as Isobel Forrester remarked in 'A Cousin's Memories' (the biographical sketch which she wrote for the posthumously-published volume of John's addresses, *Christian Devotion*), "These bare facts can do no more than suggest what he contributed in vision, in wisdom, in constant travel, in administrative ability, in prayer and in a great wealth of personal friendships, to the drawing together of the separated parts of Christ's Church on earth." Certainly the esteem in which he was held world-wide cannot have been surpassed by many church leaders in the first half of this century, as the tributes which poured in to Scotland on his death bear ample witness. A leader of the American Lutherans began his letter of condolence with the words, "A hallelujah and a sigh went up all over the world at the news of Dr Baillie's translation", and the then Archbishop of Canterbury, Geoffrey Fisher, expressed himself in terms such as do not often flow from Anglican pens when they are writing about Scottish Presbyterians: "What a glorious man - and many will tell you so - as a divine, a teacher, a man of vision, of prophecy, of friendship and of wit. So many here, in the U.S.A., and in the World Council, owe him so *much*. Never was a man more beloved for his good graces."

Donald likewise was much involved in the affairs of the ecumenical movement, prompted (as John put it) by his eirenic temper and his concern for Christian unity. His particular interest was in that aspect of the movement which found its focus in the Faith and Order Commission of the World Council of Churches. He played an important part in the Edinburgh Conference of 1937; attended many Faith and Order committee meetings in Europe over a number of years; and made an especially notable contribution to the Conference held at Lund, in Sweden, in 1952 - not least by the pre-communion sermon which he preached in the Cathedral on that occasion. As convener of the sub-commission on *Intercommunion*, he co-edited the weighty volume with that title which appeared under its auspices in that same year. And like his brother he gave much time to the ecumenical cause within his own country. Indeed, at the time of his death he was serving as convener of the Church of Scotland's Inter-Church Relations Committee, and had been named as one of the representatives appointed by the Kirk to confer with the Church of England in the interest of closer relations. In Hugh Montefiore's words, he "was not just a Presbyterian divine: like all the saints he belongs to the whole Church of God."

Much, assuredly, has still to be said about the Baillies' services to the ecumenical movement, and I can imagine a doctoral thesis or even a book being written on the subject in course of time. While happily leaving this task to others, I should simply like to observe that the brothers' involvement in the work of the British Council of Churches and the World Council of Churches was scarcely surprising in view of the catholicity which they displayed in so many areas of life: in the world of theology and the world of literature, in things ecclesiastical as in things cultural. Appropriately enough for one whose years at New College had been spent under the principalship of the remarkable Alexander Whyte, a man who delighted both in Puritan divinity and in the whole range of literature from Dante to Rabelais and from Milton to Tennyson, John Baillie could declare - and there is no doubting his sincerity: his own writings proclaim it at every turn - that "my interest in poetry, in the general literature of the few countries whose languages I could command, in history, in various forms of art, as well in nature itself, has not lessened but rather increased as the years have gone by." And Donald too, though often beset by ill-health and depression, could be a witty and even hilarious companion, with the wide interests and generous sympathies of a truly cultured person. Inevitably, therefore their catholicity extended to the realm of religion. Though true in essentials to the faith in which they had been nurtured in the manse at Gairloch and in the family home in Inverness and

Edinburgh, they grew and broadened steadily as fresh influences came to play upon them. We have seen how they exchanged the Free for the United Free church and the old sacramental traditions of Scottish Calvinism for what John described as "the more liturgical mode" - without jettisoning anything of first-class importance. And if time permitted I should like to have paid some attention to Donald's sensitive and penetrating treatment of such deeply contentious subjects as the Real Presence and the Eucharistic Sacrifice, as well as to the exceptionally wide range of authors (though with a distinct preponderance of Catholics, Roman and Anglo!) whose writings he discusses in *The Theology of the Sacraments*.

(iii) Piety

Of the brothers' personal piety, time would fail me to tell. In John's case, let me simply refer you to his *Diary of Private Prayer* (which since its first publication has sold more than 125,000 copies in Britain alone, and has been translated into over a dozen languages) and to Isobel Forrester's reference in "A Cousin's Memories" to the "three clear focal points" in his study at Whitehouse Terrace, in Edinburgh: "the big uncluttered desk by the window", "the big leather chair, where he often sat far into the night reading" - and "the prayer desk by the window with its little pile of well-worn versions of the Scriptures and of devotional books" where in solitude he read and thought and worshipped. As for Donald, John Dow has a few sentences whose truth many from those days have confirmed: "Nothing but the peremptoriness of an early morning train could persuade this man of God to omit family worship at his own table. Unfailingly by 8.40 each week day down College Street came the familiar figure in the old mackintosh, gown over his arm, often looking pale, ill and fragile, on his way to morning prayers in the University Chapel: others might steal a morning off, he with more excuse would not. When he was a worshipper, there was the promptness of the real participant in every response. When he himself conducted the service, we could not but be drawn closer by the tones of his voice and the sincerity of his words. In addressing a newly-ordained minister his final stress was on the danger of letting carefulness about many things cut out the one thing needful - personal devotion..."

I have done. But how fittingly to bid these teachers of our farewell? Some of you may recall the concluding paragraph of Lytton Strachey's biographical essay on *Queen Victoria*, where he calls up the various images from the past which may have flitted through the aged monarch's mind as she lay dying at Osborne. Just a few weeks ago, a friend of mine (a fellow-student at New College in John Baillie's time as Principal) told me that in the last year of his life John, with Jewel his wife, motored from Inverness on a last visit to Gairloch. Can we, like Strachey, imagine some of the pictures which his mind conjured up out of the past as they travelled West? - The places, first: that beautiful room in the old College at Edinburgh, its walls adorned with Raeburn's portraits of dignitaries of the University's Athenian age, where he had attended so many Senatus meetings in his time; the Senate Room at New College, with its portraits - of George Adam Smith, A.B. Davidson, Adam Welch and the rest - and its memories of colleagues and friends like John Burleigh, Norman Porteous, James S. Stewart and Willie Tindal; those other *foci* of New College life, the Martin Hall, the Rainy Hall and the Library (its pride and joy, where the Baillie Papers now rest); the large grey-stone house in its quiet tree-girt setting in the Grange district of Edinburgh, long the home of John and Jewel and of their son Ian, where they had entertained generations of students with good food and good talk and ridiculous party games; those other homes and workplaces, also, at Union Seminary, New York, (with all the remembered excitement of the nineteen-thirties, as the liberal tide retreated and news came in of political and religious revolution in Europe), at Emmanuel College, Toronto, and at Auburn; as well as all the cities and peaceful country areas visited, on lecture tours or on vacation, in Europe, America and Australia. Still more, the people: his colleagues at New College from 1934 to 1956, together with those in North America (particularly the "six in New York" - Henry and Dorothy Coffin, Reinhold and Ursula Niebuhr, Henry and Betty Van Dusen - to whom he had dedicated his *Invitation to Pilgrimage*); his old teachers at New College - Sandy Martin, Harry Kennedy and Alexander Whyte - and at Old College (Pringle-Pattison in particular); the school-masters at Inverness Royal Academy, with the august W.J. Watson at their head; and of course his early friends and his brothers Donald and Peter - Donald above all, and their innumerable walks and talks together (in which the views of each had been aired and modified, rejected or confirmed), and the continuing sorrow that he had been taken from him just when they were looking forward to even closer association in retirement, Donald in St Andrews, in Kilmacolm, in Cupar, in Bervie, in St Boswells, in Edinburgh at Braidburn Crescent, in Inverness...But now the rich farming country of Easter Ross would be yielding to the heatherclad moorlands of the West, and the great peaks would be appearing on the skyline, and the elderly professor's thoughts would home in on Gairloch and the gaunt little church there, and the lamp-lit nursery of the manse, and his mother's face and his father's voice, and the old catechetical question and answer, "What is man's chief end? Man's chief end is to glorify God and to enjoy Him for ever"; and perhaps as the well-remembered township on the Atlantic coastline came into view a prayer from his own *Diary of Private Prayer* (or one not unlike it) may have risen to his lips: "To thy care, O God, I commend my soul and the souls of all whom I love and who love me: through Jesus Christ our Lord. Amen."

VIII. THE CHRISTOLOGY OF DONALD BAILLIE

"A TALE OF TWO EXCHANGES"

- John McIntyre

An immediate impression gained from a re-examination of the Christology of Donald Baillie after forty years is the fact that so many of the issues which he raised, and to which he proposed solutions, are still with us.   Indeed, such a re-examination forms an excellent introduction to this most central of theological disciplines and to an assessment of what has been happening within the discipline in the years between.   The late Pitney Van Dusen, President of Union Theological Seminary in its great days, said of Donald Baillie's *God Was in Christ*, that it was the most outstanding work on the subject in the English-speaking world, since H.R. Mackintosh's *The Person of Jesus Christ* (1912).   The joint-mention of these two works is not a little significant, as we shall see later.   The statement is no exaggeration - Van Dusen had himself researched the field - and his view was reinforced when Bultmann, in 1955, said that it was the 'most significant book in Christology in our time'.

My plan for presentation is as follows: (1) to set forth Donald Baillie's christological views, mainly found in his *God Was in Christ*, relating them to the history of christology in the 20th century; (2) to outline the criticism of his position, as I saw it when reviewing the book in 1948, in *The Reformed Theological Review*, Vol. 7, No. 2 November 1948, pp.11-19; (3) to report Baillie's reply to me in a letter which he sent to me in Sydney at the time, dated 12 March 1949; (4) to take up the issues explored by John Hick, in an article in *The Scottish Journal of Theology*, Vol. 11, No. 1, March 1958, pp.1-12, entitled 'The Christology of D.M. Baillie';   and finally, (5)   John Baillie's spirited defence of his brother, in *Scottish Journal of Theology*, Vol. 11, No. 3, September 1958, pp.265-270, entitled, 'Some Comments on Professor Hick's Article on "The Christology of D.M. Baillie"'.   These form 'the two exchanges' of the sub-title.

I

While Donald Baillie, in his historical introduction to the exposition of his own view of christology, shows mastery of the minutiae of the thought of such theologians as Leonard Hodgson, H.M. Relton, L.S. Thornton, and Karl Heim, it is when drawing with large strokes on the big canvas that he is at his most penetrating in definition, and predictive in his judgements.

1.1 Beginning with the 'Jesus of History movement', which has become the conventional point of departure for all christological investigators more or less ever since, he emphasises as few others have done the genuine achievement of the movement, in establishing the humanity of Christ, in a manner which makes - or should make - it unacceptable for theologians to show any sympathy for docetism. This point he holds to very stubbornly, and I believe, very rightly, against two movements which now appear in his discussion, namely, the Formgeschichte School of criticism, which he sees as an extension, if refinement and a high sophistication, of the historico-critical method, which the 'Jesus of History' writers had been employing according to their lights; and on the other hand, Barth, Brunner and Bultmann, who for all their ill-concealed disagreements, could be relied upon to agree upon an almost total historical radicalism, as Baillie calls it sometimes, and at others, downright scepticism. Such scepticism, he rightly indicates, in its reaction against the 'Jesus of History' presuppositions, goes so far in the other direction as to compromise belief in the Incarnation, and in the humanity of Jesus. Baillie could here have extended his case by noting the uniform influence which Kierkegaard had upon the whole Dialectical and Existentialist schools. What he could not have anticipated was the fresh light thrown upon the historical dimension of the Incarnation and the Gospel records by the so-called 'New Quest'. The most important resultant issue which remains unsolved for us now, however, is whether the study of what has come to be called 'the analytic philosophy of history' has changed the character of the old controversy about faith and history which lies at the back of all contemporary analyses of the historicity of the Gospels and the humanity of Our Lord. That discussion is for another day.

1.2   There are two christological positions upon which Baillie reflects, which deserve special comment: *anhypostasia*, and kenoticism, both interesting in very different ways because of the involvement of H.R.Mackintosh.   *Anhypostasia* is the theory that the divine Person of the Logos, who by definition had a divine nature, assumed a human nature which did not have a human personality, a *physis anhupostatos* - a theory affirmed by Cyril of Alexandria (if not even anticipated by Apollinarius) - in Cyril's case in opposition to the thorough-going dualism of Nestorius.   It was a position which was engrossed in the Chalcedonian christology, and which was sharply criticised by H R Mackintosh, who protested against the 'impersonal humanity' which it seemed to be ascribing to Jesus Christ.   Baillie followed his old teacher in this rejection, saying that few theologians would now defend the phrase, since it appeared to deny that Jesus was a man, or a human person.   He was wrong here for, in fact, at least two major theologians did come to use the phrase and even to make it an article of faith in their christology.   His treatment of *kenoticism* is almost lethal.   He rejects it, on several grounds: it falls foul of the old charge that it does not explain what was happening to the providential care of the rest of the universe while the self-emptied Creative Word existed only in the infant Jesus; kenoticism describes not an Incarnation but a theophany or a kind of pagan metamorphosis of God into a man; and, alternatively, what kenoticism is speaking of is not a God-man, but one who is successively God the Word, then the man Jesus, and finally again God the Word.   There is no room left for the doctrine of the eternal humanity of Christ.   This demolition of a theory which had dominated Scottish christology for thirty-five years, and influenced it for up to fifty years, for Mackintosh was a prescribed book for the BD still in the 'sixties, is remarkable, in view of the high regard in which Baillie held Mackintosh.   It also reveals that if, as Charles Raven said, Apollinarianism was the heresy of twentieth century English christology, no less was kenoticism the specially Scottish heresy.   A final word for kenoticism: in fact it was attempting to do justice to the achievements of the 'Jesus of History' school and their emphasis upon the humanity of Christ, while holding on, however tenuously, to the affirmation of the deity of Christ.

1.3   When Baillie approaches his own account of the Person of Jesus Christ, he does so by means of the concept of *paradox*, which he illustrates first briefly, showing how it arises from the application of the 'spectator-attitude' to a God who cannot be spoken of in objective terms, and who by his infinite nature eludes the control of our words and categories; and then by referring to the paradox of the idea of *creatio ex nihilo* and to that of providence. His main interest is in what he calls 'a far greater and deeper paradox than those', namely, the paradox of grace, familiar to us from the words of St Paul: '...I laboured more abundantly than them all: yet not I, but the grace of God which was with me' (I Cor 15.10); and from the words of St Augustine's prayer, 'Give what thou commandest, and command what thou wilt'; or Harriet Auber's hymn,

> 'And every virtue we possess, and every victory won,
> And every thought of holiness are his alone'.

What has been true of the saints is authenticated in the life of all Christians who are deeply aware both that in a sense everything depends upon their choice and upon their effort when confronted by some great task, and yet that success when it comes, is due to the prevenient grace of God, 'the good which was his before it was ours' (pll6). This paradox we are told points better than anything else in our human experience to the mystery of the Incarnation, to the way in which in Jesus Christ there takes place the perfect union of God and man. What we experience in a fragmentary way is a reflection of the union in Jesus Christ of the perfection of humanity and the very life of God himself.

1.4 The soteriological segment of Baillie's christology is somewhat briefer than the rest, but it carries its own originality, particularly in two respects. After observing that 'the moral failure complex' has come to replace 'the guilt complex' of an earlier generation, and that when it becomes a repressed complex, the solution will not lie on the level of psycho-analysis. First, in answer to the question, 'Why atonement?', he finds what he calls 'a faint analogy' (pp.173f) from a situation in everyday life, in the way in which a true friend sustains some very serious wrong, but who nonetheless forgives, to the kind of love which George MacDonald had in mind when he said of the love of God, 'nothing is inexorable but love'. If I were to commit some grave offence against such a friend without his knowledge initially, and he subsequently finds out, the more deeply he cares for me, the less likely is he to shrug the matter off lightly. Nor will he be slow to forgive me, but such forgive-ness will never take the form of pretending that the offence had never happened. On the contrary, he will bear the shame of my wrongdoing much more intensely than I do, and this suffering will be a part of the forgiving process, not because of any self-pity, but because of the inexorable quality of his love for me. What is true in this context of the forgiving love of a human friend, who like myself is imperfect and who has himself committed wrongs, is pre-eminently true of God and of his forgiving love towards sinners. If we as sinners disobey and are disloyal to God, it is sin against the perfect love that created us and all the world and its creatures that we offend, and that must be the ultimate betrayal. Because of the intensity of his love, his forgiveness is no easy amnesty. There is an 'atonement, an expiation, in the heart of God and out of that comes the forgiveness of sins', (p.175). Secondly, and rather ingeniously, Baillie then sets out to show how the ancient Israelite sacrificial system, which embodied all the terminology of atonement, expiation, propitiation and reconciliation, reaches its climax in the death of Christ in the New Testament, where it is transformed in a notion of atonement in which God himself and alone bears the cost. To substantiate his thesis, Baillie suggests that there have been two strands in Old Testament thinking about sin and guilt and forgiveness. On the one hand, offerings and sacrifices came to be regarded as the means of expiating ritual offences rather than the great sins of violation of the Decalogue, for the forgiveness of which in fact there was no provision. God might be hoped to be merciful. Generally, sinners could only expect punishment. But, on the other hand, in the great Prophetic movement of the eighth century B.C., two new notes were heard. First, there was widespread declaration that the truly great offences were not the ritual ones, but the moral offences - of injustice, dishonesty, bribery, violence, oppression. Secondly, however, the great affirmation is now made that God will freely forgive, if sinners will repent and return to God. Given this second theme, the student of theology would expect that the sacrificial system would come to an end. On the contrary, in the post-Exilic period, the sacrificial system becomes more sophisticated, extending now to include both ritual and moral offences. When we come to the Christian era, a climax occurs, in which absolutely free forgiveness is offered to the repentant sinner by a loving Father, who will also go out to find the sinner who has not repented; while the sacrifice which is offered for the sinner comes from God; he bears the brunt and he pays the price. The Lamb, who takes away the sin of the world is none other than the Eternal Word, God of God. No sacrifice could be more costly. Even in using this language of sacrifice, and later of propitiation, Baillie continually emphasises the 'remarkable identification' of the love of Christ which brought him to the cross, and the love of God, whose will it was that Jesus should die. So, to bring together the main themes of his christology, Baillie declares that 'as God was incarnate in Jesus, so may we say that the divine Atonement was incarnate in the passion of Jesus' (p.191).

II

The Reformed Theological Review Vol 7, No 2, November 1948, pp.11-19.

I turn now to certain criticisms which I made in my review of Baillie, after having made unambiguously clear my appreciation of the many qualities of his work, which incidentally I still admire.

1. At the start, in view of the enormously important role which the concept is going to have in his christology, I wondered whether Baillie might not have examined more closely what is involved in the notion of *paradox*. Even in 1948, it had almost been worked to death, having been widely employed by Karl Heim, Daniel Lamont, John Baillie, and Reinhold Niebuhr, and the explosion of Kierkegaardiana in the forties made it all the more important that the meaning and implications of the term be no longer taken for granted. Kemp Smith used to say that paradox is truth standing on her head and it is the duty of a gentleman to assist the lady to her feet. Even in the Theological Society of those days, the mere utterance of the word, 'paradox', was an accepted conversation-stopper; whereas, in fact, it should have been an invitation to further examination and exploration. With the hindsight of forty years on, I have to confess that maybe we still have not taken the question of the nature of paradox much farther than equating it with a kind of logical contradiction, which of course it

cannot be *simpliciter*. Certainly some of the uneasiness that a modern reader may feel with Baillie's position may be found to derive from the unexamined implications of the use of the term 'paradox'. The brief examples which he gives - religious discourse, the doctrine of creation, and even the doctrine of grace - do not evince any single conceptual pattern.

2. The central thesis of Baillie's christology is that 'our experience of grace is a reflection of the perfect union of God and man in Jesus Christ'. This thesis rests on the assumption that 'God is in Christ' in the same way as God is in us, when we experience grace, an experience expressed paradoxically by St Paul, 'I, yet not I, but the grace of God'. So Baillie asks the question (p. 16), 'Is it not the same *type* of paradox taken at the absolute degree, that covers the whole ground of the life of Christ?' I wonder whether it is not a fundamental *given* of christology that God was not in Christ in the same way as he is in Peter, James and John; and it is exactly this fact that constitutes the christological problem. Certainly, if the thesis were misunderstood (cf. Hick), it could be taken as a form of the heretical view that 'Divinity is humanity writ large'; and I am sure that Baillie would have none of that. We have in fairness to notice that Baillie, having spoken of our experience of God's grace being a *reflection* of the perfect union of God and man in Jesus Christ, also, if fleetingly, suggests that there is an *analogy* between the two; and I do wonder whether it might have been more profitable to have taken that interpretation of the situation farther. The notion of the *analogia gratiae* has an honourable theological history.

3. To follow another of my lines of criticism: if the paradox of grace be taken as the clue to the understanding of the Incarnation, could it not be argued that our author has committed the logical error of *metabasis eis allo genos* or, as we are more accustomed to saying, committed a category mistake? When Christian people come to right decisions, and achieve noble ends, and confess that they do so not of themselves, but 'by the grace of God', Christian theology has on the whole affirmed that the Holy Spirit is indwelling their lives and inspiring their actions. Accordingly, to take the argument to the next stage, we might appear to be justified only in saying that in Christ there was fulness of grace; or alternatively, that it was the Holy Spirit

who was incarnate, rather than the Word of God. Agreed: we read at St John 1.14, 'The Word became flesh, and dwelt among us, full of grace and truth'. It is an interesting exercise both in theology and in exegesis to determine the relationship of the sentences 'The Word was made flesh' and 'He dwelt among us, full of grace and truth'. But I doubt if anyone would want to equate them with one another, so that one could be said to be resoluble without remainder into the other. What is appearing, as we examine the implications of Baillie's use of the paradox of grace in constructing his christology, is the beginning of serious confusion about the part played by one person, namely, the Holy Spirit, in the *opus ad extra* of another person, namely, the Word.

4. There is one position which as stated gives me cause for uneasiness. At p. 149, after suggesting that the Incarnation did not come at an earlier stage in the history of mankind, because men and women were not likely to be sufficiently responsive, he deduces, from the *fact* that God did eventually invade human life and become incarnate, the *conclusion* that it was because *here* finally was a Man who was responsive. The reason for this contention is a desire to avoid docetism, and to secure genuine responses in the Word made flesh. In the review I made the point that as stated, the view commits a hysteron-proteron, the cart before the horse fallacy, for surely, the perfect responsiveness of Jesus derives from the fact that in him the Word has been made flesh.

5. Perhaps we may now raise a methodological question, relating to the practice of using the paradox of grace as a hermeneutical principle. It could be said that this method substitutes a problem in moral psychology for one in metaphysics and logic. What Baillie has done is to describe how the way in which we make moral and religious decisions and strive for good objectives and in so doing receive the gift of God's grace, is a clue to the compresence of the human and the divine in Jesus Christ. But the question which Baillie himself touched upon when examining the notion of the *anhypostasia* remains unsolved. It is the question of who is the subject of the experiences which we describe as having a human and a divine nature. The Chalcedonian formula, with its *anhypostasia* theory, was affirming that the Person of the Logos was the subject of the divine nature but the human nature had no person or logical subject. Accordingly, Leontius of Byzantine,

followed by H.M.Relton in the present century, sensing that Chalcedon represented an unstable position, proposed that the human nature should find its person or its logical subject in the Person of the Word, the position known as *enhypostasia*. As I have said elsewhere, *The Shape of Christology* (1966) pp.99ff, Ephraim of Antioch seems to me to give the most satisfactory answer to that whole crop of questions, by saying that in Jesus Christ the human and the divine persons (*hypostaseis*) are fused, so that the subject of the divine and human natures, as of the experiences appropriate to both, is Jesus Christ. I have no intention of pursuing this theme. I only mention it here to indicate that Baillie's Christology does not in fact solve the main problems raised by Chalcedon.

6. I would still have, as I had in 1948, misgivings about the relation of Baillie's christology to his soteriology. Then my concern had been about the absence from the main presentation of the christology, of a strong *emphasis* upon the central theme of the Word being made flesh, or of the only-begotten Son being sent to fulfil the will of the Father, a strong emphasis which would be required to sustain the firmly advanced contentions that the death of the Son was the high price paid by the Father for the sins of the world. In fact, as I can see now, the soteriological position which Baillie is proposing falls into two parts: the first, which draws on the analogy of what happens when I offend a friend who loves me and forgives me, and which is very close to the soteriology of McLeod Campbell, with its doctrine of vicarious repentance; and secondly, a more traditional soteriology, which speaks of sacrifice, propitiation and reconciliation, but which employs the imagery which McLeod Campbell was endeavouring to replace. The question then arises whether Baillie has succeeded in welding those two kinds of soteriology together. My own judgement is that he comes very close to success, and I know that it is a stance which is supportable. My problem of the relation of the christology to the soteriology would, of course, remain.

III

The earlier sections of this paper have unavoidably had to be longer than the ensuing, for it has been obligatory upon me to provide for you the basic structures of what is a fairly complex system, despite its clarity and definition.   In his letter to me of 12 March 1949, Baillie made the following points:

1. As regards the use of the concept of 'paradox', he pointed out that he himself had introduced it into his book, *Faith in God* as far back as 1927, and that therefore originally he depended in no way upon Heim, Lamont, Niebuhr, or even Kierkegaard, though by 1949, he admitted that their influence, and especially that of his brother, John, would be present but not overwhelming.   He was therefore using it in a rather unsophisticated sense, which would bring it near to meaning logical contradiction.   It would be no longer open to us to ignore the history of the term.   He added a comment, which will be seen to be important later, namely, that the retention of an emphasis on paradox in theology serves to stave off Pelagianism or its half-brother, semi-Pelagianism, especially in the case of the paradox of grace.

2. He illustrated the way in which paradox may be applied in the doctrine of creation with its talk of *creatio ex nihilo,* and of the creation of time, which would lead to our saying that there was a time when time was not.   That point is not, I feel, at issue, and need not detain us.

3. Baillie then takes me to task over my drawing attention to the sentence 'When God at last broke through into human life and became incarnate, must we not say that in a sense it was because here at last a Man was perfectly receptive?' (p.149), and over my commenting upon what seemed to me to be a wrong order.   Quite justifiably, he points out that at the foot of the same page, he makes the very claim that Jesus lived as he did because he was the Son of God. 'The divine is always prevenient' (p.150).   Incidentally, it is here that Baillie elects to draw out the full incarnational features of his christology, arguing that from the human life of Jesus upon earth, we are led 'paradoxically but inevitably' to its eternal origin in the life and heart of God.   So the orthodox statements find their immediate expression, 'When the fulness of time was come, God sent forth his Son', who had been with him from all eternity.   In this sending forth God manifested his love to us.

Two remarks to round off this section. One: I still feel that Baillie, while endeavouring to do justice to the human element in choices taken within the context of divine grace, both in ourselves and in Jesus Christ, has over-stated his case in saying that the Incarnation took place because finally a Man was receptive, though he does make every attempt to correct any false impressions thereby created. Two: Baillie must surely have provided us with one of the earliest examples of christology 'from below', in fully orthodox terms. The nineteenth century saw christologies 'from below', but they were not designed to maintain, but rather to refute, traditional positions. But in Baillie, as a quite explicit methodological procedure, we have someone setting out from the human situation, and yet ending up with most of the orthodox affirmations, a long time ahead of Pannenberg, Moltmann and Sobrino. Full recognition of that fact should be made, and that is something that we could not have done in 1948, without an unusual gift of prophecy. Also, it provides us with a fresh perspective in which to view our theologian.

IV

John Hick: *Scottish Journal of Theology*, Vol 11, No 1, March 1958, pp.1-12: 'The Christology of D. M. Baillie':

Hick sets himself the task of appraising the christological theorem as we have seen propounded by Donald Baillie, that the Incarnation 'was the supreme instance of the "paradox of grace"'. May I in parenthesis protest at the start that nowhere does Baillie speak of the Incarnation being either an instance, or even the supreme instance, of this paradox, so maybe things are going wrong from the start. Hick is concerned with four subjects:

1. He defines the central task of christology as being that of defining what is meant by saying that Jesus of Nazareth was both God and man. Conceding that the statement that Jesus was man 'is clear enough' - though the history of christology would not altogether bear out such optimism, but we shall let that pass - Hick turns his attention to the statement that Jesus was God. Hick confirms what Baillie has already said, namely, that the word, 'God', is not the title of a class,

or even an individual of a class, but the proper name for a certain being. So, though text books often refer to Jesus as 'divine', and seem thereby to imply that Jesus has the universal characteristic of divinity, which he might be thought to have in a higher degree (even an infinitely higher degree) than others, it is much more appropriate to refer to the 'Deity' of Christ, which has substantival rather than adjectival logical status. The orthodox language of *homoousios to patri* was intended to convey the identity and continuity of being and nature between Jesus Christ and the Father; but he was also continuous as regards his human nature with human beings. Hick sets as the criterion for a valid christology that it should illumine for modern man the conception of the deity of Christ as substantival and not adjectival.

2. Hick next reminds us of the structure of Baillie's christology, with its use of the paradox of grace as the best clue to the understanding of the Incarnation, and as in its fragmentary form in our lives, the reflection of the perfect union of God and man in the Incarnation. A very interesting suggestion, but does it meet the criterion of the first paragraph? It would seem not; for, according to Hick, the paradox of grace which covers the whole of the life of Christ is the same *type* of paradox taken to a supreme degree, which is encountered in the lives of men and women inspired by God's grace. 'What in other men is inspiration amounted in Christ to Incarnation' (p. 6), so that the case has been made only for the adjectival concept of divinity.

3. Hick now draws attention to a refinement in Baillie's position, which we have not so far found it necessary to notice, but mention now because John refers to it. Baillie had said that there is in fact a difference between the presence of God in believers and in Christ, in so far as it is because of the presence of God in Christ that he is in us, because we are 'in Christ'. Hick seeks to dispose of this suggestion as 'a rather central inadequacy' (p. 8), by pointing out that the paradox of grace is not peculiar to Christian moral experience, but can be observed in other moral systems, even pagan in character, and hence the connection solely of Christians with grace in Christ is forced, if not inaccurate. Hick now seeks to present Baillie with a dilemma, both horns of which grow out of the predestinarianism which Hick highlights in Baillie. On the one hand, there is, he alleges, a kind of

what I shall call 'hard' predestinarianism, which loads the paradox of grace on the side of the divine prevenience, in the form of irresistible grace. This view is said to imperil human freedom, by denying human co-operation in moral achievements. There is just enough textual evidence for this position to justify Hick's charge, though he constantly says that Baillie would not subscribe to such a view. So, on the other hand, he offers Baillie the horn of adoptionism, extracted from a text (which I fear does not support it, viz., p.116) which speaks of every good action being the genuinely free choice of a person with a will. Hick wants to oppose this view, which he interprets as saying that what good people do is to allow the divine grace to work within them, to his paraphrase of the previous predestinarianism, which says that God *causes* men to choose rightly (p. 9). So the adoptionism comes in sight, for the paradox of grace is now being used as the combination of prevenient grace and free moral choice which takes up the offer of that grace, what I would call 'soft' predestinarianism. Jesus' life consisted of the conjunction of divine grace and perfect receptivity, but, so Hick argues, any man who lived such a perfect life could and would equally be God incarnate. In short, Incarnation has been construed, not substantivally as deity, but adjectivally as divinity; and so, Baillie's christology fails Hick's test.

V

John Baillie: *Scottish Journal of Theology*, Vol. 11, No. 3, September 1958, pp.265-270: 'Some Comments on Professor Hick's Article on "The Christology of D. M. Baillie"':

Naturally, John Baillie could not be expected to allow such strictures to go unrecognised as a virtual debunking of Donald's very carefully argued theory, and within a very brief time replies.

1. As regards Hick's main criticism that, whereas for Donald, God's presence in Christ was admittedly in a higher degree, and to a greater extent, than in other men, for classical Chalcedonian christology, God is thought to be in Christ in a totally unique way, unparalleled in any other human life, John quotes a statement of H.R.Mackintosh, that God's immanence in Jesus so transcends his presence in other

men as to be absolute, singular and totally unique. A difference of degree becomes a difference of kind. Reflecting upon Hick's suggestion, that we seek some more 'dynamic' concept to construe the uniqueness of God's presence in Christ than the idea of *homoousios to patri*, which is too 'static', John rightly points out that that is exactly what Donald has done in describing the Person of Christ in terms of the Work. The presence of God in Christ would then be defined in terms of the special vocation of Christ, namely, to save the world; while God's presence in us would relate to the task which God has in store for each of us. John, therefore, suggests that Donald's view of the uniqueness of the presence of God in Christ is to be accepted in the sense that his vocation was unique.

2. In reply to Hick's criticism that the paradox of grace alleged by Donald to be peculiarly evident in Christian experience, and so a derivative from the supreme mystery of grace in the Incarnation, is a much wider phenomenon, exemplified in all good deeds; John affirms very vigorously that certainly God's enabling grace has been available to men and women in every age, but that it has proceeded from the Son, as well as from the Father and the Spirit. He claims also that Donald's very strong insistence on the pre-existence of Christ, to which he traces back the human life of Christ, guarantees within all human history the presence of the grace of God.

3. Finally, as regards the dilemma of adoptionism and predesti-narianism, with which Hick confronts Donald, John quite firmly rejects the dilemma, and holds that Donald would certainly have inclined to the 'hard' predestinarian view, and I should have thought that that assessment would have been totally correct. There are several occasions on which he affirms strenuously the prevenience of divine grace in human moral action, and in the offer of salvation, to which men and women can only respond through the enabling grace of God - all of which takes us immediately to the paradox of grace and the doctrine of predestination in some form.

To conclude briefly: if I were now to be reviewing *God Was in Christ* with the hindsight of our discussion and exchanges, I would say something like the following: If it is our intention to construct a christology on the basis of the paradox of grace, then we really must give closer attention to the concept of paradox and what is involved in it. I think that John Hick has been able to make so much play of the dilemma of adoptionism and predestinarianism because of an initial unclarity on Donald's part of what a paradox is all about, if you like, how it works. Next, I do think that it may just be possible to construct a doctrine of the two natures in Jesus Christ, using the paradox of grace; but again, one or two controls have to be observed. It must be shown that the paradox as found in human beings is being employed *analogically*, so that Hick's attempt to charge Baillie with a confusion of deity as a substantive and divinity as an adjective is frustrated at the start. Also, provision must be made to ensure that the category mistake between logico-theology and psychology is not committed; and that provision would involve a longer discussion of the state of play in the logic and metaphysics of substance, and also in what has come to be known as philosophy of mind, which involves so many problems on the borderline between philosophy and psychology.

So if there is to be any single tribute to Donald Baillie it must surely be that forty years after he was writing his book, we should still be discussing the questions he examined, as relevant to our time; and considering his answers as genuine intellectual possibilities for us.

IX. D. M. BAILLIE AND THE PREACHING OF CHRISTIAN DOCTRINE

- J.A.Whyte

I did not have the privilege, as some here had, of studying under Donald Baillie.   He taught for a year in New College, during his brother's moderatorial year.   That happened to be the year when I was being introduced by Professor G.T. Thomson to the mysteries of Reformed Dogmatics - a memorable experience, indeed, but it prevented me from sitting under Donald Baillie as a student.   I did hear him deliver the occasional paper, and, like everyone else, I was charmed by the shy strength of his personality.   John Baillie was then, and remained for ever, my teacher, whose openness of mind and clarity of thought delighted and inspired, even though they remained an unattainable ideal.   In my student days, Donald was a more shadowy figure, though it was not long after, as an Army Chaplain attending the Summer School of Theology in 1947, and as a Territorial Army Chaplain on courses thereafter, that I had the opportunity to appreciate the penetration of his mind.   The subjects on which I remember him lecturing were Baptism and the Theology of Worship: which shows, I suppose, that the boundaries between Systematic and Practical Theology have a way of becoming blurred.   I noticed when I was preparing this lecture that the book which my wife gave me to mark my induction to Oban: Dunollie Road, on 15 April 1948, was the newly-published *God Was In Christ.*   That book, of course, established him in all our eyes as a major theologian, and brought him out from the shadow of his brother.

I did not encounter Donald as a preacher until one morning which I vividly remember.   It was Passion Sunday, 5 April 1954, and at 9.30 I turned on the wireless in our kitchen in Oban and heard Donald Baillie preaching on "Why did Jesus die?"   I had intended to go into the study and make ready for my own service at 11.00 - I had a sermon on Matt. 19:30, "Many that are last shall be first, and the first last" - but I was held there, because here was profound truth being expressed by a theologian in the most clear and simple way.   I never forgot that sermon.   I used it in my teaching of First Communicants, and many years later when I had to do a Broadcast Service on The Cross and Forgiveness, I turned to Baillie's sermon (it was published in *To Whom Shall We Go*) and quoted from it.

It is interesting to reflect that during his lifetime Donald Baillie published two substantial works of theology - *Faith in God and Its Christian Consummation* (1927) and *God was in Christ* (1948)[1]. The first book to be published after his death was a volume of sermons, *To Whom Shall We Go?* (1955)[2], followed in 1957 by *The Theology of the Sacraments*[3], and then in 1958 another volume of sermons, *Out of Nazareth*[4]. So many of us have become acquainted with his preaching only after his death.

It happens that we have here in St Andrews the papers and sermons of D.M.Baillie. They used to be housed in St Mary's and are now in the University archives under the guardianship of Mr Smart. A little more than twenty years ago I had an American research student, Nicholas van Dyck. His attention had already been drawn to the Baillie papers, and we agreed that since we had many, though not all, of Baillie's sermons, and his unpublished lecture-notes and papers as well as his published work, we had an unusual opportunity to compare the preaching of a theologian with his writing and lecturing. Did he preach his theology, or did he leave it behind when he went into the pulpit? Did he have to censor and simplify his theology when he came face to face with a congregation? Were there matters explored in the theology on which he kept a discreet silence in his preaching? And vice versa? These questions seemed worth asking, and we were fortunate to have the material from which to answer them. In 1965 Dr van Dyck's thesis on "Theological Themes in the Preaching of D.M.Baillie"[5] was approved for the degree of Ph.D. It has rested in the University Library, undisturbed, as far as I know, from that day until recently, when I consulted it as a source for this paper. I am very

---

1 Hereafter referred to as **GWiC**

2 Hereafter referred to as **TW**

3 Hereafter referred to as **TS**

4 Hereafter referred to as **ON**

5 Hereafter referred to as **NvD**

grateful for Nick van Dyck's permission to quote from his thesis. I have looked at some of the archive material, but since it is uncatalogued and there is a great deal of it, one would need the time available to a research student to find one's way through it.

One of the sources I looked at is Baillie's Register of Sermons, dating from 1913 to 1934 - i.e. from his time as an assistant in North Morningside, Edinburgh, through his period as a *locum tenens* in St Boswells, and his ministries in Bervie, Cupar and Kilmacolm, until his appointment to the newly founded Chair of Systematic Theology in St Andrews. For reasons known only to himself it stops there. He did not stop preaching when he became a Professor - few of us do.

Apart from the occasional preaching and broadcasting to which he was invited, there was the pulpit of the Collegiate Church of St Salvator, where he preached at least once each session. Baillie preached 29 sermons in the Chapel in the 20 years he was in St Andrews, ending with a broadcast sermon from the Chapel on Easter Day 1954, on "Thanks be to God, who giveth us the victory, through our Lord Jesus Christ". (I Cor. 15:57, see *TW*, p.144ff.).

The Register of Sermons is interesting. It lists 652 sermons. (Not all of these can now be found: some may have been reconstructed for later use.) It is an encouragement to those of us who preach here and there to know that Baillie had some "travellers", as preachers call the sermons they carry around from place to place. The sermon which gives the title to the book *Out of Nazareth* was first preached in Kilmacolm in 1932, and in the next 9 years it was preached 12 times, being altered only minimally to allow for the passage of the years. (An illustration in the original was introduced by the words "Last Sunday"; later altered by Baillie himself to "A few summers ago", and finally by the editor of the book to "Many years ago". Tempus fugit.)

In a paper to a conference of ministers on The Preaching of Christian Doctrine, Donald Baillie said, "When I look back to the days of my regular pastoral ministry, one of the things I regret is that I did not more faithfully try to make my ministry a *teaching* ministry." (*TS*, p.141). But when you examine the Register of Sermons, you see that the note of doctrine was by no means absent. Some of the sermons of this young man may not have been different in theme and approach from those of other young ministers: devotional sermons, appeals to the young to follow Christ, comfort to those in trouble. In 1915 he preached a series of sermons on The Character of Jesus, and later one on the Story of Jacob and one on the Book of Jonah. In 1922 he preached 15 sermons on the Life of St Paul. In 1923 there is a series on Great Christian Doctrines - the Doctrine of God (I Cor. 8:6); Sin and Forgiveness (Col. 1:14); Grace (I Cor. 1:4); the Holy Spirit (Jn. 14:26), and from then on the note of doctrine is never long absent from the sermon titles. The Animal and the Divine in Man (Jer. 2:25); the Healthiness of the Doctrine of the Forgiveness of Sins (Is. 1:18); The Necessity of the Cross (Gal. 6:14). A series on Christianity and Human Nature in 1925 had 3 sermons: The Christian View of the Body (I Cor. 6:9); the Christian View of the Intellect (I Cor. 14:20); and The Christian Control of the Imagination (Phil. 4:8). There are also series on The World's Great Religious Sayings, on How Jesus Dealt with Human Ills, on Questions People are Asking and on What We Believe - about God, about Creation, about Providence, about Jesus Christ, about the Forgiveness of Sins and about the Atonement. And we meet the sermons which gave the titles to his books - God Was in Christ, Out of Nazareth and To Whom Shall We Go?

It seems then that, however he might accuse himself for not doing enough, Baillie himself was far from those whom he criticises for preaching "general moral and religious reflections ... without any firm content of the Christian message." [1]

One of the interesting results of Nicholas van Dyck's research was the discovery that the themes which appear in Donald Baillie's lectures and published work on Christian Doctrine appear also in the sermons, with only very few exceptions. Among these is the doctrine of *creatio ex nihilo*, creation out of nothing. In his lectures he maintains that this doctrine is important in order to avoid Pantheism on the one hand and Manichaeism on the other, but it does not seem to appear in any of the sermons which deal with creation, as though, whatever its intellectual justification, the idea that creation is out of nothing is a relatively abstruse point that he was not able to relate to Christian experience. Another point which van Dyck notes is that while Baillie uses the first

---

[1] **The Content of Preaching Today**, Book 50, p.13. NvD, p.3.)

three chapters of Genesis in his academic treatment of Creation and Fall, "there is no record of any sermon preached by Baillie on a text from these passages." (*NvD*, p.311) That is not to say that there is no mention of man's creation or of man's sin in the sermons . There is a great deal about both, but for reasons which we may be able to suggest later, he chose not to base his sermons on the Genesis stories.

The other discovery is the extent to which the very same language in which Baillie's own positive teaching is given in the academic work is to be found within the sermons - sentences, paragraphs, pages. It may be, of course, that in some instances the traffic is not from theology to sermon, but the other way round, and that some thought, imagery, form of expression, argument, first developed in a sermon finds its way later into the theological teaching. It would require a careful comparison of the dating of the lectures and the first versions of the sermons to determine that. I suspect it worked both ways. In a sermon preached in 1937-38 he uses the idea of the "inferiority complex", in a way which is further developed as "the moral inferiority complex" in *God Was in Christ* and in the later sermon on Sin and Forgiveness. [1]

At the beginning of his lectures on Systematic Theology Donald Baillie warned his students:

> There is a danger of ministers ... going out into the world with a considerable knowledge of how to put a sermon together and how to preach it, but with little knowledge of *what to preach*, because they have not taken their theological study seriously enough, they have not thought out what they believe, certainly they do not know it clearly enough to be able to help the people in the pew to think out their faith.[2]

Baillie himself had been educated in that most systematic of all schools, the Shorter Catechism. He was very fond of telling one story which occurs in some of his lectures and in at least one of the sermons.

---

[1] See **GWiC** pp.160-167, **TW**, p.117 ff. **NvD**, p.359, n.1

[2] Systematic Theology, vol.I, (Bk. 8), p.14; **NvD**, p.5

I give it in his words.   When D.L.Moody, the great American evangelist, was in Edinburgh he held a meeting for children and addressed a vast congregation of them in the Assembly Hall.   "He had chosen 'Prayer' as the subject of his address, and he began by asking, as a merely rhetorical question, 'What is prayer?', not expecting an answer and never thinking that these were the exact words of a question in the Shorter Catechism.   No sooner were the words out of his mouth than a hundred hands shot up all over the hall.   Moody picked out a boy at random to give his answer.   Without a moment's hesitation the boy stood up and said 'Prayer is an offering up of our desires unto God, for things agreeable to his will, in the name of Christ, with confession of our sins, and thankful acknowledgement of his mercies.'   They were the words of the shorter catechism, and any one of these other hundred boys and girls could have said the same thing.   Moody listened, and then said, 'Thank God, my boy, that you were born in Scotland.'" [1]

Baillie went on to say that he was not defending the Shorter Catechism as a doctrine or as a method for children.   But, he said, "I do like the story as illustrating the ideal of a virile, intelligent Christianity that knows what it believes and can give an answer to anyone who asks for a reason."   He himself believed strongly, and often maintained that Christian Doctrine must be a coherent system, but he saw that not in terms of the Federal Calvinism in which he had been brought up, which tends towards abstract timeless truth, but rather in terms of a story that has been told and has to be told again.   And he was convinced that if we are to have a "virile, intelligent Christianity" that story has to be preached.   How does he relate the work of the theologian and the work of the preacher?

In his lecture to ministers on The Preaching of Christian Doctrine, Baillie said,

> "I believe that there is a great difference between what a
> professor of theology ought to be doing in his classes and

---

[1] "What is Christian Doctrine?", Book 71, p.17-19, **NvD**, pp.106-107. cf. **TW**, pp.63-64)

what a preacher (perhaps that very same professor) ought to be doing in his pulpit; and it would be a dreadful mistake for the latter to adopt precisely the same method and technique as the former."[1]

But he goes on to show that it is a matter of method rather than of content:

"That is why so many theological professors, who may once have been fairly good preachers, become very dull and heavy in the pulpit, a weariness to the flesh of the man in the pew. But that is a matter of method, and I am convinced that the preacher, always remembering that he *is* a preacher to the great mixed body of the people, ought also to be a teacher: and still more he must remember that what he has to preach is not simply fancies or even whatever great thoughts come into his head, but the *Christian message* - and that really means Christian doctrine."[2]

Perhaps the easiest and most accessible place to illustrate and test what he says here is his treatment of the Doctrine of the Trinity. We have in *Out of Nazareth* some lectures on The Trinity, and in the same volume a sermon on The Mystery of the Trinity. In *To Whom Shall We Go?* there is a sermon on The Doctrine of the Trinity, and in the lecture from which I have just quoted he gives a possible outline of a sermon on the Trinity, an outline which corresponds very closely, in places word for word, to the actual sermon we have in *To Whom Shall We Go?*

In the lectures on the Trinity, Baillie begins "Hardly any part of Christian dogma is more continually present in the worship of the church than the doctrine of the Trinity" (*ON*, p.179). He refers to the three-fold Benediction, the Baptismal formula, the Gloria. "Yet", he says, "hardly any part of Christian dogma is less present and real to the actual religious consciousness of the ordinary devout Christian."

---

[1] TS, p.142

[2] Ibid.

He approaches the question "What does the doctrine mean?" by asking first "On what is it based?" He looks at, and rejects, two answers to that question:

1. First, it is based simply on revelation: it is a given, a starting point for Christian thought and experience.

2. Second, it is based on "a natural necessity to think in a triadic way". He spends what may seem to you, and does to me, an unnecessarily long time examining this view, from speculations about early Babylonian religion down to Hegel's thesis/antithesis/synthesis, and gently refutes it, though he says there is some truth in both these views.

He then comes to a third answer to the question on what is the doctrine based:

3. Third, it was "based on Christian history and experience ....: on historic facts and experiences which had to be interpreted by the Christian church." This is the approach he follows.

So he looks, in the lectures, at the "historic facts". First, the fact of Jesus, "so stupendous a fact ... that his followers were faced with an urgent task of explanation. He had made everything different for them, had brought God into their lives in a wholly new way - and forgiveness and joy and power and victory over sin and care and death." His own death was not defeat, for it had won them the greatest thing of all ... "Only one explanation could suffice: that *God was in Christ* ... But how? Was Jesus simply identical with God? Is 'Jesus' simply another name for God? No, that could not be the truth, for Jesus was a man ...." And here he deals, in passing, with Patripassianism and Sabellianism. Was he a second God?: no, he says, for that would run counter to monotheism. Was he a demi-god or a semi-divine being? Then you would have neither incarnation nor atonement, and here in passing he criticises Arianism. "So the church", he says, "was driven to the conviction that while Jesus was not identical with God, God was incarnate in him." To explain this he uses the Greek word *hypostasis* and its Latin translation *persona*. "God existed in more than one *hypostasis* or *persona*." He refers to the concept of Logos or Word as the name given to the Second Person, then points out that there was another expression more akin to Jesus' own way of talking - that of Son. "So there was God the Father and God the Son, not two Gods but one."

He then turns to the fact of Pentecost: how the disciples had felt that if Jesus was taken from them "God would fade out of their lives": but now "Jesus seemed nearer than ever and God had come into their lives as never before." This is the fact of experience, and in explaining it they looked back to the Old Testament, to Joel, and said "This is the Holy Spirit". So, the orthodox statement of "Three persons in One God" grew naturally "out of the historic facts and experiences."

Baillie then has dealt with the basis of the doctrine and now considers the meaning of the doctrine. He examines the terms *ousia* and *hypostasis*, and the development of their meanings before, at and after Nicaea. He refers to Origen, to Theodoret, to the Arians and to the Cappadocian Fathers, and, at some length, to Tertullian. The idea of *perichoresis* or *circumincessio* (interpenetration) is briefly explored in relation to Athanasius and Hilary of Poitiers. Augustine's view of the Trinity in terms of love is appreciated. He quotes Augustine "We say three Persons, not in order that such a statement may be made, but in order to avoid saying nothing." (And I have to say that I think that is the most sensible word about the Trinity that has ever been uttered.) We meet also the other old Latin tag "opera trinitatis ad extra sunt indivisa". Baillie returns to the Biblical evidence when dealing with the Holy Spirit (most of his treatment is concerned with the relation of the Father and the Son). He sums it all up with reference to Arianism, Ebionite and Adoptionist Christologies, and Modalism. But, he insists, however abstract all this seems, it stands "at every point for some vital concern of our faith."

In the concluding section of the lectures, Baillie deals with the question "whether the doctrine is a natural or necessary expression of our Christian faith today". Here he deals mainly with the Holy Spirit, which has received scant attention in his historical survey, and relates that to Christian experience. He rather neatly jinks the question which has divided East from West for 900 years - whether the Spirit proceeds from the Father or from the Father and the Son. "Christianity", he says, "has always taught that the Son existed from all eternity, coeternal with the Father: and the same is true of the Holy Spirit": which seems to be nearer the Eastern position than the Western. He stresses the personal character of the Spirit, and adds a brief paragraph on The Mystery of the Trinity.

That thought is taken up and very much developed in his sermon on The Mystery of the Trinity (I Tim. 3:16; *ON*, p.69). The sermon has two points. (How original for a sermon on the Trinity to have two points and not three!) The first is How mysterious God is, and the second is How accessible God is. Here we see him grounding the doctrine of the Trinity in Christian experience. "The Doctrine of the Trinity tells us all that (i.e. the accessibility of God) only when it comes at the end of the Christian story. If it came at the beginning it would be merely a mathematical puzzle about Three in One and One in Three." Now this is precisely the criticism which he makes in the lectures of the traditional approach, which takes the Trinity as given by revelation, a starting-point for Christian thought and experience, rather than a conclusion to it.

Also in this sermon, his description of the experience of the disciples after Calvary and at Pentecost is very close to the account given in the lectures, if somewhat briefer.

It is in the sermon on the Doctrine of the Trinity (*TW*, p.73) that one sees best the points of difference and also the close correspondence between the theology and the preaching. The two sermons have an almost identical beginning, but in this he proceeds to take three points.

(1) "First of all, One God." "Anything more than One is too many. For there is only one true God." Here there is an argument for monotheism, very similar to that of Richard Niebuhr, but put very simply in terms of the divided loyalty, idolatry, superstition, materialism, "then life is distracted, your heart is torn asunder, because you have too many Gods." This is a point which is taken for granted or glossed over in the lectures: but the word "monotheism" which is used as shorthand in the lectures, never appears in the sermon. It seems that in his preaching Baillie is determined to eschew the technical terms of theology, though the reality which they represent may be solidly expressed.

(2) "The fact of Jesus Christ". Here we have a passage, describing the career of Jesus, his impact on the disciples and their reaction to his death - all this is almost word for word as in the corresponding passage in the lectures, closing with the realisation that *God was in Christ* and the same series of questions asked in the lectures, "Was Jesus identical with God?" "Is Jesus just another name for God?" and so on. But where the lectures thereafter contain references to Patripassianism, Sabellianism, Arianism, *hypostasis* and *persona*, none of these terms is to be found in the sermon. Yet the questions are the same and the answers are the same and the language is the same, right down to his discussion of the terms Word of God (he doesn't use the Greek word *Logos*) and Son of God.

(3) His third point is "The Fact of Pentecost". Here again his description of the disciples' experience and the reference back to Joel is almost word for word what is given in the lectures. He ends the sermon with a point made at the beginning of the lectures, that the Doctrine of the Trinity is not the starting point but the conclusion of the story of our faith. "To say merely three-in-one and one-in-three - that in itself means nothing. But when it comes at the end of the story, it tells you everything."

It is interesting to note that the passage in the lectures which dealt at some length with The Meaning of the Doctrine finds no parallel, as far as I can see, in either sermon. But this section, though he justifies it by saying that at every point it stands for some vital concern of our faith, is really a survey of the thought of the Early Fathers, and an attempt to teazle out the tangled use of Greek terms by Creeds and Councils and heretics. Perhaps he found it too daunting to try to translate all of this into simple terms. Perhaps he wasn't so sure after all that the vital concerns of our faith were still wrapped up in these matters; at any rate he passed it all over, and with it also the question of the eternity of the Son and the eternal procession of the Spirit.

I have to say that I think his sermon is all the better for that, and it remains one of the most beautiful gems of preached theology that you may find anywhere.

A word might be said about Baillie's treatment of Sin and Forgiveness. Van Dyck points out that "these two terms are never found apart from each other in the sermons. The Doctrine of Sin is not preached without reference to the Doctrine of Forgiveness." In his lectures he deals with the two topics separately, presumably because this is the way in which the theological tradition is accustomed to deal with them. One may regret this, and consider that the instinct of the preacher is truer than the tradition of the theologian.

Dr van Dyck points out that in his sermons Baillie makes no use of the term "original sin". "This omission, he says, "can be criticised on the grounds that Baillie missed an opportunity to specifically clarify a much misunderstood concept. But, on the other hand, its omission is doubtless due to Baillie's concern to avoid clouding the sermon with a theological phrase so easily misunderstood." (*NvD*, p.360).

Baillie took scrupulous care to avoid technical terms in his sermons. Even the word "paradox" which he used in God Was in Christ, and the term "the paradox of grace" does not occur in the sermon where he is saying precisely the same thing and using the text "Not I, but the grace of God which was with me" (I Cor. 15:10). However, he clearly thought that the term "inferiority-complex" had enough currency in popular use to allow him to use it in a loose and popular way - without reference to Adler or anyone else. He coins the phrases "moral inferiority-complex" and "moral failure-complex" and these are to be found both in his theology and in his sermons. Van Dyck points out that the whole treatment of forgiveness in God Was in Christ "parallells, often sentence for sentence, the sermon presentation in 'Sin and Forgiveness'". [1]

I have heard it said that a criterion of a sound theology is that it is able to be preached. A somewhat loose statement, which can be criticised on many grounds. Presumably one means by a sound theology one that is true - and Donald Baillie would have agreed with that, because time and again he insists that truth and truth alone is what matters in theology. But it would be a strange criterion of truth to say that

---

[1] **NvD**, p.359,n.l, referring to **GW**, pp.160-167 **TW**, pp.117-123

anything that can be preached is true: and it would go against all our experience of preaching. For indeed an awesome lot of nonsense has been and is still poured forth from some pulpits. It is possible to preach almost anything, however silly or abstruse, though it may be that sometimes the congregation is neither edified nor kept awake by it. The Anglican rector who looked down on his slumbering rural flock and said, "At this point I fear some of you may be suspecting me of Eutychianism", was preaching theology. Whether he was preaching effectively is another matter.

On the other hand, when you had a Scots congregation drilled in the Shorter Catechism and thoroughly educated in the Westminster standards, you were in trouble as a preacher if your sermon did not contain "points of doctrine" suitably elaborated, and in deeper trouble if that doctrine did not conform precisely to the Federal Calvinism of the Westminster Divines. The question that was asked then about any preacher was not "Is he eloquent?" or "Is he helpful?", not even "Is he an honest exegete?" (For how could anyone who preaches for three months on a single text, which he calls 'his ordinary', be an honest exegete?). The question asked about the preacher was "Is he soond?". Soundness of doctrine was what mattered. So there was no problem of using theological language. The congregation was familiar with it and expected it. Times have changed. The other day I went in to School III to lecture to the 1st Arts and 1st Divinity Class in Theology. On the board someone, lecturing before me, had written the single word "infralapsarian". I felt like one of the three bears. "Who's been doing theology in *my* classroom?". I asked the Theology class if any of them knew what the word meant. One did, and he because he happened to have a dictionary in his bag and had looked it up before I came in. Now, I am sure that there have been times in Scotland when you could not only have used that term in a sermon, knowing that your congregation would understand it, and also when, whether you used the word or not, your congregation would have detected when you were putting forward infralapsarian views of election.

Preaching itself then can scarcely be a criterion for theology. Perhaps theology is more fittingly a criterion for preaching. Since all preaching should be the proclamation of some aspect of the Christian message, and since theology is an attempt at a reasonable and systematic understanding of that message, theology is precisely what ought to be preached.

That may account for our sense of the close relationship between theology and preaching. But it is also true that the Christian message is not an abstract message but a message of salvation, a message that relates to human life. Perhaps the demand that theology should be able to be preached springs from the assumption that theology is more likely to get out of touch with human reality than preaching is. It is certainly true that some speculative theologies seem to lose all contact with human experience. Whether preaching can be relied on to maintain that contact is another matter. One difference between them may be that theology has always a more general context than preaching. Preaching is, or should be, to this congregation with its particular needs and capacities, and at this particular time. This may determine in what ways the language of preaching has to differ from the language of theology.

One could rephrase that last point and say that preaching should relate theology to the actual or possible experiences of this particular congregation. It may illumine their experience; it may enlarge it; but in some way it must speak to them as they are in time and space. "If the doctrine we preach does not bear upon daily human life, then it cannot be the real thing at all."[1]

I have sometimes wondered if Donald Baillie revised theology enough in the light of his own insights. Although he insisted that the finer points of Trinitarian doctrine touched vital concerns of our faith, he did not preach them all. I could wish that he had been more critical of the philosophical and cultural presuppositions which had determined the way in which these concerns were expressed. In the same way it seems to me that his refusal to separate Sin and Forgiveness in the sermons has a sound *theological* basis: but this is obscured when he continued to treat them separately in his theology, in the manner of the theological tradition.

---

[1] The Content of Preaching Today, Book 50, p.4. NvD p.3.

If your theology is derived from revelation, or authority, or if it is a rationalistic and speculative theology (I am thinking here of the two approaches to the doctrine of the Trinity which Baillie rejects in his lectures) then the task is how to relate that or apply it to human experience. If, however, you believe, as Baillie does, that theology has its roots in experience (the experience of the first disciples) then it can appeal to experience at every point. The task of preaching theology becomes that much easier.

Baillie repudiates any isolation of Doctrine and Experience to the detriment of either. He will not say that Christian experience is the real warm heart of the matter, and that doctrine is simply the reflection on it afterwards. "The mistake here lies in thinking that religious experience is merely a matter of feeling, when in fact it is an experience of believing." "Religious experience is a faith experience: it is an experience of being constrained to believe."[1] Again, "Christian doctrine is not simply a subsequent reflection upon the experience: it is in the experience."[2] Again, his insistence that the Christian message is not a system of timeless truths, but a story with a plot (which is another way of saying that doctrine is rooted in experience) leads him easily from theology to preaching. "That is what we have to preach," he says, "if we do not preach that, we might as well close our churches altogether."

In his hands this meant a theology that could be preached, and a preaching that was always simple and clear, never insulting the intelligence of his hearers, and never losing touch with basic human experience. Donald Baillie, and, if I may say so, his brother John, both of them achieved the simplicity which is the result of clarity of thought, and were superb preachers of Christian doctrine.

When a church was skailing after one noted theologian had been preaching, a member of the congregation said, "Ah, but he was deep." To which another replied, "No deep, but drumly." The brothers Baillie were deep, but never drumly.

---

[1] "What is Christian Doctrine?", Book 71, p.12. **NvD**, p.103.

[2] ibid.

X. WHEN DID JEREMIAH BEGIN TO PROPHESY?

- W. McKane

I shall avoid some older forms of the debate about Jeremiah's call, but I shall remind you that according to 1.2 the word of Yahweh came to him in the thirteenth year of Josiah, that is, 626 B.C. This is also the date indicated by 25.3 and Jeremiah's activity is more generally connected with the reign of Josiah in 3.6 and 36.2. Dates which appear at 25.1, 26.1 and 36.1 are not manifestly given as dates of his call or of his first public utterance, though they are claimed as such. The date given at 26.1 is 609 B.C., the year of Josiah's death at Megiddo, and at 25.1 and 36.1 605 B.C., the year when Nebuchadrezzar crushed the Egyptians at Carchemish. The claim that evidence is provided in the text of these passages that Jeremiah began to prophesy in 609 or 605 is without foundation and is even contradicted by the extant text at chapters 25 and 36, since both 25.3 and 36.2 state that Jeremiah's prophetic activity began in the reign of Josiah.

You might suppose that these attempts to find new dates for Jeremiah's call are frivolous, but they are far from being that. They are rather unsuccessful efforts to come to grips with serious problems of interpretation, and more can be done to bolster their credibility than I have yet indicated. For example, it can be argued that 25.3 and 36.2 are not stumbling-blocks: they are indications of the same Deuteronomistic tendency as pushed the beginning of Jeremiah's activity back into the reign of Josiah at 1.2 and paved the way for the representation that he was a crusader for the Josianic reform. In that case neither 25.3 not 36.2 would be original in the contexts where they now appear - they would be elements of the Deuteronomistic redaction of the book of Jeremiah. The dates on which we have to focus are then either 609(26.1) or 605(25.1?36.1) and these are moments of crisis and disaster when the first public intervention of Jeremiah as a prophet is understandable. But notice I am still maintaining there is no evidence in the text that the dates 609 or 605 are being offered as dates of Jeremiah's call.

The scholars whose thoughts run along these lines have, therefore, to enrich the credibility of their case by introducing less direct considerations. The word against Jerusalem and its temple (ch.26) is the kind of explosive, prophetic utterance with which Jeremiah might well have inaugurated his prophetic activity and the sharpness of the reaction which it aroused is then an indication that it was being heard for the first time. There was a demand from the priests and prophets of the Jerusalem temple for capital punishment from which he was shielded by the statesmen of Judah. The exegetical detail does not concern us, only the argument that these developments are inexplicable, unless Jeremiah was making this kind of utterance for the first time. It is argued that he was firing the opening shots in his prophetic campaign against Judah and Jerusalem in the year 609, when Judah's political ambitions disintegrated with the fall of Josiah at Megiddo and when Jeremiah first declared publicly that his religious legacy, the centralized cult at Jerusalem, had encouraged shallowness and error and blocked the path to a deeper understanding of how Judah stood with Yahweh.

The argument which presents 605 as the date of Jeremiah's call has a similar character, but it is more difficult to conduct and to make it credible we have to banish 36.2 from our minds. It was not a collection of oracles which Baruch read in the temple, containing Jeremiah's prophetic output from 626 to 605. Rather it was a single, specific, oracular message, spelling out the consequences of Nebuchadrezzar's victory over Egypt and declaring that Jerusalem lay defenceless before the Babylonian king. This may be gathered from Jerusalem's instructions to Baruch in vv.27ff., in which Jehoiakim's reaction to the contents of the first scroll are reproduced *verbatim*: 'You burnt this scroll and said: Why have you written that the king of Babylon shall come and destroy this land and exterminate both men and beasts?' The scroll as reinstated is to contain a threat directed at Jehoiakim and his offspring. According to this view of the matter, the oracle which Baruch read was Jeremiah's first prophetic utterance and so he opened his prophetic career by proxy. The statesmen of Judah were alarmed because they had not heard these threats before. The thought that Jeremiah opened his prophetic career by proxy I find particularly odd. Whatever reason is then offered for his exclusion from the temple area it cannot be that he had given offence by prophetic utterances.

We have to enquire more closely what are the general reasons for dissatisfaction with the year 626 which spur scholars to demonstrate that Jeremiah's prophetic career began in the reign of Jehoiakim. The kind of critical activity directed to chapters 26 and 36 which we have been reviewing arises from a prior dissatisfaction. It is held that the evidence supplied by the contents of the book of Jeremiah locate the activity of the prophet mainly in the reign of Jehoiakim and that those who maintain that he received his call in 626 have to tolerate a long period of inactivity between 621 and the reign of Jehoiakim. Moreover, it is urged, that evidence of prophetic activity before the reform of Josiah are not so firm as have been supposed, and that the lack of any mention of the prophet in connection with the events recorded in 2 Kgs 22 casts doubt on the assumption that he was already a prophet in 626. References to the idolatry of Baal worship may indicate that the reform of Josiah was not so thoroughgoing and successful as has been supposed or that by the beginning of Jehoiakim's reign its effectiveness had worn off and there had been a regression to pre-reform abuses. Moreover, the effect of a Deuteronomistic redaction on the present shape of the opening chapters has to be weighed. The prose passages which connect Jeremiah with the reform of Josiah and the book of Deuteronomy (especially chapter 11) are not to be regarded as historical sources. They do not show that the historical prophet Jeremiah participated in the programme of the reform, only that the book has been redacted by Deuteronomists whose concern was to present the prophet in this light. In view of all these considerations there is a clear case (so it is argued) for the application of Occam's razor and the conclusion that Jeremiah did not begin his prophetic activity until the reign of Jehoiakim.

I intend to pursue this matter further by glancing at the poetry in the opening chapters which has not featured largely in this discussion. But for the moment I turn aside to look again at 1.1-3. In my first volume of Jeremiah I did not give much consideration to the claim that 1.2, which places Jeremiah's call in the year 626, is an aspect of a Deuteronomistic redaction. I was, however, in a more general regard, impressed by the lateness of 1.1-3 and also the lateness of the call narrative, both of which seemed to me to reflect the final and extant form of the *corpus* of Jeremiah. Roughly speaking we may regard them as a table of contents, or, in the case of the call narrative, we may say that it is an account of Jeremiah's prophetic career which has the advantage of hindsight and is founded, in important respects, on the extant *corpus*. For example the phrase 'prophet to the nations' (v.5), about which there has been much debate, is simply a recognition that oracles against foreign nations are a substantial part of the *corpus*.

I am urging that the call narrative, along with vv.1-3, is an introduction to the book of Jeremiah and that the introduction is constructed from the evidence supplied by the extant book. In that case the call narrative is retrospective rather than proleptic. It does not come from the historical prophet Jeremiah, but it is an estimate of him after he has run his course. It affirms that notwithstanding the opposition which he aroused, the hostility which he awakened and the rejection which he suffered, he was indeed a prophet called by Yahweh. The lack of inner consistency is caused by the concern to include all the contents of the book and to do justice to them. The literary history of the book of Jeremiah is long and complicated and it did not achieve its extant shape until late in the post-exilic period.

A more particular implication of this view, applied to 1.2, is that the fixing of Jeremiah's call in 626 B.C. is possibly a *consequence* of the influence of the Deuteronomistic redaction on the final shape of the *corpus* rather than an element of that redaction. This is perhaps rather a fine critical point which does not amount to much in practical effects, except that 'in the thirteenth year of Josiah' would not be a deliberate signal from a Deuteronomistic redactor that this is the historical background against which the early chapters are to be read. It is rather a conclusion made by someone who had read the extant *corpus* that Jeremiah's prophetic activity must have begun before the reform of Josiah. I am not, of course, denying that in the prose of the early chapters there are places where the Deuteronomistic redactor has indicated a historical background in the reign of Josiah, for example, at 3.6, 'In the reign of King Josiah, Yahweh said to me'.

I should say, however, that 1.2 has been explained by some scholars as a consequence of Deuteronomistic intervention. As far back as 1923 Horst argued that a more original text ran from v.1 to v.3, so that the beginning of Jeremiah's prophetic activity was set 'in the days of

Jehoiakim'. More recently (1981) Christoph Levin has urged that 1.2 is a Deuteronomistic addition which achieves the round number of 40 years - a significant period of time in Biblical tradition - for the duration of Jeremiah's prophetic career and which enables the redactor to present him as a forerunner of the Josianic reform.

I am adopting an agnostic stance on the question of the date of Jeremiah's call, but I am leaning towards the view that he first made his prophetic intervention in the reign of Jehoiakim. I am, however, unconvinced that either 26.1 or 36.1 intend to supply us with dates of Jeremiah's call or with dates when he made his first public utterance. I am inclined to discount the date in 1.2 and 25.3 and I doubt whether the poetry of the early chapters necessarily points to a historical background which pre-dates the reform of Josiah. The last matter is the one on which I now wish to dwell. I argued in the first volume of Jeremiah that it is not a straightforward task to discover precise historical settings for units of poetry in the book of Jeremiah and that exegesis which relies too much on the firmness of these correlations is ill-founded. I am not surrendering this attitude, but I am relaxing my caution to some extent, and perhaps even taking some risks and chancing my arm.

The first point is that Jeremiah's indebtedness to Hosea for the imagery of chapters two and three seems a reasonable assumption. He represents the relation between Yahweh and Israel in the desert as a honeymoon period (2.2f), but notice that the desert itself is portrayed as a grim place (2.6) and that he does not blame Canaan for Israel's apostasy. Just the reverse! It was not the culture of Canaan which demoralized Israel. It was Israel who polluted Yahweh's gift of the Promised Land (2.7). Hence Jeremiah employs this imagery with considerable freedom. The same may be true of the harlotry/apostasy imagery on which our attention should now focus. We should not readily assume that the situation towards which the harlotry/apostasy imagery necessarily points in these early chapters is the one with which the reform of Josiah sought to deal: that the reference is always to Baal sactuaries in Judah where Baal worship has made inroads into Yahwism.

I should like to make it clear, however, that I am not closing my mind to the possibility that there may be poetry in the *corpus* which is not attributable to Jeremiah. There has perhaps been a tendency to take it for granted that the poetry of the opening chapters derives from Jeremiah and to concentrate critical enquiry on the prose, as if metrical form itself settled the issue. On the other hand, the metrical form of the oracles against foreign nations has not discouraged scholars from dissociating them from the prophet Jeremiah.

Chapter 2 is saturated with harlotry/apostasy imagery, with allusions to Baal shrines on the hill-tops and in the valleys, and the same state of affairs continues in chapter 3. This hardly needs illustration, but a few examples may be offered:

2.20:   On every high hill and under every leafy tree you lay down and fornicated.

2.23:   How can you say, I am not defiled. I have not gone after the Baalim? Look at your track in the valley. Consider what you have done.

3.2:   Look up to the hill-tops! Is there any place where you have not fornicated?.....You have defiled the land with the evil of your harlotry.

3.13:   You have spread your legs for strangers under every leafy tree.

3.21:   A sound is heard from the heights. Israelites are wailing as they pray; they have corrupted their way of life, they have forgotten Yahweh, their God.

It might be supposed in view of this concentration on Baal worship that these chapters should be disengaged from the prophet and regarded as an aspect of a Deuteronomistic redaction whose precise function is to represent that Jeremiah participated in the reform of Josiah. The principal reason why I resist this conclusion for chapter 2 is that it is a history of apostasy which extends from the settlement in Canaan to the contemporary conditions which the prophet confronts.

It is not precisely an account of the religious situation in Judah between 626 and 621. Some would say that the prophet is obsessed by sexual imagery. What at least must be said is that he was using harlotry/apostasy imagery as a paradigm to describe Israel's lack of constancy in her relationship with Yahweh through the centuries. But it is evident that this chapter does not always refer to conditions in Judah between 626 and 621, and if it sometimes does, this does not necessarily establish a special connection between the prophet Jeremiah and that period. He is recalling a long history of apostasy and he can incorporate in it the recent past just as he employs the distant past. Moreover the harlotry does not always refer to Baal worship. It can be directed towards the diplomatic manoeuvres of the statesmen of Judah who suppose that their dalliance with great powers can assure Judah of survival in a dangerous world. That too is harlotry. This passage (2.36-37) leads on to a prediction of doom - surely a characteristic of Jeremiah: You will be let down by Egypt just as you were by Assyria. You will go out from here (that is from Jerusalem) into exile, with your hands on your heads - as a train of prisoners. Yahweh has rejected your security pacts and they will avail you nothing. Or harlotry can be associated by Jeremiah with oppressive behaviour: There is blood on your skirts, the blood of the innocent poor. You did not catch them in the act of housebreaking.'

I do not, however, feel disposed to argue seriously that chapter 2 derives from the reign of Jehoiakim rather than the reign of Josiah. I do not see on what grounds one could consistently exercise such discrimination, though it was argued long ago by David Kimchi that the words 'Egypt will fail you as Assyrian did' (2.37;cf. vv.16-18) is a reference to the pro-Egyptian policies which were pursued by Jehoiakim. Rudolph apparently agrees with Kimchi's exegetical judgement, but he dissolves its critical significance by urging that vv.16-18 and 37 are later additions to chapter 2.

The ground is somewhat firmer when we come to consider the war-poetry of the opening chapters. According to an old view the 'enemy from the north', mentioned as early as 1.13-15, was originally the Scythians and Duhm singled out a number of passages to which he gave the title 'Scythian Songs'. These were 4.5-8, 11-17, 19-21, 23-26, 29-31; 6.1-5, 22-26; 8.14-17; 10.9-22. It may be helpful to reproduce a few of these, so that we have in our minds the kind of thing which is being discussed:

4.5-8 :   Go to the fortified towns and assemble there,
          put up a signal - to Zion!
          Make for safety without delay,
          for I am bringing disaster from the north,
          a great disaster which will crush you.
          A lion has come out of its lair,
          A destroyer of nations is on the move,
          he has come out of his camp
          to lay waste to your land:
          your towns will be destroyed and deserted.

4.13   He rises like the clouds,
          his chariots are like a whirlwind,
          his horses are swifter than eagles.

6.1   Make for safety, men of Benjamin,
            get out of Jerusalem,
          blow the trumpet in Tekoa,
          kindle a beacon on Beth-Hakkerem,
          for disaster peers out from the north -
          a shattering defeat.

The view that passages like these referred originally to the Scythian invasion of the region was encouraged by the assumption that the early chapters as a whole are set in the reign of Josiah. With the view that the Scythians were the original enemy from the north was coupled the qualification that when the enemy from the north emerged clearly as Nebuchadrezzar, these passages were reinterpreted and that the sense which they now have in the *corpus* has to be related to the threat presented by Babylonian after Nebuchadrezzar had crushed the Egyptians at Carchemish in 605. Among the more recent defenders of the Scythian hypothesis are H.H. Rowley (1961) and H. Cazelles (1967). Cazelles supposes that Jeremiah is drawing on recollections of a Scythian domination of Syria-Palestine which obtained when he was a boy and lasted until 611. The view that these passages referred to the Scythians and then were transferred to the

Babylonians in cumbersome and unconvincing, and there is a suspicion that it is influenced by the prior assumption that the opening chapters deal with events in the reign of Josiah. There is a case for cutting the knot and arguing that these passages never referred to the Scythians and therefore did not have to be transferred to Nebuchadrezzar and the Babylonians by a process of reinterpretation. There was no enemy from the north other than Nebuchadrezzar and this poetry emerges for the first time in the reign of Jehoiakim when this threat was perceived. Thus an important constituent of the contents of the opening chapters locates the activity of Jeremiah not in the reign of Josiah but in the reign of Jehoiakim and lends no support to the 605 date of his call.

A particular aspect of the war-poetry is descriptions of invasion and I end this lecture by making a point which is both historical and theological. First of all I furnish you with a few examples:

4.15-17   A messenger has just come from Dan
           another brings bad news from Mount Ephraim.
           Make the nations aware of these things,
           Announce them to Jerusalem.
           Besiegers are coming from a distant land,
           and threaten the towns of Judah
           They have encircled her borders as men encircle a field,
           for it is against me that she has rebelled.

4.19-22   Oh the writhing of my bowels!
           Oh the pounding of my heart!
           Feelings overwhelm me.
           I cannot keep silent.
           I hear the blast of the trumpet,
           the battle-cries are raised.
           News comes in of one disaster after another,
           the whole land is in ruins.

8.16   The snorting of their horses is heard from Dan,
           while their stallions neigh, all the land shakes.
           They come and devour the land and all it contains.
           towns and their inhabitants.

10.22   News is coming in:
          a great commotion, an army from the north,
          to lay waste the towns of Judah,
          to make them the homes of jackals.

My position on these passages is that they are not to be understood as descriptions of an invasion which is actually in progress. We cannot attach precise dates to them, whether 597 or 587. They are prophetic premonitions of the end, at a point when it is not very far away, probably after 605. Judah's attitudes to Babylon are fundamentally flawed, the inevitability of disaster and the imminence of attack are felt so intensely that they are translated into a graphic account of an enemy advance. To convey this overwhelming proleptic assurance in an English translation, this prophetic grasping of a future outcome, is not easy. The present tense is the best that we can do, but more is needed to convey the intensity and complexity of the prophetic premonition. These events are not actually happening, so that the present tense is in a measure deficient. Neither have they happened, so that the past tense is defective. Yet something of pastness is needed to catch the emphatic prophetic foreclosure of the imminent future. And a future tense is too weak, although the reference is to the future.

I should attempt very briefly to draw together what I have said in this lecture. I have not reached a firm conclusion about the date of Jeremiah's call, but I have argued against the view that the poetry of the early chapters requires a historical background in the reign of Josiah. I have contested the view that this poetry is part of the Deuteronomistic redaction of the book of Jeremiah and is designed to support the representation that the prophet was active in the cause of the Josianic reform between 626 and 621. I have urged that the Scythian hypothesis should be abandoned and that the war poetry should be set in the reign of Jehoiakim. I note in closing that despite the concentration of harlotry/apostasy imagery in chapters 2 and 3 and numerous references to the Baalim, Jeremiah's principal conflict was not with syncretism - not with the invasion of Yahweh sanctuaries by Baal religion - but with Jerusalem institutional orthodoxy. Jeremiah is mostly concerned not with conditions in Judah before centralization of worship in the Jerusalem temple but with the kind of Yahwism which centralization of worship produced. It was against the shallowness of this Jerusalem orthodoxy that he unsuccessfully strove. It was difficult to nail this lie, because he appeared to be arguing against Yahweh rather than for him.

XI. HOW REVOLUTIONARY WAS JESUS?[1]

- Ronald A. Piper

The 1980's have signalled noteworthy events not only in the life of St Mary's College, but also in the development of some of the disciplines represented there. In particular, this decade has brought stimulating new approaches to the search for the historical Jesus. One of the most fascinating aspects of this research has been the optimism that can now be found in scholarly writings about being able to reconstruct the main features of the ministry of Jesus—the Jesus behind the gospels, behind the faith of the earliest Christians who had begun to mould and adapt his teaching to their new situations. But equally fascinating has been the portrayal of Jesus that has emerged from these new reconstructions, which has revived a recurring debate about Jesus as a political revolutionary.[2] Before turning to this, however, it is helpful briefly to indicate how scholars in the 1980's have felt able to attempt a reconstruction at all.

METHODS IN THE QUEST FOR THE HISTORICAL JESUS

In previous decades, Bultmann and his followers had persuaded nearly all but the more conservative investigators that it was no longer possible to find the real 'historical' Jesus from the gospel records.[3] Form criticism had demonstrated the extent to which the synoptic tradition had been adapted and changed by the early church. For Bultmann himself this did not have catastrophic consequences for faith because it is the Christ of faith, not the Jesus of history, who

---

[1] This essay is based on a lecture given at St Mary's College on 16 November 1988.

[2] For the history of this theory, cf. E. Bammel, 'The Revolutionary Theory from Reimarus to Brandon' in E. Bammel & C.F.D. Moule (eds.), **Jesus and the Politics of His Day** (Cambridge University Press, 1984) 11-68; and I.M. Zeitlin, **Jesus and the Judaism of His Time** (Polity Press, 1988), 129-62.

[3] Notable exceptions included J. Jeremias in Germany and C.H. Dodd in Britain.

challenges people in the present. Some of Bultmann's later students, such as Käsemann and Bornkamm, however, recognized that theologically it might be dangerous to say that the historical Jesus did not really matter for faith, and they tried to launch a 'New Quest' for the historical Jesus.[1] But they still faced the obstacle of not being able to describe very much more of the historical Jesus than Bultmann had.[2]

This obstacle centres around the methods used for gaining access to an historical understanding of Jesus. Bultmann had advocated the idea of testing every individual tradition about Jesus to see if it was sufficiently unique to make it reasonable to suppose that it originated from Jesus and not someone else. If a saying too closely reflected Jewish ideas or attitudes found in the early church, then there was no certainty that it did not get introduced later by the church. In a state of uncertainty, one effectively had to put the saying to one side. This became known as the criterion of dissimilarity.[3] Of course, attempts were made subsequently to add further criteria for testing whether gospel traditions were authentic. N. Perrin[4] formulated three other criteria—coherence, multiple attestation and linguistic or environmental tests—in an attempt to widen the base for discovering Jesus' message. But these in fact had only limited effect. The criterion

---

[1] Cf. E. Käsemann, 'The Problem of the Historical Jesus' in his **Essays on New Testament Themes** (SCM, ET: 1964) 15-47, and 'Blind Alleys in the "Jesus of History" Controversy' in his **New Testament Questions for Today** (SCM, ET: 1969) 23-65; G. Bornkamm, **Jesus of Nazareth** (Hodder & Stoughton/Harper & Row, ET: 1960); J.M. Robinson, **A New Quest for the Historical Jesus** (SCM, 1959); and articles by Bultmann and Bornkamm in H.K. McArthur (ed.), **In Search of the Historical Jesus** (Scribner's/SPCK, 1969/1970) 161-3, 164-73, 209f.

[2] Cf. Bultmann's own work, **Jesus and the Word** (Scribner's/Collins, ET: 1934 & 1958).

[3] R. Bultmann, **The History of the Synoptic Tradition** (Basil Blackwell, ET: 1968) 101-108 *et passim*. Also cf. the critiques by R.S. Barbour, **Traditio-Historical Criticism of the Gospels** (SPCK, 1972); H.K. McArthur, **Search**, 137-44; C. Tuckett, **Reading the New Testament** (SPCK, 1987) 104-6.

[4] **Rediscovering the Teaching of Jesus** (Harper & Row/SCM, 1967) 39-49; **The New Testament. An Introduction** (Harcourt Brace Jovanovich, 1974) 280-2.

of coherence is ultimately dependent upon the criterion of dissimilarity.[1] Multiple attestation can sometimes point to sayings which conflict with the criterion of dissimilarity.[2] And, what is recognized as being absolutely unique to Jesus depends heavily on the state of knowledge at any given time about Judaism and early Christianity.[3] Material identified by Bultmann as 'unique' or 'characteristic' was sufficiently limited in any case that careful critical scholars have been hesitant to voice many opinions at all about 'the historical Jesus'.

Until now, that is. In the view of some observers[4], we are now entering a new phase in the quest for the historical Jesus, perhaps a 'Third Quest'. With it has also come a revised method of study, a greater optimism about results and a fresh assessment of the first-century world in which Jesus lived.

What is this revised method? There has been a nagging worry for some time about the use of the criterion of dissimilarity. When this criterion becomes the guiding principle for testing the sayings of Jesus in the gospels, Jesus is made to appear to be a figure who shared almost nothing with the beliefs of his fellow Jews. It creates a lop-sided and historically incredible Jesus.[5] Jesus was born and raised as a Jew; he used the Old Testament; he lived and taught virtually exclusively in Palestine. So how valid is a description of his teaching in which he shares hardly anything at all with his Palestinian companions, family and even opponents? Surely it is intrinsically more likely that Jesus and his message must be firmly located in first-century Judaism, and that means a considerable measure of overlap with the teaching of Judaism. It does not imply that Jesus would have

---

[1] Cf. C. Tuckett, **Reading**, 106, who also notes the problem of judging 'consistency' of traditions.

[2] Cf. G.N. Stanton, **The Gospels and Jesus** (Oxford, 1989) 160-3.

[3] Cf. E.P. Sanders & M. Davies, **Studying the Synoptic Gospels**(SCM/TPI, 1989) 316ff; G. Theissen, **The Shadow of the Galilean** (SCM, ET: 1987) 141.

[4] Cf. S. Neill & T. Wright, **The Interpretation of the New Testament. 1861-1986** (Oxford, 1988) 379; G.N. Stanton, 'Historical Jesus' in Coggins & Houlden (eds.), **A Dictionary of Biblical Interpretation** (SCM, 1990) 289.

[5] E.P. Sanders & M. Davies, **Studying**, 316ff; E.P. Sanders, **Jesus and Judaism** (Fortress, 1985) 16, 18ff; G. Theissen, **Shadow**, 141; H.K. McArthur, **Search**, 137-44.

agreed with known Jewish views in every respect. But it does mean that he would have been interacting with the groups of first-century Palestine and that his teaching and activities would have reflected this. The realization of this has led to a series of recent scholarly works with titles that emphasize the 'Jewish' roots of Jesus:[1] Geza Vermes, *Jesus the Jew* (1973) and *Jesus and the World of Judaism* (1983); A. E. Harvey, *Jesus and the Constraints of History* (1982); John Riches, *Jesus and the Transformation of Judaism* (1980); Ed Sanders, *Jesus and Judaism* (1985); Gerd Theissen, *The Shadow of the Galilean* (ET:1987); J. Charlesworth, *Jesus within Judaism* (1988) and I.M. Zeitlin, *Jesus and the Judaism of His Time* (1988). These writers are all pressing for an evaluation of Jesus which would be credible in a first-century Jewish context.

But to obtain such a portrait of Jesus new methods of reconstruction are needed. Bultmann's means of sifting authentic traditions are not adequate alone—indeed, as has been shown, they worked towards an opposing conclusion. In this respect, at least two developments have been important.

Firstly, the context in which Jesus lived is being given more weight, and this has been accompanied by fresh assessments of first-century Palestinian society and religion. The impetus has been provided in part by recent sociological analyses of the New Testament. These studies attempt, using sociological models, to do more than just confirm what was already known—that there were various Jewish religious groups around in the time of Jesus, such as the Pharisees and Sadducees and Essenes. They have focussed attention more clearly on the *economic, social and political* groups of the day. To what economic and social groupings did Jesus' message appeal, and which did Jesus criticize? What were the economic and political characteristics of the Pharisees and Sadducees? Which groups were involved in resistance to Rome at this time? How did Jesus' teaching address concerns that rural peasants, merchants and other groups must have had?[2] In other

---

[1] Vermes and Sanders have also re-examined Jesus' attitude to the Jewish law and have concluded that Jesus' opposition to the law was much less marked than often suggested.

[2] Cf., for example, how teaching against sabbath observance must have seemed to the poor for whom this was a welcome day of relief from work, as noted by G. Theissen, *Shadow*, 104f.

words, to see Jesus in the context of first-century Judaism, a better picture of first-century Roman Palestine itself is required.[1]

Josephus, of course, still provides the scholar with one of his most useful sources for the situation in Palestine at this time. Yet Josephus must be used with great care, and fresh assessments of his evidence are currently being undertaken.[2] A wider range of primary sources is also now available, and these have been helpfully presented in J. Charlesworth's recent book.[3] Perhaps the most accessible presentation of the world in which Jesus lived, however, has been written almost like a novel rather than a scholarly tome by Gerd Theissen in his popular book, *The Shadow of the Galilean.*

Alongside the re-evaluation of first-century Palestinian society has also come a re-evaluation of Judaism as a religion in this period. Neusner's studies of rabbinic traditions[4] and E.P. Sanders' works on Judaism have been particularly significant.[5] Sanders observes that Bultmann himself worked with an inaccurate description of Judaism, largely derived from Bousset and Billerbeck.[6]

Secondly, a more comprehensive view of Jesus' ministry is being sought. The attempt to reconstruct even a partial description of the ministry of Jesus by testing individual gospel sayings for authenticity and then piecing together the 'genuine' sayings into some kind of patchwork is increasingly being viewed as an unsatisfactory method. The difficulty of applying criteria for authenticity has already been noted above. Furthermore, the sayings material can be subject to so

---

[1] Cf. recently, D. E. Oakman, **Jesus and the Economic Questions of His Day** (Edwin Mellen Press, 1986).

[2] On the matter of the Zealots, for example, see especially the works by Hengel and Horsley below.

[3] **Jesus within Judaism. New Light from Exciting Archaeological Discoveries** (SPCK,1989).

[4] These are too numerous to list in full, but many of his views are conveniently summarized in **First Century Judaism in Crisis** (Abingdon, 1975).

[5] Cf. his **Paul and Palestinian Judaism. A Comparison of Patterns of Religion** (SCM, 1977); **Jesus and Judaism**; and the forthcoming work **Jewish Law from Jesus to the Mishnah** (SCM, 1990).

[6] **Jesus and Judaism**, 29.

many different nuances of meaning that conflicting estimates of its import can easily emerge. Most importantly, the perception of the whole may differ from that of the individual parts.

As a result, an historical approach which has proved more attractive in recent studies is to extrapolate from known facts and probable traditions to a hypothesis for Jesus' ministry as a whole. Such hypotheses may go beyond the individual traditions to the extent of trying to provide a credible framework for explaining the traditions, but any hypothesis must also meet certain requirements. Amongst these, E.P. Sanders lists:

(1) 'It should situate Jesus believably in Judaism and yet explain why the movement initiated by him eventually broke with Judaism.'[1]

(2) 'It should offer a connection between his activity and his death.'[2]

Hypotheses do not emerge out of nothing, however, so the starting point has been to fix upon certain firm details about Jesus, particularly *events* rather than teaching or sayings. A.E. Harvey begins with a consideration of Jesus' trial and crucifixion under Pontius Pilate.[3] E.P. Sanders takes Jesus' activity in the temple prior to his execution as 'the surest starting point' for his investigation.[4] How is 'firm' evidence found? In addition to adapting many of the earlier criteria for authenticity, Sanders and Davies suggest the process is also largely one of 'cross-examination' of the gospel evidence—treating the gospels as 'hostile witnesses in the court room'.[5] They look for material which is 'directly against what the evangelists wished to be so'.[6] If the authors of the gospels preserve traditions that 'go against the grain', then those traditions may well be genuine. Similarly,

[1] **Jesus and Judaism**, 18.

[2] **Ibid.**, 22.

[3] **Jesus and the Constraints of History** (Duckworth, 1982).

[4] **Jesus and Judaism**, 61.

[5] E.P. Sanders & M. Davies, **Studying**, 301.

[6] **Ibid.**, 330-3.

attacks on Jesus by his foes in the gospels may point to genuine traditions. For example, the charge that Jesus performed exorcisms by the power of Beelzebul (Mk 3:22ff) provides persuasive support for the view that in his own day Jesus was believed to perform many exorcisms.[1] Often the evaluation of a tradition about Jesus is not clear-cut, though, so that one has to assign a degree of certainty or probability to the tradition. Eventually, one reaches the stage of trying to extrapolate from the more probable traditions to a hypothesis— asking questions about what the 'sure' points imply. For example, what is implied by the fact that the method of Jesus' execution was crucifixion? What is the implication of Pontius Pilate being the agent in Jesus' execution? What can one infer from Jesus' disciples not being arrested with Jesus? Who precisely was offended by Jesus' actions in the temple and why? What is implied by Jesus' choice of *twelve* disciples? By tackling these questions a hypothesis can develop about the nature of the confrontation between Jesus and his opponents. This hypothesis can then be tested against other traditions about Jesus and the known situation in Palestine. Thus the method is to extrapolate from a small pool of evidence towards a larger view that makes sense of the whole of Jesus' ministry in the times in which he lived.[2] The result is not a complete 'life of Jesus' in the style of previous centuries, nor is it exempt from alternative interpretations. But it offers a much fuller picture than has been attempted for most of this century, and an impressive amount of common ground does seem to have emerged in many of the studies listed above.[3] In particular, Jesus is seen as one who sought the renewal of Judaism, not the establishment of a new religion or community.[4] Most of the current discussion is in terms of defining more closely what kind of renewal was envisaged.

---

[1] **Ibid.**, 304-15.

[2] **Ibid.**, 335-44.

[3] Another feature which marks these scholars is their purported theological disinterest or neutrality. Unlike Bultmann and his followers, they do not raise the question of how Jesus' message applies today. The Christ of Faith is a theological construct. These scholars are ostensibly interested simply in history as ordinary history, in a ruthlessly honest way: cf. **ibid.**, 302f. But also note the comments by G. Theissen, **Shadow**, 153, 164.

[4] See recently also G. N. Stanton, **Gospels and Jesus**, 274.

R.A. Piper

JESUS—WHAT KIND OF PROPHET?

When Jesus' ministry is viewed in relation to other Jewish social, religious and political groups of his day, further questions arise. What exactly was his intention within this context? Hardly anyone denies that Jesus' message was prophetic. He proclaimed the dawning of the kingdom of God, a new age and a new order. Since the works of J. Weiss and A. Schweitzer, the eschatological import of this proclamation has been widely accepted. Yet when this message is examined from 'the ground' of first-century Palestine, it raises important questions about what Jesus thought of the old order, the 'present' order of his day, marked by varied vested interests. Jesus proclaimed that God's kingdom would belong to the poor (Lk 6:20-22 par). Those on the fringes of society—including beggars, those in despised trades, demoniacs and the sick—drew special attention during the course of his ministry. [1] Jesus declared that the first would be last and the last first (Mt 20:16 par), the proud would be humbled and the humble exalted (Lk 14:11 par). A great reversal was envisaged. Whereas Bultmann's outlook inclined him towards interpreting this radical reversal in terms of individual, existential decision, when viewed in social, economic and political terms it becomes a 'revolutionary' message of a rather different kind. The challenge which is presented entails not just a change in the inner life of the subject but also outward and objective changes.

Political revolt did of course come to first-century Palestine in AD 66-70 when many Jews finally took up arms against those who governed their society, the Romans. These Jews were themselves inspired in part by eschatological hopes for a divine intervention.[2]

---

[1] **Ibid.**, 202f. Douglas Oakman (**Jesus and the Economic Questions of His Day**, 182-98) rightly notes, however, that Jesus is also often portrayed in the company of wealthy individuals. Oakman suggests therefore that Jesus played the role of 'patron-broker' between the wealthy and the destitute.

[2] Cf. R. Horsley, **Bandits, Prophets and Messiahs. Popular Movements in the Time of Jesus** (Winston Press, 1985), 118-27, 182-5; M. Hengel, **The Zealots** (T & T Clark, ET: 1989; first German edition 1961, revised 1976), 229ff.

Although these sentiments erupted so dramatically in the 60's, similar feelings seem to have led to smaller demonstrations in 4 BC upon the death of Herod the Great, when the Jews made another bid to be released from their subjugation. In AD 6, when Quirinius attempted to count the people so as to extend the imposition of taxes, hurting the poorest classes most of all, popular resistance appeared again. Is it possible, then, that these sentiments were also present in the 20's and 30's when Jesus was travelling around the rural villages of Galilee making statements that might have further fuelled such revolutionary hopes? And if so, Jesus could hardly have done so blindly, oblivious to the implications. What was his relationship to other groups pressing for the establishment of God's kingdom and for an end to Roman rule? Is it significant that his message was delivered largely in the rural parts of Galilee and, so far as our records tell, never in the more prosperous Hellenistic cities in Galilee, such as Sepphoris (within only a few miles of Nazareth) or Tiberias?

But let us go to firmer ground. One of the most firmly attested gospel traditions is that Jesus was crucified by Pontius Pilate. Even the Roman historian Tacitus[1] testified to this. But why did Pilate *crucify* him? M. Hengel has argued that crucifixion was the supreme Roman penalty, normally reserved for slaves, robbers, hardened criminals and political rebels.[2] In the gospels, however, a rather conflicting picture emerges at this point.

Mark's gospel seems to suggest that Pilate's action was simply the result of being pressed by the Jewish authorities (Mk 15:1-15). Pilate himself apparently had no direct interest in the matter and just wanted to mollify the crowds, which were stirred by the Sanhedrin's decision that Jesus fell foul of *Jewish* law[3] in a way deserving death. But there

---

[1] *Annals* 15.44; cf. also the Syriac letter by Mara bar Serapion.

[2] *Crucifixion* (SCM, ET: 1977) 33-63.

[3] A charge of blasphemy is recorded in Mk 14:64, but this too is not without difficulties. If Pilate was merely confirming the Sanhedrin's condemnation of Jesus for blasphemy, execution would have been by stoning. The puzzling tradition about Barabbas, a rebel who 'committed murder in the insurrection' (Mk 15:7) also points towards a political threat rather than religious error, despite Mark's apparent efforts to play down any political implications.

are problems with this view. (1) If all four gospel accounts agree on anything about the trials of Jesus, they agree on the inscription which Pilate insisted be put on the cross: 'The King of the Jews'. It is quite likely that Pilate meant this to be taken seriously as the charge on which Jesus was being put to death. He had questioned Jesus about just such claims (cf. Mark 15:2, 9; and especially in Luke 23:1-5).[1] (2) This concern is also reflected in the fact that the method of execution was by crucifixion, which (since there is no evidence that Jesus was either a slave or hardened criminal) was especially suited to one who was felt to pose a political threat. Pilate could have had Jesus executed by other means, if more appropriate, or have imprisoned him. Crucifixion was not the only option, so it is all the more significant for what it implies. (3) Luke himself suggests that when the Jewish hierarchy handed Jesus over to Pilate it did so by offering political rather than religious charges against him. Luke writes in ch. 23: 'And they began to accuse him saying, We found this man perverting our nation, and forbidding tribute to Caesar, and saying that he himself is Christ a king.' Soon afterwards they say, 'He stirs up the people, teaching throughout all Judaea, from Galilee even to this place'. Luke therefore suggests that Pilate acted not simply in response to Jewish religious charges, but with political implications in mind. (4) The implication of Mark's account is that Pilate was a weak figure whom the Jews were able to manipulate at will. This is not the impression that one gets from Josephus' record of Pilate's governorship, however.[2] Josephus showed Pilate ready to have his soldiers beat to death unarmed protesters who opposed his use of Temple funds to build an

---

[1] Urging caution on the interpretation of the *titulus*, however, is E. Bammel, 'The *titulus*' in E. Bammel & C.F.D. Moule (eds.), **Jesus and the Politics of His Day** (Cambridge University Press, 1984) 353-64.

[2] Cf. also S.G.F. Brandon, **The Trial of Jesus of Nazareth** (Batsford, 1968) 99: 'We are asked to believe that a tough-minded Roman governor bargained with a Jewish mob for the release of a prisoner in his custody, whom he knew to be innocent. This governor, moreover, possessed a strong military force, capable of backing his decision to release the prisoner, if he so chose, or to transfer his case to Caesarea for re-trial. And that is not all: we are told, without explanation, of the chief priests' ability to persuade a crowd, whose support of Jesus a few days before they had so greatly feared to demand his crucifixion.'

aqueduct for Jerusalem.[1] Pilate also offended Jewish sensitivities by having Roman military standards, bearing the effigies of the emperor or deities, displayed in Jerusalem, in marked contrast to the custom of former governors.[2] G. Theissen observes:

> Pilate was the first prefect of Judaea who dared to use pagan symbols on his coins: the augurs' staff and a libation vessel. The prefects before and after him carefully avoided hurting the religious feelings of the Jews with pagan emblems, which were associated with idolatry.[3]

Furthermore, Pilate ruled over a very troublesome state for some 10-11 years (AD 26-36), while many of his predecessors and successors were fortunate to last half that long. Is it really credible to portray him as a weak or indecisive leader? Ruthlessness and arrogance seem more characteristic of his rule.[4] He was not compelled to execute people whom the Jewish leaders found offensive. It seems more likely that Pilate acted in the way that he did on account of his own concerns—and his fundamental concern was to deal with any spontaneous or organized activity which potentially could have threatened or challenged Roman rule over Judaea. So, the manner of Jesus' death seems most reasonably explained by Jesus having been perceived by Pilate as one who posed just such a challenge.[5]

This then leads to a further question. How far was Jesus indeed just that—not simply a spiritual revolutionary, but someone who posed a real threat to the authorities of his day on the socio-political level? It has been suggested that his teaching did indeed have 'revolutionary'

---

[1] **Antiquities** 18.60-2; **War** 2.175-7.

[2] **Antiquities** 18.55-9; **War** 2.170-4.

[3] **Shadow**, 198 n.12.

[4] Cf. R. Horsley, **Bandits**, 38, 66.

[5] This is not necessarily to deny that there was a Jewish trial or to affirm that there was an official Roman trial. Pilate could have confirmed Jewish charges, but for his own purposes. Cf. E. Bammel, 'The Trial before Pilate' in E. Bammel & C.F.D. Moule (eds.), **Jesus and the Politics of His Day** (Cambridge University Press, 1984) 413-51.

ingredients and that Palestine may have been ripe for responding to such sentiments. Did Jesus also have a political programme for moulding such sentiments into a reality?

JESUS AND POPULAR RESISTANCE IN ROMAN PALESTINE

Gerd Theissen

There have been several recent, influential attempts to answer these questions. The first to be considered is Gerd Theissen's *The Shadow of the Galilean.* Theissen would seem to be in agreement with the stage of argument that has been reached thus far. But at this point he introduces an important distinction. Jesus' proclamation was certainly not apolitical. Yet there is a difference between actions and teachings having *political implications* and actually pursuing a *political programme*.[1] Theissen suggests that Jesus' teachings to the poor, who in his day were under increasing burdens of debt and were oppressed even by Jewish masters (not just by the Romans), could not help but have been perceived as calling into question the current economic and social structures of his society.[2]   In so far as these were maintained by Roman rule and by the collaboration of the Jewish (priestly) aristocracy, then inevitably Jesus also called into question the validity of the political rule of the land. The *implications* of his teaching thus had social and political dimensions, and Jesus could hardly have been unaware of these. Yet Theissen argues that Jesus himself offered no political *programme* by which change would come about. This is probably because of Jesus' eschatological perspective. Jesus believed that God himself would act decisively to bring in his kingdom on earth, the complete renewal of Israel. Jesus' own action was in anticipation and preparation for this cosmic intervention, but no one knew the day or hour of God's action, not even the Son (Mk 13:32). It is interesting that Luke records in the early chapters of Acts how the

---

[1] **Ibid.**, 95. Cf. also the essay by E. Bammel, 'The Poor and the Zealots' in E. Bammel & C.F.D. Moule (eds.), **Jesus and the Politics of His Day** (Cambridge University Press, 1984) 109-28.

[2] Theissen also describes the polarization of rich and poor at this time in his **The First Followers of Jesus** (SCM, ET: 1978) 39-46.

early Christians shared all goods in common and in effect instituted a new social structure among themselves. It is not certain how seriously Luke's portrayal of this period should be taken, but it may represent an early ideal which derived from Jesus' own teaching.

But if Jesus had no programme of violent opposition to the State, why was Pilate concerned about him? Perhaps, as Luke suggests in the charges against Jesus, Pilate felt that the political implications of such teaching, even without a political programme, could easily have stirred dangerous sentiments among the populace at large. Pilate had little to fear in this respect from the Jewish authorities, because the leaders were too much in league with him and would suffer as much as Rome in any uncontrolled mass uprising.[1] But wider unrest in Palestine, and especially in the hinterlands of Judaea, would have been a cause of concern. The potential for unrest would have been even greater if there were Zealots or other armed resistance groups active in Palestine in the time of Jesus. Theissen suggests that this was the case, and that they shared a great deal in common with Jesus. They addressed the same social groups. They shared an anticipation of the kingdom of God. They opposed the priestly hierarchy in Jerusalem. Therefore the feelings and hopes which Jesus stirred up in his teachings, healings and other actions[2] could have played directly into the hands of these violent nationalist groups. Theissen suggests that this directly contributed to the threat that Jesus posed in the eyes of the Romans.

How do we know that Jesus was not a Zealot sympathizer himself? Presumably for the same reasons that this thesis, advocated earlier by S.G.F. Brandon[3], was rejected by M. Hengel in his book *War Jesus Revolutionär?*[4]. How could one who sympathized with such violent

---

[1] It is noteworthy that after the revolt in AD 66-70, the Sadducees and priestly aristocracy were so effectively removed from power that it was left to the Pharisees to lead the Jews and reformulate Judaism through the emerging rabbinic movement.

[2] Most notably in his attack on the Temple in Jerusalem.

[3] **Jesus and the Zealots. A Study of the Political Factors in Primitive Christianity** (Manchester University Press, 1967); also cf. his **The Trial of Jesus of Nazareth** (Batsford, 1968).

[4] ET: **Was Jesus a Revolutionist?** (Fortress, 1971). Recently, also cf. I.M. Zeitlin, **Jesus**, 130ff.

activists preach unconditional love for one's enemies, prayer for one's persecutors, and turning the other cheek when wronged?[1] Moreover, why was Jesus alone arrested and his followers left alone, if the Jesus movement was known to be in sympathy with armed resistance to Rome?[2] Hengel himself goes so far as to conclude that Jesus directly *opposed* the Zealot movement. Jesus may have shared certain ideas that were made familiar by the activity of the Zealots, and he may have been executed as an alleged Zealot messianic pretender, but Jesus himself actually opposed the violent tactics of the Zealot group(s). The Zealots were of course never explicitly named in Jesus' teaching,[3] but they probably represented the 'left wing of the Pharisees'.[4] The absence of reference to them may simply be a method of Jewish argument and in Hengel's view does not undermine the case for Jesus' conscious opposition to them.[5]

Marcus Borg

Hengel's argument that Jesus consciously opposed the activity of the Zealots[6] implies a stronger contrast between Jesus and the Zealots than that suggested by Theissen, but a theory of Jesus' opposition to

---

[1] See chapter 10 of G. Theissen, **Shadow**.

[2] Other arguments against Brandon's thesis are detailed by D. Catchpole, 'The Problem of the Historicity of the Sanhedrin Trial' in E. Bammel (ed.), **The Trial of Jesus** (SCM, 1970) 51-4; and J.P.M. Sweet, 'The Zealots and Jesus' in E. Bammel & C.F.D. Moule (eds.), **Jesus and the Politics of His Day** (Cambridge University Press, 1984) 1-9. For a defence of the view of Jesus as a pacifist, cf. J.H. Yoder, **The Politics of Jesus** (Eerdmans, 1972).

[3] The old issue of whether Simon ὁ ζηλωτής (Lk 6:15; Acts 1:13) was a 'Zealot' continues to be debated: cf. M. Hengel, **Zealots**, 392-3. Theissen believes Simon was truly a 'Zealot': cf. **Shadow**, 205.

[4] Hengel, **Zealots.**, 378-9.

[5] Ibid., 339. Brandon (**Jesus and the Zealots**, 200-1) had argued that the silence of the synoptic gospels about Zealots showed that Jesus was in sympathy with them, in contrast to his polemical attacks on the Pharisees and Sadducees. A further possibility is discussed below: that there were no Zealots at the time.

[6] **Ibid.**, 337-41, 378-9

militant resistance movements has been developed further by Marcus Borg in his work, *Conflict, Holiness and Politics in the Teaching of Jesus* (1984).[1]   Borg argues that the ideological touchstone of Jewish renewal groups in the first century was the concept of 'holiness', which required separation from Gentiles and sometimes separation from other Jews. This exclusivism was expressed in table fellowship, sabbath observance, and Temple practices. The Jewish liberation movement was another manifestation of the desire for separation from non-Jews and from their influence on Jewish life. According to Borg, Jesus himself directly opposed such separatist ideas on the grounds that true holiness involved imitation of the *mercy* of God (cf. Lk 6:36), which was not exclusive but extended to all peoples. Accordingly, Jesus attacked Pharisaic observances, the Temple practices of the priesthood[2], and, of course, any who supported armed insurrection. The Temple was not just dominated by the priestly class; it had also become a den of λῃσταί (violent ones) rather than a house of prayer for all τὰ ἔθνη (nations, Gentiles).[3] Jesus was a 'political' figure in the sense that he was critical of the institutions which preserved Israel's cohesion and of all groups which represented resistance to non-Jews; but his main motivation was the reform of Jewish religion away from its exclusivist ideology.[4] However, why

---

[1] In his article 'The Currency of the Term "Zealot"' in **Journal of Theological Studies** n.s. 22 (1971) 504-12, M. Borg argues that there is no evidence for a group called the 'Zealots' before AD 66, yet he accepts that religiously-inspired opposition to Rome did exist much earlier and that it was a feature of all major groups of Judaism (especially the Pharisees), not just of one group. This resistance was not always violent, but could be so at times.

[2] The attack on the money-changers is explained in relation to the issue of 'holiness'—they protected the Temple's exclusivism by exchanging profane (secular) coinage for holy (Temple) coinage: M. Borg, **Conflict, Holiness and Politics in the Teaching of Jesus** (Edwin Mellen Press, 1984) 170ff.

[3] **Ibid.**

[4] The limitation of Jesus' ministry to Israel would apparently be explained by Jesus' concerns with the internal factors in Judaism which were so exclusivist. Why gather Gentiles if Israel was not ready to receive them? The crisis was Israel's crisis: **ibid.**, 219-20.

such an anti-insurrectionist, pro-Gentile Jesus should have been crucified by Pilate remains, it seems to me, a difficulty.[1]

Richard Horsley

Thus while Theissen emphasizes how much Jesus shared with the revolutionary sentiments of the Zealots (apart from the means by which renewal would be brought), Borg places emphasis on the contrast between the fundamental goals of the two. The reconstructions of Theissen, Borg and Hengel, however, are all implicitly challenged in a provoking study by Richard Horsley entitled *Jesus and the Spiral of Violence. Popular Jewish Resistance in Roman Palestine* (1987). Horsley has devoted several studies to the question of the nationalist resistance in first-century Palestine[2] and has argued for the view that there were no 'Zealot' groups in the time of Jesus and, even more significantly, no *sustained* insurrectionist movements at all running through the first century. Josephus indicates that there were Zealots active against Rome in the late-60's[3] and assassins (*sicarii*) operating

---

[1] On the question of Jesus' attitude to Rome, Borg (**ibid.**, 235) argues that there was no 'positive evaluation of the Roman imperial order'. Borg does not show that Jesus was a credible threat to Roman rule, though.

[2] 'Josephus and the Bandits' in **Journal of the Study of Judaism 10** (1979) 37-63; 'The Sicarii: Ancient Jewish "Terrorists"' in **Journal of Religion** 59 (1979) 435-58; 'Ancient Jewish Banditry and the Revolt against Rome, A.D. 66-70' in **Catholic Biblical Quarterly** 43 (1981) 409-32; 'Popular Messianic Movements around the Time of Jesus' in **Catholic Biblical Quarterly** 46 (1984) 471-95; (with J.S. Hanson), **Bandits, Prophets and Messiahs: Popular Movements in the Time of Jesus** (Winston Press, 1985); 'High Priests and the Politics of Roman Palestine. A Contextual Analysis of the Evidence in Josephus' in **Journal of the Study of Judaism** 17 (1986) 23-55; 'The Zealots: Their Origin, Relationship and Importance in the Jewish Revolt' in **Novum Testamentum** 28 (1986) 159-92.

[3] M. Hengel (**Zealots**, 62) also notes: 'He [Josephus] never applies the name οἱ ζηλωταί to all the rebels....He in fact uses it only when speaking of a special group confined to the followers of John of Gischala, Simon bar Giora and the Idumaeans. Their leader was the priest Eleazar b. Simon, who began to play a distinctive part as the head of the radical wing after the victory of Cestius Gallus

in the 50's and 60's[1]. Some Pharisees seem to have been involved in a disturbance following Herod's death in 4 BC, which included the occupation of the Roman armoury in Sepphoris by a certain Judas.[2] Judas 'the Galilean' and a Pharisee called Saddok waged sporadic battles against the Romans in protest to the census under Quirinius in AD 6. But there is no *direct* evidence that any of these attempts at resistance formed an ongoing violent movement that would have been active during the time of Jesus' ministry in the 20's and 30's. This is not to deny oppressive activity on the part of the Roman authorities during this time. The *pax Romana* was maintained by repression, and Horsley describes this in detail. There were also periodic outbursts of protest when Pilate did something outrageously insensitive, such as bringing the banners with the emperor's insignia into Jerusalem. But any active protest was largely spontaneous, in reaction to individual Roman atrocities. It was not organized, despite widespread social discontent. In contrast to Hengel, who in effect traces the founding of the Zealot movement to Judas the Galilean in AD 6,[3] Horsley argues that no such 'sustained movement' linked the events of protest throughout these decades and that it is strictly incorrect even to talk about Zealots as a recognized party before late AD 67.[4] Introducing

---

in Jerusalem.' Hengel also notes the application of the term to Phinehas in the rabbinic literature and in 4 Macc 18:12 (**ibid.**, 393).

[1] The term is first mentioned in Josephus when referring to the period of Felix (**War** 2.254f); cf. also Acts 21:38.

[2] Hengel (**Zealots**, 331) identifies this Judas with 'Judas the Galilean', active in AD 6. Horsley disagrees (**Jesus and the Spiral of Violence**, 53; 'Popular Messianic Movements', 471-93).

[3] **Zealots**, 330ff. Hengel draws attention to how Josephus describes the main figures in the Jewish Revolt as descendants of Judas the Galilean. Cf. also E. Bammel, 'The Poor and the Zealots' in E. Bammel & C.F.D. Moule (eds.), **Jesus and the Politics of His Day** (Cambridge University Press, 1984) 113; and I.M. Zeitlin, **Jesus**, 29-37 (who appears to rely heavily on Hengel, but shows no knowledge of Horsley's works).

[4] **Jesus and the Spiral of Violence**, 318; **Bandits**, 216-59. Horsley draws attention to the diversity of forms of popular unrest in the first century: 'The Zealots proper were a totally separate phenomenon, historically, from the Fourth Philosophy mentioned by Josephus as active over sixty years earlier. Moreover, not even the Fourth Philosophy, led by a "teacher" and a Pharisee, advocated armed rebellion against the Romans' (**Bandits**, 241).

further regional distinctions, Seán Freyne has argued that Galilee in particular was relatively peaceful during the long reign of Antipas in Galilee (4BC - AD 39), which served 'to shield the province from Roman procuratorial rule for almost half a century'.[1]

The consequences of these views for a reconstruction of Jesus' ministry are considerable. Previously, it has been common to appeal to alleged armed resistance movements as a foil against which to contrast the teaching of Jesus. Either Jesus was unwittingly playing into the hands of these groups, or he directly preached against them. But if the existence of these violent groups is called into doubt, then the nature of Jesus' message must also be re-examined. Horsley's analysis might explain, for example, why Jesus' disciples were never persecuted by Pilate and indeed why the early church could even establish its early centre in Jerusalem itself. If there were no organized movements which Pilate had to dismantle, then there would be less cause for concern about the immediate followers of Jesus. If there were just sporadic outbreaks, then dealing with the leader of the outbreak alone might well be sufficient. This would also explain why Jesus never directly refers to the Zealots or any other such groups. No such violent organized groups existed.

But at this point it is necessary to return to an earlier question—why did Pilate crucify Jesus? Theissen had answered this by assuming that Jesus gave rise to certain sentiments that might all too easily have been used by groups advocating armed resistance to the Roman government of Palestine, even though Jesus did not share their political programme. But if there is no clear evidence for such violent groups at the time, then this explanation comes into question. Pilate himself could hardly have confused Jesus with Zealots or other established insurrectionist groups if they did not exist. In other words, if the Palestinian revolutionary threat was less clearly focussed, then it is only logical to assume that *Jesus' own political threat was more direct*. This is what Horsley argues. Jesus himself was perceived as a

---

[1] S. Freyne, 'Bandits in Galilee: A Contribution to the Study of Social Conditions in First-Century Palestine' in J. Neusner *et al.* (eds.), **The Social World of Formative Christianity and Judaism. Essays in Tribute to Howard Clark Kee** (Fortress, 1988) 53f. Freyne contrasts the relative peace in Galilee with the situation in Judaea.

direct threat to the Roman and Jewish authorities, and this perception must have had some genuine basis in his proclamation. Jesus' vision of the kingdom of God must have threatened the very political and social stability of Roman Palestine.[1]

How can such a view of Jesus' message be reconciled with the love-of-enemies teaching, or the non-retaliation sayings, or the message of giving tribute to Caesar ('unto Caesar the things that are Caesar's')? Do not these teachings work against the hypothesis of Jesus as a direct political threat? Horsley argues, however, that these teachings and others like them have often been misinterpreted. After all, Jesus not only advocated a radical reversal of the roles of rich and poor,[2] he was even disruptive of family structures when the patriarchal family seemed to hinder a sense of solidarity with God's people (Mk 3:32-5; 10:29-31; Lk 9:59-62; 12:51-3; 21:16). Loyalty to him could set family members against one another (Mt 10:35f). He demanded that one leave 'the dead' to bury the dead, even if it should be one's own father (Lk 9:59f), when it detracted from recognizing one's higher obligations.[3] Jesus' sayings about taking up the sword have also been a recurring focal point of discussion (Mt 10:34 par; Lk 22:36-8).[4] From this catalogue of sayings, it is at least clear that Jesus did not hesitate to oppose deeply-rooted structures of his society when necessary.

Horsley's analysis of other gospel sayings is also significant. Regarding the teaching on love of enemies in Mt 5:39-48/Lk 6:27-36, not only is it striking that no other teaching in the gospels implies that this is the proper attitude towards a real oppressor or persecutor, but even in the cited passage the examples of non-retaliation apply only to minor insults (slaps on cheeks or walking two miles instead of one). Horsley argues that these refer to personal animosities within local

---

[1] Jesus and the Spiral of Violence, 285ff.

[2] R. Horsley, Jesus and the Spiral of Violence, 209ff, 240ff.

[3] Ibid., 232-40.

[4] Cf., however, M. Black, "'Not peace but a sword": Matt 10:34ff; Luke 12:51ff' and G.W.H. Lampe, 'The Two Swords (Luke 22:35-38)' in E. Bammel & C.F.D. Moule (eds.), Jesus and the Politics of His Day (Cambridge University Press, 1984) 287-94, 335-51.

(village) contexts, but they do not apply to oppressive rulers.[1] There is no encouragement here, Horsley argues, for the follower of Jesus to allow an unjust and oppressive power to do whatever it wishes to the socially oppressed. There is no passive toleration of this kind anywhere in Jesus' message. On the contrary, Jesus is critical of social institutions. Even the famous tribute saying should not be interpreted as lending tacit support to the State. Since Jesus argues elsewhere that you can only serve *one* master (Mt 6:24/Lk 16:13), and since Jesus preached that God's demands were exclusive, radical demands that had priority over anything else in life (cf. Mt 6:33f par; Lk 9:59-62), surely when Jesus says to give 'to God the things that are God's' he not only avoids the trap set for him by the Pharisees and Herodians (Mk 12:13ff) but also makes clear to anyone of perception that *all* things are ultimately God's and *nothing* is ultimately Caesar's.[2]

Jesus may indeed have lacked a political programme, expecting that the political upheaval accompanying the kingdom would take place when God himself directly intervened in the last days. But Jesus proclaimed uncompromisingly that such a renewal would take place, and he made no attempt to hide the implications that this would have for those in power. The reversals of the kingdom would result in real reversals within society. The implications of this were sufficiently near the surface to put in motion the hopes of many who were subject to the oppression of Roman Palestine. This is would explain why Jesus was perceived as a real threat by Pilate. Jesus may have led no armed group of revolutionaries, and no armed group may have appealed to his teachings, but he nonetheless directly attacked what the authorities represented, and this was thinly concealed. Jesus' calling was to

---

[1] R. Horsley, **Jesus and the Spiral of Violence**, 255-73. For a contrary view, cf. M. Borg, **Conflict**, 129-34. Brandon (**Jesus and the Zealots**, 309-10) had argued that the love of enemies teaching was created later by the church.

[2] R. Horsley, **Jesus and the Spiral of Violence**, 306-17; so also S.G.F. Brandon, **Jesus and the Zealots**, 345-9. But against M. Borg, **Conflict**, 376 n.21; I.M. Zeitlin, **Jesus**, 161; and F.F. Bruce, 'Render to Caesar' in E. Bammel & C.F.D. Moule (eds.), **Jesus and the Politics of His Day** (Cambridge University Press, 1984) 249-63. Hengel argues that in this saying Jesus simply expresses *disinterest* in the State and places emphasis on the latter part of the saying (**Revolutionist**, 33f).

proceed with the social revolution, the transformation of social relations, 'in anticipation of the completion of the political revolution' that could only be implemented by God directly.[1]

THE SIGNIFICANCE OF THE DEBATE

Which reconstruction of Jesus' ministry is correct? Clearly the question is one that is quite central to the interpretation of the historical Jesus. The main thrust of his message and ministry is at stake. How far was his prophetic preaching of the God's kingdom concerned with renewing the religious ideology of Judaism, and how far with renewing the social and political context in which he lived? How real a political threat did he present to Pilate?

In the first place, it is striking that an answer to these questions seems to lie at least as much in a clear reconstruction of Palestinian *context* in which Jesus lived as in the recorded gospel sayings of Jesus. For example, the debate can be as much over whether violent resistance movements operated in the 20's and 30's as over the interpretation of Jesus' sayings about non-retaliation and tribute to Caesar. In this respect closer attention to regional distinctions in Galilee and Judaea, to the different periods of Roman rule in first-century Palestine and to social models have taken the debate beyond the earlier one involving Brandon and others in the 1960's.[2] Ultimately, though, the context and Jesus' message are interrelated. The context is what helps to interpret the teaching. The agenda is therefore clearly set for a fresh and more intense investigation of Roman Palestine in the time of Jesus in an effort to understand Jesus himself better. But perhaps it should not be surprising that renewed emphasis on the socio-political background has been accompanied by the rediscovery of a socio-political Jesus.

---

[1] R. Horsley, **Jesus and the Spiral of Violence**, 324.

[2] A brief review of the earlier debate can be found in John Reumann's introduction to M. Hengel, **Was Jesus a Revolutionist?**; see also O. Cullmann, **Jesus and the Revolutionaries** (Harper & Row, ET: 1970).

More specifically, though, I believe Horsley has rightly warned us against too uniform an image of the decades of Roman Palestine. Many studies, including those of Theissen, Hengel and even Borg, seem prepared to assume that the evidence points to violent resistance movements having been active at least from the time of Judas the Galilean in AD 6 until the Jewish Revolt in AD 66-70. The few fixed points of rebellion are linked to suggest an ongoing movement. Josephus himself may suggest this,[1] but the evidence for an ongoing movement is slight. Lines of 'trajectory' too easily become drawn over a few fixed points, resulting in a misleading portrait of the times. Surely Horsley is correct to call this into question.

Secondly, the new debate about the historical Jesus illustrates how a patchwork of individual sayings, even if accepted as authentically from Jesus, cannot in itself satisfactorily describe the aims of Jesus. While scholars will continue to struggle to assess individual sayings in an effort to put a reconstruction of Jesus on a 'firm' grounding, the area of firm ground is always likely to be small. To succeed in a reconstruction of the ministry of Jesus, there is a need to move from such isolated sayings and events towards an overall hypothesis for Jesus' aims and ministry. Sanders has not only ably described the procedure to be followed, but also he has highlighted many of the key features which any good hypothesis must answer.

This also leads to more specific observations. A credible explanation for the death of Jesus at the hands of Pilate is essential. It seems to me that this poses a serious problem for those scholars, such as Hengel and Borg, who argue that Jesus consciously *opposed* Jewish insurrectionist groups. It would appear that they must appeal either to considerable ignorance on the part of Pilate or to considerable weakness on his part. Hengel asserts that 'Jesus himself was handed over to the Romans by the leaders of the Jewish people as [sic] alleged Zealot messianic pretender and condemned and executed as such', even though Jesus' proclamation was 'directed against the Zealots'.[2] It is not impossible for these views to be reconciled, and Hengel

---

[1] Cf. p.202 note 3 above.

[2] **Zealots**, 378

207

himself believes that Jesus' claim to the title Messiah contributed to the threat posed to Pilate and his Jewish accomplices, despite Jesus' anti-insurrectionist stance.[1] But one again is faced with the implied ignorance or weakness of Pilate in the situation. The strength of the theses of Theissen and Horsley is that such a view of Pilate, which has little else to support it, is not essential.

Finally, much of the discussion above has shown how Jesus' message itself is increasingly being examined for its social and political dimensions. Is this a one-sided approach to Jesus' message? Sanders and Davies note that the context for Jesus' message of renewal could be determined by Jewish hopes for a future cosmic event, or the hopes of protest movements for the restoration of society or even hopes for spiritual renewal.[2] Sanders himself opts for relating Jesus' message mainly to Jewish hopes for a future national restoration of Israel, in which the twelve tribes would be reassembled with a new temple and with Jesus and his disciples in a leading role. This would be dramatically implemented by God, since 'Jesus seems to have had no more socio-political ambitions than did his predecessor [John the Baptist] or his followers'.[3] Yet this could be misleading. As T. Wright observes[4], Sanders is mainly opposing a view of Jesus as intending *violent* revolution against Rome; he fully accepts that the execution of Jesus demands more of a threat to Jewish and Roman authorities than

---

[1] **Christ and Power** (Christian Journals, 1977) 17; and more recently, I.M. Zeitlin, **Jesus**, 159-61.

[2] He rejects the idea of Jesus seeking to reform Jewish Law, however: cf. his **Jesus and Judaism**, 267-9; also E.P. Sanders & M. Davies, **Studying**, 341-4. I.M. Zeitlin (**Jesus**, viii and 159) apparently views Jesus as an anti-Zealot 'charismatic leader', but recognizes 'charismatic leadership' as always presenting a challenge to traditional authority.

[3] **Studying**, 343. There is no reason, however, why Paul's attitude to state and society must reflect that of Jesus. It is not unlikely that a more cautious attitude towards the State followed both the Gentile mission and the fate of Jesus. Concern about social tensions in Palestine was apparently replaced with the problem of social tensions within the church itself. With respect to John the Baptist, the fact of his execution at the hands of Antipas may not preclude a socio-political dimension to his message.

[4] **Interpretation of the New Testament, 1861-1986**, 394.

that which a wandering charismatic alone would pose.[1] Jesus' talk 'about another kind of kingdom, not one that depended on force of arms'[2] must not be assumed to be devoid of political significance.[3] Theissen has rightly shown how a message can carry real socio-political threats without necessarily entailing a personal programme of violence or reform. Any new model for Jesus' role and message must recognize such distinctions when defining the nature of the threat that Jesus posed to those responsible for his execution.

Of course, it might be objected that the growing interest in socio-historical models and political portrayals of Jesus gives too little attention to the eschatological nature of Jesus' kingdom announcement, which has dominated discussions of his message throughout this century. The difficulty of relating eschatological concepts to the present day and the attraction of a more socially-oriented Jesus for liberation theology and other socio-political interests in our own day might seem to be a hidden agenda behind these discussions.[4] There is, however, no necessary polarization between the social preaching of Jesus and an eschatological outlook. It is likely that Jesus believed that only the intervention of God himself would make Jesus' promises to those on the fringes of society into a reality. The kingdom of God can be understand as a dramatic event of restoration, but one which leads to a new social order.[5] In the context of Jesus' own times, this would still have posed a threat to the authorities of his day who had much invested in the present or 'old' social order and institutions.

It might also be objected that the trend of these recent studies reduces Jesus too much to a first-century figure. Few could deny that the message of Jesus has in fact transcended the situation of first-century Roman Palestine. To consider Jesus virtually on par with other

---

[1] **Jesus and Judaism**, 329.

[2] **Ibid.**

[3] Sanders and Davies (**Studying**, 343) recently allow that Jesus expected the kingdom 'either as a dramatic cosmic event, or as a new social order—or both, one leading to the other'.

[4] But see page 192 note 3 above.

[5] E.P. Sanders & M. Davies, **Studying**, 343.

popular prophets or popularly acclaimed 'kings'[1] in his own day hardly does justice to the influence of his message on subsequent centuries of Christians. Yet such problems are common to most historico-critical studies of Jesus. The studies that have been investigated in this essay seek less to detract from the impact of Jesus' message than to insist that the revolutionary ideas within it are not limited to the spiritual life of individuals. The very fact that these ideas address corporate and social as well as personal aspects of life must widen our perspective to appreciate the whole situation within which Jesus worked. It is only there that the full force of his revolutionary message can be appreciated.

---

[1] R. Horsley, **Bandits**, chs. 3 and 4.

XII. ST ANSELM - MEDIAEVAL AND MODERN

- D.W.D. Shaw

If any of you have been lucky enough to drive through France to Italy, you may have gone by that marvellous creation, the new road tunnel under Mont Blanc Travelling south, as you emerge out of the tunnel into the sunlight of Italy, you find yourself in the beautiful Val d'Aosta. That is where Anselm was born in 1033, and that is where he was brought up. His mother died when he was young - she came of a well-to-do family from Burgundy. He did not, apparently, get on too well with his father, himself related to the House of Savoy, but now of somewhat decayed nobility, and, after several years of what one authority rather primly calls 'undisciplined life'[1], in 1056 he crossed over into France, never again to return to his home town. Three years' wanderings in France, presumably as a scholar, ended at the Benedectine Abbey of Bec, in Normandy (which still stands, and still receives visitors). The great attraction there, for Anselm, was Lanfranc, known throughout Europe as one of the leading scholars and philosophers of his day. It was as a scholar that Anselm went to Bec and Lanfranc in 1059, a 'mature student' as we would now say, and study he did under Lanfranc, who became his great mentor and exemplar. Under Lanfranc's influence, - 'my will was not yet tamed', Anselm explained, - in 1060, after three years' study, he himself became a monk at Bec, throwing himself wholeheartedly into the corporate life of religion, above all learning the principle of obedience to authority which was to be so important to him throughout his life. Three years later, Lanfranc left - eventually to become Archbishop of Canterbury - and Anselm became prior of Bec, at the age of thirty. After fifteen years he himself became abbot at Bec, and abbot he remained until 1093, when he was elected - and eventually - consecrated Archbishop of Canterbury. He was Archbishop for sixteen years, which included, in all, six years of self-imposed exile, until his death in 1109 at the age of 76.

---

[1] 1 F. L. Cross, ed. **Oxford Dictionary of the Christian Church**, Oxford, (1958)

These are the bare bones of his *curriculum vitae*, but they tell us little enough about Anselm the man or scholar or saint. It was at Bec that he found his true niche, his calling as a monk first and last. The corporate life of the monastery provided for him the ideal environment for the development and cultivation of both the spiritual and the intellectual life. Not all monasteries, incidentally, would have provided this; Anselm had at one time considered becoming a monk at Cluny, but turned down the idea because the routine there was too arduous to allow time or energy for such scholarship. At Bec, things were different, and he was able to steep himself in learning. The learning he did steep himself in - and here he was no different from his contemporaries - were the works of St Augustine. He knew him backwards and all his theological writings testify to this. Scripture and Augustine - these were to be his guides. And in a defence of an early work, he claimed to be doing little more than re-thinking the thoughts of St Augustine: 'It was my intention', he says in a letter to Lanfranc, 'throughout the whole of this disputation to assert nothing which could not be immediately defended either from the canonical writers or from the words of St. Augustine. And however often I look over what I have written, I cannot see that I have asserted anything other than this'.[1]

But Anselm also studied that other great patristic guide for the whole mediaeval period: Boethius. Anselm apparently knew no Greek, and it was through Boethius that he became acquainted with Aristotelian logic. It is also clear that he was well versed in the classical Latin poets, and that he knew Bede's *De ratione temporum* (and, incidentally took the trouble to get from England a more reliable text than the library at Bec could provide). He was in no hurry to commit his thoughts to paper. Indeed, if he had been not at Bec in the 11th century but an American University in the twentieth he would certainly have been in trouble over tenure. He was, in fact, at Bec for seventeen years before he wrote his first treatise. But he was by no means idling. He was studying - and thinking, getting his ideas sorted out in a way which was to prove of enormous benefit to their eventual presentation and to posterity. He was playing his full part in the leadership of the

---

[1]   R.W. Southern, **St Anselm and His Biographer**, Cambridge, (1963), p.31.

life of a great monastery. That included teaching: first, children, and there is evidence that his educational theory was much more humane, much more advanced than that which lay behind the harsh regimes of the schools of his time; then, teaching monks and visiting scholars, who would come to discuss problems with him; also advising the neighbourhood and, as his reputation grew, far beyond the neighbourhood, on problems spiritual and pastoral. He was also praying.

It is, I think, significant that it was his prayers which received the widest circulation during his lifetime and during the hundred years that followed his death. They circulated in the monasteries of Europe, but not only there. Indeed, it seems that many of the recipients of his prayers were ladies of the nobility. He wrote prayers, for example, at the beginning to Adelaide, William the Conqueror's daughter; and the last recipient we know of was Matilda, Countess of Tuscany and, according to Sir Richard Southern, the greatest woman of her time.[1] For the benefit of TV addicts among you, this does *not*, repeat *not* imply that there was any similarity between Anselm's situation and that of 'The Thorn-Birds'. It does, however, correctly imply the importance and influence of Anselm among the great ones of his day, an implication supported by the vast correspondence he conducted with the nobility, as well as with brother monks, letters which have survived brimming over not just with spiritual wisdom but with a deep and moving spirit of real friendship as well.

But why were his prayers so popular? First, because of the care and skill he employed in the language he used. Some have claimed them as literary masterpieces. Second, and more important, because, compared with what had gone before, he left behind the austerity which up to that time had been the rule. Instead of just quoting biblical texts, he threw himself into them, existentialising them, as we might say now, so that they were applied directly to his own situation, giving full rein to his emotions, in a profusion of imagery, before him unknown. Take this prayer to St. Peter, long recognised as the shepherd, with the sinner his sheep: 'The sheep is sickening to death:

---

[1] Southern, op.cit., p.375.

his ulcers swell, his wounds are reopened and grown putrid. The wolves have tasted blood. They are waiting for him to be cast away. Faithful shepherd, turn your eyes on him; see that he is one of yours. If he has strayed, still *he* has not denied his lord and shepherd. If, through the filth, you cannot recognise the face of one washed white in the fountain of Christ, at least see that he confesses the name of Christ, who thrice asked "Lovest thou me?" and then said "Feed my sheep"'.[1] Sometimes, it may seem to us that he goes 'over the top' with his outpourings of emotion, his extravagant confessions of sin, and fervid, personal devotion (especially to the Virgin Mary). But the fact that they may not be to our taste is beside the point: Anselm's prayers undoubtedly met the devotional needs not only of the religious but of the educated laity of his day, and were an influential foretaste of many of the chief characteristics of later mediaeval piety.

Given this emphasis on prayer, it is perhaps not surprising that the two earliest works he produced (1077/78) are extended meditations which can be and often have been read as religious exercises. These were the *Monologion* (1077) and the *Proslogion* (1078), and the circumstances of their composition have been so vividly recorded by Anselm's contemporary biographer that the account is worth repeating. Eadmer wrote: 'He also composed another small book, which he called the *Monologion* because in this he alone spoke and argued with himself. Here, putting aside all authority of Holy Scripture, he enquired into and discovered by reason alone what God is, and proved by invincible reason that God's nature is what the true Faith holds it to be, and that it could not be other than it is. Afterwards it came into his mind to try to prove by one single and short argument the things which are believed and preached about God - that he is eternal, unchangeable, omnipotent, omnipresent, incomprehensible, just righteous, merciful true, as well as truth, goodness, justice and so on; and to show how all these qualities are united in him. And this, as he himself would say, gave him great trouble, partly because thinking about it took away his desire for food, drink and sleep, and partly - and this was the more grievous to him - because it disturbed the attention which he ought to have paid to Matins and to divine service at other

---

[1] op.cit, pp.44f.

times. When he was aware of this, and still could not entirely lay hold on what he sought, he supposed that this line of thought was a temptation of the Devil, and he tried to banish it from his mind. But the more vehemently he tried to do this, the more these thoughts crowded in on him. Then suddenly one night during Matins, the grace of God shone on his heart, the whole matter became clear to his mind, and a great joy and jubilation filled his inmost being'.[1] It is not my intention to offer now a detailed critique of these two decisive early works, nor of the works that followed during his time at Bec, *De Grammatico*, *De Veritate*, *De Casuviaboli* (1080-1085), *De Incarnatione Verbi* (1092-4). But I do want to make some general remarks on these two first works, the *Monologion* and the *Proslogion* which will, I hope, throw some light on Anselm's originality and influence. The *Proslogion* I shall return to later, because it is on this that his philosophical reputation today principally rests. The first general remark is that they are both mediations, indeed the *Proslogion* is presented entirely as a prayer. Meditation hitherto had meant learning passages of scripture, preparing lessons or music for the offices. It had not meant a vehicle for philosophical or theological argument. Yet by the twelfth century, Hugo St Victor could classify it as one of the arts, thus: 'meditation has its foundation in reading, but is constrained by no rules or order of reading. It rejoiced to run freely in an open space, where it can gaze on the truth without hindrance, and investigate now this, now that problem until nothing is left doubtful or obscure'. It was Anselm, more than anyone else, who exploited and developed this form, showing that meditation could be a most fruitful basis for extended private prayer as well as rigorous philosophical enquiry.

Secondly, both are attempts to bring to light the rationale of Christian faith. Both are examples of philosophy or reason being employed in the interests of faith, or, in his own words, which make more concise an emphasis which he had found in St Augustine, of faith seeking understanding: *fides quaerens intellectum*. The relation between faith and reason has preoccupied philosophers of religion since the earliest times, and the pendulum seems to swing between two extremes: those

---

[1] Southern, op.cit., p.50

who think that reason is all, if you are clever enough and have enough common sense you will discover all you need to know about God and his relation to the world; and, at the other extreme, those who think that in matters of faith, reason is more of a hindrance than a help, or worse, a dangerous diversion, these latter pinning their colours to that famous dictum of Tertullian, *Credo quia absurdum,* I believe because it is absurd. In modern discussions, the pendulum is still swinging. For Anselm, there could be no conflict between faith and reason, because both were the gifts of God and ultimately both had the same object, God. For him, faith is both the mode by which one holds to the truth as it has been given by God and the Faith, the Catholic faith, the propositions of which it was obligatory on all baptized persons to hold. Thus he writes in a letter: 'Our faith is to be defended by reason against unbelievers, not against those who profess to rejoice in the name of Christians. From the latter it may justly be demanded that they hold inviolate the pledges made for them in baptism...The Christians ought to progress through faith to understanding, and not through understanding to faith. Let him rejoice if he is able to attain understanding, and if he cannot, let him revere what he cannot apprehend'.[1]

But faith is not purely passive, nor reason purely defensive. Whoever believes is impelled to raise his mind to God, and this he does by means of reason. As Southern puts it, 'reason is itself a spiritual gift, by which man is made in the image of God: reason is not a machine for performing a plodding series of mechanical acts; it is a kindling of the spirit, a throwing off of the chains of the flesh, a rising above the world of material things'.[2] So, for Anselm, reason can never supplant faith or make it superfluos. In this he was unlike St. Thomas for whom once a thing was proved it ceased to be an object of faith. For Anselm, as far as the believer was concerned, reason's role was to make faith intelligible, to enrich it by relating one article to another, and to think through apparent inconsistencies. As far as the unbeliever was concerned, on the basis of the common philosophical assumptions of the day - and for Anselm and his contemporaries these included the

---

[1] Southern, op.cit., p.54

[2] op.cit. p.55

reality of universals, and the acceptance of incorporeal essences - the role of reason was to demonstrate the rationale of the tenets of faith. So, putting faith seeking understanding to work, in the *Monologion*, Anselm mediates on the Being of God, drawing heavily on the thought of St Augustine and demonstrating that God is the Supreme Goodness and Justice, and Trinitarian in nature. In the *Proslogion*, however, he leaves Augustine far behind, and is out on his own. Here he constructs a logical argument for the existence and principal attributes of God which will refute even the Fool in the Psalms, who says in his heart 'There is no God'. I want to go into this argument in a little detail in a few minutes, but for the moment, I want to draw attention to a third characteristic of St. Anselm's works which is so clearly evident in these two treatises. And this third element is the method employed here, from which he never departed. He is explicit, in the opening words of the *Monologion*: 'Some of my brethren have persistently asked me to write down some of the things which I have proposed to them in talk for meditation on the divine essence and certain associated topics...with this condition, that I should persuade them of nothing on the authority of the scripture, but plainly and simply put down whatever the argument might require, without overlooking any objections, however, fatuous'[1] *'Nothing on the authority of scripture'*. It is almost impossible to exaggerate what a break this represents from the theological method of his predecessors and his contemporaries. For them, theological knowledge was to be advanced only by the compilation of authorities, scripture first, with such patristic authors as they knew almost on an equal footing. A theological statement or position was to be judged true or false depending on the authority you could quote for it. And now, here was Anselm, proposing to proceed without the aid of authority, by philosophical argument alone. This was new. I do not mean, of course, that prior to him theologians had not used philosophical arguments - this would be patently untrue - from the earliest times. To give but one pertinent example, Augustine without his neo-Platonic framework of thought would simply not be Augustine. (Indeed, Anselm seems to have got from Augustine most of the Platonic conceptuality on which he relied so heavily). The point is that before Anselm, philosophy had been used as a supplement to

---

[1] Southern, op.cit. p.51

the authority of the scriptures and the fathers. Now with Anselm, it is solely on the correctness of his reasoning that he asks to be judged. He did not of course deny the authority of scripture, the wisdom of the fathers who had been responsible for formulating the faith. Rather he refused to use them as a substitute for philosophical argument and enquiry. And in this resolve, consistently carried through in his works, he opened the door to the rigorous application of critical thought which was to make of theology a scholastic enterprise and the science which, in the later Middle Ages, it became.

These three features which characterised his first two treatises - the meditational quality, the exercises of 'faith seeking understanding', his 'philosophic mission' as some-one has called it, which made him eschew the authority of other men's words - these three features are evident in all his subsequent work. To them we could well add clarity of vision, and orderliness, as he proceeded, usually in response to some-one else's questions, rather than his own, to discuss major topics of the faith. Gillian Evans has drawn a useful distinction: 'In Anselm's day', she says, 'and immediately after, the principal division' (in theology) 'which theologians perceived was that between the subject-matter which pagan philosophers and Christian thinkers had in common (questions to do with the existence and nature of God) and the theology of Redemption. It became something of a commonplace in the first half of the twelfth century to remark on the principle adumbrated in Romans i. 19-20: even pagans have no excuse for not worshipping God the *Creator* because they can learn of his existence and nature by studying the created world' - she might have added 'or by the right use of reason'. 'The work of God as *Redemptor* (Redeemer) is another matter. The reasons why God redeemed the world as he did are not to be found in Creation'.[1] There is an orderliness with which Anselm moves from topics of the first kind - God, his being and attributes, the Trinity, freedom of the will, the devil and evil, - to topics of the second, Incarnation and Atonement, a deliberate orderliness, in virtue of which Anselm takes it for granted that the points that he had made in previous works were accepted by those who were reading those which followed. The work which was

---

[1] G.R. Evans, **Anselm and a new Generation**, Oxford, 1980, p.5.

to have the greatest theological influence in the centuries which followed was his *Cur Deus Homo? (Why the God-man?)*, completed in 1090 when Anselm, now Archbishop, was in exile in Capua. In this he set himself to answer the question, 'Why was it necessary for the salvation of the world that the God-man (Christ) should die?', and in answering it, he provided the Church with the first systematic treatment of the Atonement, a treatment so successful that it dominated Christian thought and teaching until this century. For this reason, it is worth saying a little more about it.

Here he is true to the method he followed in the earlier works, taking as a starting point premisses which his opponents could accept, and eschewing appeals to authority. In the *Monologion*, his starting point was the empirical generalisation that 'all men seek to enjoy things which they think to be good', and by reason, with liberal use of the Platonic Doctrine of the Forms, proved not only the existence and attributes of God as the *summum bonum* but also his three-in-oneness.[1] In the *Proslogion*, he starts from the premiss (G.R. Evans, *Anselm and a new Generation*, Oxford, 1980, 5). that even the Fool can understand what he hears when God is defined as 'That than which a greater cannot be thought', and goes on from there to show the rationality of accepting the existence and attributes of God. In our *Cur Deus-Homo*, written for those who accept some of the tenets of Christian faith - the existence of God, his nature, the fact of sin and evil, the need for forgiveness - but who do not see the necessity for the Word to become flesh, the 'God-man', he makes what they accept his starting point, and, setting Christ aside as if he never had been, *remoto Christo*, he seeks to prove that for the salvation of the world it was necessary that there be the God-man (Christ) and it was necessary that he should die.

An outline of the argument might interest you: Man was created for eternal blessedness, this blessedness requiring the perfect voluntary submission of man to God's will. But the whole human race is guilty of disobedience. Any deviation of man's will must either be punished by deprivation of blessedness or rectified by an offering greater than

---

[1] See J. McIntyre, **St Anselm and his Critics**, Edinburgh, 1954. 12

the act of disobedience ('satisfaction'): there can be no free remission. No member of the human race can offer anything to God beyond his due obedience; there is no human capital with which to redeem the past, not to speak of present and future. Therefore the whole human race must forfeit the blessedness for which it was created. But this means that God's purpose in creating man has been frustrated. But that is impossible. Therefore a means of redemption must exist. Because man is the guilty party the necessary offering must be made by him. But man has nothing to offer. The offering required is greater than the whole existing creation. Nothing is greater than the whole creation except God. Therefore God alone can make this offering. Since only God can, and only man ought to make this offering, it must be made by a God-man. Therefore a God-man is necessary who can make this offering. Therefore the Incarnation is necessary. That is just the skeleton, and I would not blame you if you find it somewhat strange and sterile. But a couple of comments might be in order. First, you will have noticed that Anselm gives no role to the Devil. Before him, any account of the effectiveness of the work of Christ had included the defeat of the Devil and the end of his rights over sinful mankind. But for Anselm, the Devil had no claim to justice against God which needed satisfying. He could be left out of the theory. This was new, so new that most of Anselm's contemporaries did not like it.

Second, everything seems to hinge on the nature of the reparation, owing by sinful man to God. Here, Anselm drew on the notion of 'satisfaction', a Roman legal term, familiar in feudal times, which Anselm developed in his own way. If one party injures another party, compensation is due, and that compensation consists of what is necessary to make good the injury *plus* something over and above that sum to compensate for the affront to the honour or dignity of the person injured. It is this latter extra that is the satisfaction (it bears some slight resemblance to the Scots Law notion of 'solatium'). But with satisfaction, the greater the dignity or honour of the person injured, the greater the satisfaction due. Man cannot pay satisfaction to God because, as a sinner, for whom the slightest deviation from God's will, 'the merest glance', is sufficient to disrupt the moral order of the entire universe, he already owes all he has, his whole self, the whole universe is owed to God *apart* from the satisfaction that is owing. Only the sinless God-man can provide the necessary satisfaction.

Third, you may be wondering, as many critics have wondered, starting as far back as Anselm's younger contemporary, Abelard, why is it necessary to think of payments of debts, let alone satisfaction, to God at all? Why cannot God freely forgive, as we are bidden to do? The answer is two-fold: such forgiveness would place disobedience on the same level as obedience: and such forgiveness would not restore the order and beauty of the universe disturbed by sin, rather it would lead to anarchy and disorder. Only by the satisfaction offered by the God-man, adequate and acceptable to God, can disorder be restored.

I cannot discuss the details of the *'Cur Deus-Homo'* here. Anselm, with his 'satisfaction' theory of atonement has been accused by critics of every crime in the book: an impersonal and artificial transaction introduced from the law-courts, an elaborate rationalisation of the mediaeval penitential system; a competition between the honour and justice of God, without regard to his love; an objective business deal going on over the heads of humanity. Most of these objections have been answered. But the fact remains that in this work, Anselm proved his ability to provide a way of understanding the work of Christ which was to make sense for many generations, and almost acquire the status of orthodoxy. The *Cur Deus-Homo* was written, as I have indicated, when Anselm was no longer at Bec. The circumstances of his election as Archbishop of Canterbury are somewhat mysterious, but I cannot go into that now. Clearly, the influence of the monasteries, but perhaps more important, also of the Norman barons, with many of whom he was on terms of friendship, had much to do with it. I must leave to your imagination what it must have been like for him, at the age of sixty, to find himself transformed from abbot of a scholarly monastery in Normandy to spiritual head of the prime see of Great Britain, almost Pope of that 'alter orbis', Great Britain, as the Pope in Rome described it in these pre-Common Market days: and not only that but a great feudal magnate, charged with the administration of vast lands and endowments. Nor can I give an account of his disputes with King William and with King Henry over the question of investitures and homage, with important implications for Church-

State relationships. It seems generally agreed that he was much more at home in the ordered, devotional and scholarly environment of Bec than Canterbury, with its political and judicial responsibilities. That he showed great courage in resisting the royal will is not in doubt, resulting as it did in long periods of exile. Neither is his exercise, whatever the consequences, of obedience to the Pope in Rome - except where this involved some improper infringements of the privileges and primacy of the See of Canterbury, of which God had appointed him steward. Of the miracles later attributed to him - his fire-fighting success, the curative power of his girdle - I shall remain silent. It has been suggested that he saw too clearly, lacked the necessary pragmatism, moderation and political know-how to be a great archbishop. But this did not prevent his being much loved, and, after his death, venerated at Canterbury.

Looking back over his whole life, we can see that there was a great deal about him that marked him as a man of his age. His outlook on life was feudal and conservative. Evans makes much of his certainty, his freedom from anything approaching radical doubt concerning the inviolable truths of the Catholic faith. It is ironic that his greatest theological work was a systematic treatment of the Atonement, the effectiveness of Christ's sacrifice for all mankind and angels, and yet he himself saw life as a fight to preserve his soul from damnation. Few would be saved, the monastery or the convent was the place to be, and unless a monk lived as the few, he too would be damned.[1] A letter he wrote to King Harold's daughter, Gunhilda, illustrates this horribly, though well. Apparently Gunhilda had lived as a nun in a monastic foundation at Wilton. Count Alan Rufus saw her and fell in love with her, and persuaded her to leave Wilton to marry him. He died before the marriage. This is what Anselm then wrote to Gunhilda: 'You loved Count Rufus, and he you. Where is he now? What has become of the lover whom you loved? Go now and lie with him in the bed where he now lies; gather his worms into your bosom; embrace his corpse; kiss his bare teeth from which the flesh has fallen. He does not now care for your love in which he delighted while he lived; and the flesh which you desired now rots'. Not the sort of letter of condolence

---

[1] Southern, op.cit., p.102

I would like to receive. But for Anselm, Gunhilda had turned her back on the monastic life for an impure love, and only damnation was assured. In most of his assumptions, spiritual, moral, philosophical, of course, secular, Anselm was a mediaeval man. But his thought, and the unique personal, prayerful way he expressed it was not. And it is to its continuing relevance today that I now turn. First philosophically and second theologically.

Philosophically, his reputation largely rests on the argument for the existence of God contained in the *Proslogion*, the 'Ontological Argument', as Kant was to call it because it did not depend on any empirical observation, a *priori*, by the use of reason alone. If ever there was a case of bringing a logical rabbit out of a hat this is it. Schopenhauer called it 'a charming joke', and as it is far clearer in Anselm's words that any paraphrase, I give them to you now:

> And so, O Lord, since thou givest understanding to faith, give me to understand - as far as Thou knowest it to be good for me - that thou dost exist, as we believe, and that Thou art what we believe thee to be. Now we believe that thou art a being than which none greater can be thought. Or can it be that there is no such being, since 'the fool hath said in his heart, "There is no God"'? But when this same fool hears what I am saying - 'A being than which none greater can be thought' - he understands what he hears, and what he understands is in his understanding, even if he does not understand that it exists. For it is one thing for an object to be in the understanding, and another thing to understand that it exists. When a painter considers beforehand what he is going to paint, he has it in his understanding, but he does not suppose that he has not yet painted already exists. When he has painted it, he both has it in his understanding and understands that what he has now produced exists. Even the fool, then, must be convinced that a being than which none greater can be thought exists at least in his understanding, since when he hears this, he understands it, and whatever is understood is in the understanding. But clearly, that than which a greater cannot be thought cannot exist in the understanding alone. For if it is actually in the understanding

alone, it can be thought of as existing also in reality and this is greater. Therefore, if that than which a greater cannot be thought is in the understanding alone, this same thing than which a greater cannot be thought is that than which a greater can be thought. But obviously this is impossible. Without doubt, therefore, there exists, both in the understanding and in reality, something than which a greater cannot be thought.

Well! Let it be admitted that at first hearing it sounds like magic. There is another, and very important part of the argument to follow, but let us pause there. What has Anselm done? By getting "the fool" to agree that he understands 'that than which a greater cannot be thought' he has shewn that because what exists in reality as well as in the understanding is greater than what exists in the understanding alone, therefore that than which a greater cannot be thought must exist in reality as well as in the understanding. Therefore, God exists. The very simplicity, almost effrontery, takes your breath away, and when you recover it, common sense tells you that it just cannot be right. Anselm's contemporary, the monk Gaunilo of Marmoutiers, complained that on this reasoning anything you cared to imagine, like the most perfect island, must exist (to which Anselm replied that God is not like an island: he alone necessarily exists). Thomas rejected it: the existence of God is not thus self-evident. But the niggling thought persisted that there might be something in it. Descartes reformulated it, followed by Leibniz and Spinoza. Descartes claimed that the idea of God must contain existence, just as in the idea of a triangle, the angles must equal the sum of two right angles. Kant appeared to deal the death blow: existence is not a predicate, you can reject a triangle with its angles as you can deny God with existence. At this level, Kant seemed to have won the day, though Hegel was to introduce a new note into the argument, and in this century, philosophers have still been discussing whether or not Kant was entirely right in saying that 'existence is a predicate' disposes of the argument.[1]

---

[1] e.g. Bertrand Russell, G.E. Moore; or in its Hegelian form, Collingwood and Ryle.

In this century, and currently, however, Anselm's argument lives on principally because of the bit that immediately follows the passage I quoted. For having shewn that 'that than which a greater cannot be thought' must exist in reality as well as in the understanding, he goes on to show that because that which *cannot* be thought of as *not* existing (i.e. must exist) is greater than that which *can* be thought of as not existing, (i.e. need not exist) then that than which a greater cannot be thought cannot be thought of as *not existing* (i.e. must be thought of as existing). So then, he concludes, 'there truly is a being than which a greater cannot be thought - so truly that it cannot even be thought of as not existing. And *thou* art this being, O Lord our God.' Anselm himself probably thought of this as an amplification of his previous argument. But in this century, nine hundred years after it was first expounded, it is being hotly debated as a second, different and more compelling form of the argument. For here the debate is not about things existing in reality and things only existing in the understanding. Now it is about two kinds of existence: things existing necessarily and things existing not necessarily or contingently, possibly not-existing or impossibly not-existing. Anselm's definition precludes God's existing contingently, "the fool", who understands the definition, is committed to acknowledge God's necessary existence. Norman Malcolm has defended this position, so, with great tenacity, has Charles Hartshorne, as has Alvin Plantinga, each in their different ways. The debate is still going on, with analysis of the concept 'necessary existence' a central one for contemporary philosophy of religion. So discussion of Anselm's Ontological Argument is by no means at an end. It cannot, of course compel anyone to believe in God. But it is *still* not clear and probably never will be that Anselm was wrong in his claim that anyone who has a really clear idea of what is meant by God cannot fail to believe in him. As Richard Taylor has put it, 'Whether or not it ever convinces a theological doubter, it will always remain one of the boldest creations of man's reason, and a credit not only to its inventor, but to human reason itself'.[1]

Anselm's claim to modernity must not be restricted to that particular area of philosophy of religion on which I have perhaps dwelt too long.

---

[1] Alvin Plantinga, ed., **The Ontological Argument**, London, 1968, xviii.

His contribution to 20th century theology extends far further than that. The fact is that the man who in the opinion of many is the greatest theologian of this century, Karl Barth, was quick to acknowledge the decisive and lasting effect Anselm had on him. An early work, *Fides Quaerens Intellectum*, an analysis and commentary on *Anselm's Proslogion*, is of the greatest possible importance for anyone wanting to understand Barth's theological method, and in it Barth virtually declares that he intends to follow Anselm's own, a declaration amply vindicated by the many favourable references to Anselm in Barth's later work. As McIntyre puts it, Barth 'is appreciative of St Anselm almost to the degree of being uncritical', and the fact that Barth, in his eagerness to avoid anything that might smack of 'natural theology', sometimes misinterprets Anselm does not detract from the determinative influence Anselm had on his massive theological achievement.[1]

But leaving Barth aside, we may agree that not only was Anselm the first to formulate the principles of theological methodology, his development of the idea of theology as 'faith seeking understanding' is as relevant today as it was in the 11th century. Like Anselm, the theologian today wants, among other things, to provide a rationale of faith. But he has to avoid two extremes: that of rationalism, and that of fideism. He does not need to pretend that he is starting from a position of neutrality, and that before he believes he has to prove it by reason alone. Neither does he need to pretend that what he believes, because God-given, is immune from outside enquiry or logical examination. Rather is he trying to understand what he believes. You see, there is no 'holy language' available to the theologian, immune from change and immune from error. What of scripture, you say? Of course there is scripture, and this is a prime *datum* of theology. And of course there are the creeds and the authoritative statements of the Church. But mere repetition of the words of scripture or of the Creeds is not theology. Circumstances change, language changes, thought forms change. That is why theology, like history, has to be written anew in every generation, addressing itself to the questions that generation is asking, and seeking answers in a language that generation

---

[1] McIntyre, op.cit. p.25

can understand. It is not just a question of persuading others, or helping them to understand, though it is a question of that. Because we are children of our own time, it is also a question of understanding better, ourselves, what we believe and why. There is no shortage of examples of theology in effect being practised as 'faith seeking understanding' today, some more successful than others; I would simply mention Bultmann, with his adaptation of the early Heidegger's existentialism, Ian Ramsey, with his use of linguistic philosophy, D.Z. Phillips, with his Wittgensteinian approach, or John Cobb with his 'Process' theology. In the attempt to use the language, the philosophy of their day, to expound and understand and so (though Barth could not agree) strengthen their faith, they are not all consciously imitating Anselm, but nevertheless they are his heirs, and to the extent that they succeed, his debtors.

Finally, and very briefly, there is the spirit in which St. Anselm wrote, a spirit which, for theologians, can never be out of date. For it was, as one of the most acute students of Anselm has put it, 'a spirit of reverent devotion towards the God whose nature and mighty acts he seeks to describe, of profound humility which recognises that theological reflection is itself a gift of God who is both *Deus absconditus* and *Deus revelatus*, and of sympathetic patience with those who have not been given to see what he has seen, (the spirit) which secures for him a place in the forefront of Christian theologians'.[1] In that spirit, let us allow Anselm, that mediaeval man who yet has something to say, to have the last word, the word with which he concluded his *Proslogion*: 'O Lord, ...let me receive what Thou dost promise through Thy truth that my joy may be full. ...Meanwhile, let my mind meditate upon it, let my tongue discourse upon it. Let my soul hunger for it, let my flesh thirst for it, let my whole substance desire it, until I enter into the joy of my Lord who is the triune and one God, blessed forever. Amen'.

---

[1] McIntyre, op.cit., p.51

XIII. KARL BARTH AND HISTORICISM

- G. B. Hall

The category of history not only occupies a very significant place in the theology of Karl Barth, it also represents an understanding of history fundamentally at odds with the philosophy and critical methods of modern historical enquiry. There has been much criticism of his refusal to admit the theological relevance of historical criticism in the examination of biblical texts while, nevertheless, insisting that the Christian is committed to the belief that certain events recounted in the biblical narratives actually occurred. This apparently arbitrary rejection of historical criticism as a check on the testimony and report of the biblical texts sometimes serves as the basis for the more general accusation that his theology represents a 'flight from history' and for that reason alone cannot be taken seriously in an age as mindful of humanity's embeddedness in history as our own.

It is not my purpose to discuss the adequacy or inadequacy of Barth's view of history. The aim here is simply to show that whatever the final judgement on his distinctive but problematical view of history, his theology cannot be represented as a 'flight from history.' In fact, Barth's understanding of history has interesting affinities and parallels with German historicism such that his own view might well be characterised as a peculiar kind of historicism.

The most general feature of the various forms of nineteenth-century historicism was the conviction that an adequate comprehension of the world of human action, value, and thought involves a specifically historical way of thinking. This allows for significant differences regarding what constitutes the proper kind of historical thinking and Barth's theology can be seen to be one such kind which he claims enables us to understand the meaning and direction of human history. From this point of view Ernst Troeltsch and Karl Barth represent radically different and incompatible twentieth-century attempts to comprehend the meaning and significance of history through history. This is obviously the case with Troeltsch but perhaps it is not apparent with regard to Barth, not least because of his frequent criticisms of historicism.

We begin with an outline of the general features of German historicism along with a brief account of J. G. Herder's philosophy of history as the background for a characterisation of Barth's understanding of history as a radical and peculiar kind of historicism.[1] Herder was one of the first to set forth the principles of German historicism and Barth's lecture on him provides a useful point of departure in drawing out the character of Barth's own historicism. The argument here does not depend upon demonstrating either the direct or indirect influence on Barth of any particular form of historicism or historicist thinker. There may well be such influences but our concern is solely with certain affinities and parallels which, when viewed in relation to his overall theological outlook, indicate the consistently historicist cast of Barth's thought.

I

The question of the precise character of historicism does not admit of a simple and straightforward answer. Historicism as an identifiable orientation to history emerged in Germany during the latter half of the eighteenth century and represents the flowering of the lengthy development of what is often called the 'modern consciousness' of history; the consciousness of human life as immersed in history, in continual change and development. There was a tendency to interpret the whole of reality, including what had previously been considered absolute and unchanging, in historical, that is to say, contextual or relative terms. Broadly speaking; the explanation and evaluation of human affairs by means of history gained acceptance as the proper basis for understanding the meaning and value of human existence.

---

[1] The studies of Maurice Mandelbaum, **History, Man and Reason** (Baltimore: The Johns Hopkins Press, 1971) and G. C. Iggers, **The German Conception of History** (Middletown: Wesleyan University Press, 1968) are complementary studies of two historicist traditions. I have relied heavily upon them though neither of them speak, as I do, of two traditions within the historicist outlook. For the background to historicism see George Huppert, "The Renaissance Background of Historicism," **History and Theory**, V, 1, 1966, pp. 48-60 and Peter Hanna Reill, **The German Enlightenment and the Rise of Historicism**. (Berkley: University of California Press, 1975).

A viewpoint as general as this can take a variety of forms and this is precisely what we find. Thinkers representing diverse and sometimes antagonistic philosophical outlooks are to be found espousing one or another form of historicism within which it is possible to identify two main traditions. Their common source was the historicism (sometimes called 'historism' so as to distinguish it from later developments) associated with J. G. Herder and, more generally, the Romantic movement.

One tradition, German historicism, maintained greater continuity with the principles of early historicism and was developed and transmitted through the German Historical School. The other tradition emerged from a complex convergence of diverse and often antagonistic systems of thought (including Hegel, the attempt to establish a science of society based on laws of social development, Marxism, and comprehensive evolutionism) to produce the historicism that dominated the outlook of the late nineteenth-century. This tradition is sometimes referred to as 'positivistic' historicism, though comprehensive evolutionism is probably more accurate. A discussion of this complicated development, though indispensble in a thorough exploration of Barth's relation to historicism, will be set aside here since the purpose of this paper is best served by considering Barth's view of history in relation to German historicism.

Maurice Mandelbaum defines historicism as "the belief that an adequate understanding of the nature of any phenomenon and an adequate assessment of its value are to be gained through considering it in terms of the place it occupied and the role it played within a process of development".[1] This definition broadly applies to all forms of historicism, although there are significant variations in the definition of 'development.'

German historicism defined development on the analogy of organic growth. G. C. Iggers brings this out in his identification of the core of German historicism with its assumption that the phenomena of history differ fundamentally from those of nature and, therefore, each requires a different mode of investigation.

---

[1] **History, Man and Reason**, p. 42

Nature, it is held, is the scene of the eternally recurring, of phenomena themselves devoid of conscious purpose; history comprises unique and unduplicable human acts, filled with volition and intent. The world of man is in a state of incessant flux, although within it there are centers of stability (personalities, institutions, nations, epochs), each possessing an inner structure, a character, and each in constant metamorphosis in accord with its own internal principles of development. History thus becomes the only guide to an understanding of things human.[1]

The basic categories of German historicism are 'individuality' and 'development.' 'Individuality' refers to what Iggers calls 'centers of stability' and was adopted because each person, nation, or other social form is a concrete and unique phenomenon possessing inherent developmental tendencies. Development here is conceived not as a sequence of related external events but as the unfolding of that which is implicit within the 'individual' in relation to its external circumstances. Iggers also provides a helpful summary of the general outlook of the earliest phase of historicism.

The early representatives of the German historicist tradition were still steeped in the belief that this was a moral world, that man possessed worth and dignity, and that an objective understanding of history and reality was possible....they insisted at the same time that all values were unique and historical, that all philosophy was national, and all understanding individual. They insisted upon the radical diversity of men and of human cultures. What preserved them from ethical and epistemological relativism was their deep faith in a metaphysical reality beyond the historical world. They were convinced that each of the diverse cultures merely reflected the many aspects of that reality.[2]

What distinguished German historicism from other forms of historicism was its emphasis on the individuality and value of the units of

---

[1] **The German Conception of History**, p. 5.

[2] **Ibid**. pp. 13-14

historical study and its conviction that the multipilicity and diversity of historical phenomena reflected a deeper metaphysical reality underlying and coming to expression in them. They were convinced "that the apparent expressions of irrationality, individual spontaneity, and will were manifestations of an underlying ethical order. This faith assumed the existence of a God who at each moment in history, actively, created the mysterious balance which linked each sovereign monad to the total whole".[1] Accordingly, the fulness of historical reality could not be contained within an abstract conceptual scheme nor its pattern apprehended through the search for universal laws of development but it could be understood through empathy, imagination, and intuition. Their faith in God as the ground of meaning and the source of unity in history obscured the relativism implicit in their contextual approach to history. If that faith is threatened, history loses its meaning and they are faced with a chaos of values.

Hegel marked a turning point in historicism. According to Mandelbaum, historicism becomes in Hegel's system the basis for a total world-view but only after he has transformed "historicism into the cardinal principle of a philosophic system, rather than leaving it as a corollary of the doctrine of divine immanence."[2] Hegel argued that Reason, not the 'feeling' of the Romantics, is the mode by which the nature of the world is apprehended. He understood reason historically and dialectically and, therefore, could not accept Herder's view "that each culture was to be regarded as an equally valid embodiment of the Divine;" rather, each succeeding culture was "a fuller embodiment of the ultimate nature of reality."[3] This process proceeded according to the judgement of reason and was, therefore, self-justifying.

The German Historical School could not accept Hegel's view that history with its variety and diversity is the manifestation of reason, of a rational principle, and reducible to a conceptual scheme.

---

[1] Ibid., p. 26

[2] History, Man and Reason.

[3] Ibid. p. 60.

Both schools shared in the conviction that behind the phenomena of historical study there was a metaphysical reality, and that the aim of all study must be the apprehension of this reality. Niebuhr, Savigny, and Ranke agreed with Hegel that true philosophy and true history were basically one. They differed from Hegel in their conviction that this fundamental reality could be approached only through historical study, for it was much more complex, vitalistic, and elusive and possessed much greater room for spontaneity and uniqueness than Hegel's panlogistic concept of the universe would permit. In brief, only history offered answers to the fundamental questions of philosophy.[1]

After Hegel, the German historicist tradition with its insistence upon the value and autonomy of every age is transmitted through the German Historical School. At the same time, the other main historicist tradition embarks upon its formation as several apparently self-contained schools of thought slowly converge through their adoption of the explanatory and evaluative theses of historicism.

By the close of the century the philosophical foundations of 'positivist' historicism were crumbling and the religious or metaphysical foundations of German historicism had virtually collapsed. The attempt to conceive universal history, or to apprehend the ultimate meaning of human history, or to discover the laws governing its single, progressive development, had all been dealt crippling blows. Such activities were no longer considered appropriate in the scientific study of history. What remained of both traditions was an empirical historiography concerned largely with 'facts' and characterised by meticulous attention to detail. As the twentieth century dawned historical-critical method stood strong and confident while alongside it historical hermeneutic staggered uncertainly and confusedly.

A deep faith in God as the ground of unity and meaning, the belief in the harmony between historical fact and metaphysical truth, had enabled German historicism to affirm the ethical meaningfulness of

---

[1] **The German Conception of History**, p. 66.

history. With the undermining of this religious foundation its philosophy of history also collapsed. Without their trust in a beneficent history, without their belief in an ultimate purpose guiding its meaningful development, there remained only their radical historicising of knowledge and value. Truth and value were now inextricably bound to their particular historical situations.

II

J. G. Herder is credited by Iggers with being the first to offer "an extensive presentation of historicist principles in Germany".[1] He is representative of the religious reaction against certain significant trends in Enlightenment thought and his view of history is based on a religious outlook that emphasises divine immanence. According to Herder, history is the unfolding of the divine purpose and God's presence is experienced in immediate intuition. Mandelbaum identifies the significance of the relationship between Herder's doctrine of divine immanence and his historicism.

> If all reality is One, and the Divine is present in all the manifestations of this One, then what occurs within the process of history is itself a Revelation. Some aspects of the historical process will more fully reveal the nature of the Divine than will others, but this is not because they conform to a human standard of goodness and evil; rather, it is because they more fully reveal the power which operates within all of the manifestations of the Divine[2]

God's plan for humankind, including each individual, is that it shall cultivate the humanity to which it is naturally inclined. When Herder speaks of Humanity as the telos of human nature he does not conceive of progress toward this end in terms of a linear development from a lesser to a greater perfection.

---

[1] **Ibid**, p. 34. It should be noted that in his later works Herder modifies the extreme views presented in his **Also a Philosophy of History**.

[2] **History, Man and Reason**, p. 55.

The fundamental principle of this divine law of nature reconciles us wonderfully not only with the appearance of our species all over the Globe, but likewise with its variations through the different periods of time. Everywhere man is what he was capable of rendering himself, what he had the power to become. Were he contented with his condition, or were the means of his improvement not yet ripened in the ample field of time; he remained for ages what he was, and became nothing more. But if he employed the instruments God had given him for his use, his understanding, power, and all opportunities that a favourable current conveyed to him; he raised himself with art, and improved himself with courage.[1]

Nations and societies pass through a life cycle and each makes its contribution to the growth of culture by its cultivation of particular human potentialities within the limits of its historical circumstances and, therefore, each must be evaluated by a standard derived from those conditions and circumstances. The perfection people should seek is not absolute but "the relative perfection which their circumstances and the standards of their times permit..."[2] Moreover, "Any body of men who achieved a form of life, a cultural configuration, was a noble manifestation of mankind, of God's creation."[3]

Though each culture is unique, it is not isolated and its achievements are transmitted to others and contribute to the 'tree' of Culture or Humanity extending through time. The history of humankind is a single history and is likened by Herder to a magnificent tree in which no two leaves are perfectly alike.[4] He was able to resist the relativistic implications of this view of history and value only because of his

---

[1] J. G. Herder, **Reflections on the Philosophy of the History of Mankind**, abridged with intro. by Frank E. Manuel from trans. of T. O. Churchill (1806) (Chicago: University of Chicago Press, 1968), p. 86

[2] **The Perfectibility of Man** (London: Duckworth, 1970), p. 223

[3] Frank E. Manuel, 'Editor's Introduction,' J. G. Herder, **Reflections on the Philosophy of the History of Mankind**. p. xvi.

[4] **Reflections on the Philosophy of the History of Mankind**, p. 3.

conviction that both history and nature form an organic unity under the guidance of divine Providence, although we cannot fully comprehend its pattern.

Herder's philosophy of history with its emphasis on the ethos, the 'spirit of a people,' raised the problem of historical knowledge since no one can understand the ethos of a people through mere description of their history. Description was indispensable but something more was required and that, Herder insisted, was empathy. Empathy enables one to interpret historical sources in such a way as to grasp fully the 'spirit' of a nation or people.

> So far as understanding the nature of anything was concerned, the doctrine of divine immanence made it imperative that one should consider all phenomena as being internally related: not merely related in the sense of being causally connected within one mechanical system but related in essence, since all were manifestations of one Divine Being. It therefore also led to the view that there were two ways of knowing that which was contained within the historical process: an outer, superficial mode, and a mode by means of which man could penetrate into the hidden springs of power from which all things followed. And so far as evaluation was concerned, the principle of divine immanence led to the belief that each thing had its own value, each was an expression of the Divine.[1]

It is interesting, in the light of this brief glance at Herder's philosophy of history, to turn to Barth's sympathetic and in many ways appreciative lecture on his thought.[2] He welcomes his emphasis on the concrete reality of history, his use of the principle of individualisation, his appreciation of the sovereignty of revealed religion, his insistence upon historical event as the basis of Christianity, his reluctance to eliminate miracle, and his general attitude to the Bible. But, Barth

---

[1] **History, Man and Reason**, p. 59.

[2] Karl Barth, **Protestant Theology in the Nineteenth Century**. (London: SCM Press Ltd. 1972), pp. 313-340

laments, these insights reflect the promise of Herder, not his achievement. In the end he failed to overcome the Enlightenment with its emphasis on the primacy and autonomy of reason.

This failure, Barth contends, follows from a fatal flaw in Herder's thought; instead of "basing theological knowledge upon the object of experience," he "bases it quite definitely upon experience itself."[1] He finds God in immediate feeling, in living experience, and what "interests him about faith is its assumedly intuitive *form* in sensation; and what interests him about the object of faith is its assumedly tangible and demonstrable *effect* in the state of mind already prevailing in the believing subject."[2] As Barth sees it, Herder's theology founders because it remains wholly within the human world "where it must be prepared to give an account of itself before self-criticizing reason."[3] Once this concession was made he was forced to fall back upon the canons of Enlightenment thought.

Barth, however, finds in Herder's thought various pointers to the need to reflect upon the presuppositions peculiar to theology, "upon the independence in authority and in faith, of revelation."[4] Unfortunately, Herder allowed his enquiry to become "bogged down in its first stage, in the hasty equation, that is, of revelation and history, of revelation and experience."[5] Barth has taken the enquiry concerning the truth and legitimacy of revelation that step further and reflected upon the basis of religious knowledge, upon the religious object rather than upon religious experience alone. Thereby, in his view, avoiding the mistake of those who fail to see that faith is not dependent on its form but on its object, the Word made flesh. God can make form and content one in effect but there can be no internal relation as such. Once this is established, Barth accepts the authority of self-critcising reason "in all circumstances primary to experience and history."[6] The

---

[1] **Ibid**. p. 338

[2] **Ibid**. p. 338.

[3] **Ibid**. p. 339

[4] **Ibid**. p. 333.

[5] **Ibid**. p. 333.

[6] **Ibid**. p. 339.

Word from beyond, the revelatory act of God, not only lies beyond the reach of self-criticising reason, it enfolds it.

Theology begins with the 'fact' of the concrete revelation of God in Jesus Christ wherein God, the Subject, is objectively present in the Word. We must, Barth says, "reject any anxiety about this occurrence as not only superfluous but forbidden" [CD II/1, p. 4]. Only God can 'prove' God and theology can do its work "only when all presuppositions are renounced which would secure it from without or within."[1] Lacking any internal or external safeguards, theology is borne and driven by the Spirit to which the theologian must simply be obedient.[2] Theology is thoroughly groundless on its human side since it is grounded in and by God alone.

This, then, is the way in which Barth safeguards the sovereignty and priority of revelation as the basis, source, and presupposition of theological knowledge. It is a radical 'corrective' to the anthropocentrism of all previous historicism and leads, I suggest, not to a decisive and sweeping break with historicism but instead establishes the basis for an admittedly radical and peculiar kind of historicism.

III

Barth endorses the verdict that unlimited relativism is the logical consequence of the historicist approach to the study of the historical, that is, to the sphere of temporal, contingent, creaturely occurrence. The radical historicising of truth and value renders them nothing more than the products of human history bound to the circumstances of their origin and development. And, yet, he insists that the meaning and value of human existence are given in history itself. He, too, speaks of a deeper reality to history but he rejects the assumption that this reality can be apprehended through the study of human history,

---

[1] **Evangelical Theology**, p. 50. It is worth noting precisely the kind of presuppostions Barth is here rejecting.

[2] **Ibid**. p. 55.

or that it is immediately intuitable, or that it can be comprehended in abstract concepts. Of course he means by history something very different from the common conception of it. 'Real' history is hidden in creaturely history which is its mirror likeness.

Our understanding of 'real' history depends wholly on divine revelation. What, then, constitutes the independence of revelation and how does it relate to history? "Revelation," Barth says, "is not a predicate of history, but history is a predicate of revelation"[1] [CD I/2, p. 58]. When he speaks of revelation he is not offering an interpretation of the idea of revelation but is attempting to draw out the meaning and consequences of the fact of the concrete event of revelation in which God "is subject, predicate and object" [CD II/1, p. 263]. Revelation is the self-contained event of God's action which brings its own history, the history of Jesus Christ, so that when we say, "God reveals Himself," it signifies that "revelation becomes history [CD II/1, p. 58]. The whole being of God is activity both in God's triune being and in relation to the creature and creation. The real but hidden truth of human history is that it is a history by God, from God, and to God [CD IV/1, p. 7]. This truth is inaccessible to human experience and enquiry but through faith in the Word of God, Jesus Christ, we receive light in the midst of darkness and "it shines over history and causes us to see at various points in its course the sway of the Creator, disclosing the masks of God as such" [CD III/3, p. 24].

In the event of the Incarnation God allows the world and humanity to participate in the history of the divine inner life just as, in this same event, God freely condescends to participate in the being of the world and so "His being, His history, is played out as world-history" [CD IV/1, p. 215]. Jesus Christ, is the 'key' to an understanding of the meaning of human existence and history for "in the most concrete sense of the term, the history of this One is world history" [CD IV/2, p. 269].

This history, and with it the true concept of history, is hidden in the midst of world history because there is no correspondence, only

---

[1] All references to the **Church Dogmatics** (Edinburgh: T &T Clark, 1963-75) are placed in brackets and abbreviated CD followed by volume number and part number.

contradiction, between the free and righteous God and sinful humankind. The true concept of history is possible "only because in the midst of all other creatures and men we have to reckon also with the fact of the existence of Jesus Christ" [CD III/2, p. 159]. It is here that we learn the real history of God and of the world. Here we learn that "the history of a being begins, continues and is completed when something other than itself and transcending its own nature encounters it, approaches it and determines its being in the nature proper to it, so that it is compelled and enabled to transcend itself in response and in relation to this new factor" [CD III/2, p. 158]. Jesus' being is this transcendence and transcending, the dynamic movement of Creator to creature and creature to Creator which is the "identity of Creator and creature." [CD III/2, p. 159].

His being as "the man Jesus, lies in the fact that God is for Him and He for God" [CD III/2, p. 159]. In this history the man Jesus is elected by God that he may elect God, is Delivered by God that he may be the Deliverer, is served in God's eternal mercy that he may serve the eternal righteousness of God, is the one to whom God is revealed that he may become the witness and revelation of God. "Jesus exists only in this history,...in the history of the covenant and salvation and revelation inaugurated by God in and with the act of creation" [CD III/2, p. 160]. Real history, including creaturely history, has no other foundation than the will and counsel of God.

Jesus' history is on our behalf for as a man he is like us and we like him. This means that what Jesus alone is, is also valid for us in the "history enacted in Jesus." He is the "one primary, direct and immediate fulfilment of the concept of history" and our being as history is dependent upon this man and his relationship to us as the one who is for us. Therefore, our being as history, in the strict meaning of history, is secondary, derived, and indirect but "in this relationship it is really history" [CD III/2, p. 161].

Here, then, is the independence of revelation and also the history of how God alone effects the unity of content and form through the Word that reconciles and unifies God with humankind. Theology must begin from the fact of this concrete event in which God is revealed. Jesus Christ grounds Christian discourse and everything that we say must be determined by his history and the biblical witness to it, which, after all, is "the history book without parallel" [CD IV/1, p. 505].

'Real' history, the history of the covenant, is grounded in the free election of grace and world history is the external basis of that history. It begins with the creation of the world, continues with its reconciliation to God, and culminates in the redemption "which consists in the general revelation of the creative and reconciling act of God" [CD II/1, p. 514]. The unity of God's history and creaturely history is grounded in the operations between the divinity and humanity of Jesus Christ. His existence for God and for us repeats and actualises the inner life of the triune God, and through his being for us, it is repeated and made effective in creaturely history. God, "in His pure, divine form of existence...is not in time but before, above and after all time, so that time is really in Him." Through God's Word and work we learn that God was not satisfied with this existence and "His inner glory overflowed outwards. He speaks His Word and acts in His work with and for 'another' than Himself. This 'other' is His creature." Thus, the inner life of the triune God is "the basic type and ground of all history" [CD III/1, p. 68].

This is the miracle. God, the Subject-in-act, speaks in Jesus Christ and though we cannot recognise this Word, we are recognised in it and the response of faith is simply acknowledgement and obedience. We hear the Word in Christ risen, present, and alive now. We know him not as one from the past but as one whose life, though it had a beginning, a duration, and an end, ended in such a way "that he is always present and still future" [III/2, p. 464]. The risen Christ is present to us through the Spirit and our acknowledgement of him is faith.

The knowledge of God, which itself is faith, is a knowledge of Jesus Christ as the centre of history. In and by him world history has acquired this new reality but apart from him it is still hidden in world history. There are, Barth grants, signs and intimations of this new reality but these are never more than meaningful gropings; at best world history appears to us only in "the twofold form of the antithesis

241

of above and below" [CD IV/3,2, p. 714]. In its light, "neither Christians nor non-Christians could suspect the reconciliation of the world to God in which the distinction between them is robbed of the sting of division, nor the divine covenant with man fulfilled by God Himself, nor the reconstituted order between the two, nor the Kingdom of God inaugurated" [CD IV/3, 2, p. 715]. Sight is not yet granted and until it is we must walk by faith but it is enough that the new reality of world history is revealed and knowable in Jesus Christ.

Barth does not want to be understood to be speaking of two histories, the 'real' history of salvation, the covenant of grace, and world history. There is but one history to which all creaturely occurrence is subordinated by being taken up into it and enclosed within it. Our knowledge of 'real' history is dependent on the self-revelation and the self-interpretation of the God to whom the Bible is the trustworthy witness since what we hear in it " is revelation, and therefore the very Word of God" [CD I/2, p. 473].

As we have seen, Barth denies to ordinary historical understanding any capacity for discerning the events of God's history with us. He speaks of the events of 'real' history, which are occurrences in time and space, as 'primal,' 'pre-historical,' or 'non-historical' history. Thus history, real history, is made up of 'non-historical' and 'historical' elements. The 'non-historical' element refers to the immediacy of God to creaturely history. Creation history is exclusively God's action and it can be the subject of only a 'non-historical' or pre-historical depiction. Subsequently, in spite of all appearances to the contrary, God rules creaturely occurrence by continually ordering it in accord with his divine plan. World History is immediate to God as well as mediate, 'non-historical' as well as 'historical'.

The identification of the historical, the sphere of creaturely occurrence, as the whole of history is what Barth refers to as the 'historicist' view of history. What it sees "is only necessity and contingency, continuity and discontinuity, law and freedom, which exist side by side with each other and in opposition to each other" [III/3, p. 160]. It fails to see "that in genuine history the 'historical'and the 'non-historical' accompany each other and belong together" [III/1, p. 80].

It cannot see that the historical or creaturely element in which there is a similarity of relationship with other historical or creaturely occurrences "may be easily and almost completely obscured," particularly in the case of miracle. "It is most apparent at the centre of the history of the covenant of grace - in the resurrection of Jesus Christ" [CD III/1, p.78]. Here the 'non-historical' element predominates and the historical element, though not wholly extinguished, occupies "a deep 'historical' twilight."

The "divine laughter," Barth tells us, "rings out over the folly of our crude or refined human imperialisms, and they will inevitably come to grief on that laughter" [III/3, p. 160]. One of these 'follies' has been our repeated attempts to discern the meaning and value of history and human existence from within the sphere of the historical. This was particularly true of the German historicists and from their 'follies' Barth drew the lesson that we cannot through our own resources of reason, experience, or intuition apprehend, let alone comprehend, the nature and meaning of world history. Historcal science is competent to deal with history considered as creaturely occurrence but this is a limited, partial view of history which we wrongly and sinfully regard as the whole of history.

'Real' history is the history of salvation and though it is for human beings, it is never through them. Rather, "God co-ordinates and integrates the history of the creature with that of His covenant of grace so that it may co-operate in this history" [CD II/3, p. 47]. Through the covenant of grace our creaturely history is taken up into 'real' history in which we participate as co-workers through faith.

IV

We began with the charge that Barth fails to take history seriously and while it may be true that he does not do justice to the historical, I do not believe that he can be justly accused of not having taken it seriously. Once his treatment of history is viewed within the context of his life-long conversation and argument with his nineteenth-century predecessors, it should be clear just how seriously he took history and how much he was indebted to an earlier generation of thinkers. Obviously, he was highly critical of much of their work but he continued to accord a similar primacy to history and to a specifically historical way of thinking.

Both Barth and Troeltsch confronted the challenge to Christian faith set by historical relativism and autonomous critical reason. Troeltsch pursued a course more in keeping with the concern of those like Herder who sought to co-ordinate and balance faith and reason, historical relativism and religious assurance. Barth pursued a very different course, one more in keeping with what he later viewed as the unfulfilled promise of Herder. Everything is to be understood in the light of our participation in the divine history and the task of the theologian is to testify to the unity and coherence of truth by showing how all things have their ground, meaning and unity in this reality. This is what is so striking about Barth's theology; not only is everything viewed from within the perspective of faith, everything that appears external to it is taken into it. Thus he does not simply deprive critical reason of its autonomy but grants it its proper relative autonomy within the framework of real history. In the same way, he seeks to overcome historical relativism, not by denying it but by subordinating it, which is to say, granting it its appropriate place in the history of God's dealings with us. A history hidden to all but those who participate in it through faith.

In many ways Barth parallels the early historicists, especially Herder. He, like Herder, affirms God as the ground of meaning and the source of unity in general history, even as his 'correction' of him renders their respective positions incompatible. Herder's doctrine of immanence and his emphasis upon our capacity to intuit divine reality in the midst of our immersion in history is far removed from Barth's theology but this should not be allowed to obscure their being at one in their emphasis on the centrality of history in speaking about God and human existence. They both affirm that the meaning of history is to be found in history, however much they differ in what they take history to be.

Thus one might conceivably characterise Barth's theology as a peculiar kind of historicism, whatever its sources. Given his declaration of the presence of the risen Lord now and in the future, it might fittingly be called eschatological historicism. Whatever the qualifier, 'real' history holds the answer to the meaning and value of human existence and must be understood by means of a particular way of historical thinking involving participation in the reality of history.

The characterisation of Barth's outlook as a radical and peculiar kind of historicism does not imply that it somehow provides the key to his thought. We recall that the historicist outlook has been closely associated with diverse and often antagonistic philosophical and theological viewpoints. Barth, like many nineteenth-century thinkers, emphasises history and a particular historical way of thinking but his is a historicism based on theological sources and cannot be understood apart from them. At the same time, it is important to recognise the consistently historicist cast of his thought. If this historicism is not a key to his theology, it does have implications for our understanding of his theology. For one thing, it may be of help in determining the precise sense in which, at least in much of the material included in this essay, the *analogia relationis* is more the *analogia historiae*. Furthermore, a recognition of his historicism and its relation to early historicism may shed some light on his relationship to Hegel. It also may help to account for his failure to engage directly those of his contemporaries who were biblical historians or were at the forefront of twentieth-century philosophy of history. Finally, Barth's historicism has a bearing on the way in which he understands time and eternity and is not unrelated to the difficulties scholars find with his treatment of it.

Barth's resolution of the problem of faith and history may be much too problematic but it is on his terms not a flight from history but the fruits of a participation in real history.

Contributors

J.K.Cameron, Professor (emeritus) of Ecclesiatical History, St Mary's College

A.C.Cheyne, Professor (emeritus) of Ecclesiastical History, New College, University of Edinburgh

G.B.Hall, Senior Lecturer in Divinity, St Mary's College

J.M.Lochman, Professor of Theology, University of Basel

D.W.Lovegrove, Lecturer in Ecclesiastical History, St Mary's College

J.McIntyre, Professor (emeritus) of Divinity, New College, University of Edinburgh

W.McKane, Professor of Hebrew and Oriental Languages, St Mary's College

G.H.M.Posthumus Meyjes, Professor of Church History, Theologisch Instituut, Rijksuniversiteit Leiden

R.A.Piper, Lecturer in New Testament Language and Literature, St Mary's College

D.W.D.Shaw, Professor of Divinity and Principal, St Mary's College

J.A.Whyte, Professor (emeritus) of Practical Theology, St Mary's College